Dental Assisting Test Preparation

Carol Giaquinto, C.D.A., R.D.H., M.Ed.
Springfield Technical Community College
Springfield, MA

Roberta Albano, C.D.A., R.D.H., M.Ed.
Springfield Technical Community College
Springfield, MA

Brady
Prentice Hall
Upper Saddle River, NJ 07458

Library of Congress Cataloging-in-Publication Data

Albano, Roberta
    Dental assisting test preparation/by Roberta Albano, Carol Giaquinto.
        p. cm.–(Brady/Prentice Hall test prep series)
    ISBN 0-8359-4944-3
    1. Dental assistants—Examinations, questions, etc. 2. Dentistry–
Examinations, questions, etc.
    I. Giaquinto, Carol. II. Title. III. Series.
    RK60.5.A43   1995   95-23664
    617.602'33'076–dc20   CIP

The following individuals and companies have generously given permission to use their material:
Pgs. vii-x, Dental Assisting National Board, Inc.; Pgs. 11, 12, 13, 15, 17, Richard Kasunick; Pg. 29,
Colwell Systems; Pgs. 90, 107, 108, 116, from *Essentials of Dental Radiography for Dental Assist-
ants and Hygienists*, Fifth Edition, by Wolfe R. de Lyre and Orlen N. Johnson, copyright © 1995,
Appleton & Lange; Pgs. 99, 102, 112, Eastman Kodak Company; Pgs. 102, 109, 110, Rinn Corporation.

We would like to express our sincere appreciation and thanks to our husbands, children and families for their support and unending encouragement throughout this endeavor.

A special thank you is extended to Ms. Kimberly DeGray, Secretary to the Division of Health/Human Services, Springfield Technical Community College, for spending countless hours typing and formatting this text.

Additionally, we acknowledge and extend our gratitude to Richard Kasunick, Professor of Human Services, Springfield Technical Community College, for photographing and coordinating text illustrations.

An American BookWorks Corporation Project
Contributing Editor: *Lyn M. Hammel*
Acquisitions Editor: *Barbara Krawiec*
Director of Manufacturing & Production: *Bruce Johnson*
Manufacturing Buyer: *Ilene Sanford*
Editorial Assistant: *Louise Fullam*
Formatting/Page Make-up: *American BookWorks Corp./JH Desktop Publishing Design*
Printer/Binder: *Banta Company (Harrisonburg)*

 © 1996 by Prentice-Hall, Inc.
A Simon & Schuster Company
Upper Saddle River, New Jersey 07632

Printed in the United States of America
10 9 8 7 6 5 4 3 2 1

ISBN 0 8359-4944-3

PRENTICE-HALL INTERNATIONAL (UK) LIMITED, *London*
PRENTICE-HALL OF AUSTRALIA PTY. LIMITED, *Sidney*
PRENTICE-HALL CANADA, INC., *Toronto*
PRENTICE-HALL HISPANOAMERICANA, S.A., *Mexico*
PRENTICE-HALL OF INDIA PRIVATE LIMITED, *New Delhi*
PRENTICE-HALL OF JAPAN, INC., *Tokyo*
SIMON & SCHUSTER ASIA PTE. LTD., *Singapore*
EDITORA PRENTICE-HALL DO BRASIL, LTDA., *Rio de Janeiro*

Contents

Preface

Dental Assisting Test Preparation is designed to help the student study for examinations and specifically prepare for the Dental Assisting National Board Examination.

Each state mandates its regulations that relate to certification areas. Individuals may be certified in the area of Infection Control, Dental Radiation, Health and Safety, General Chairside, Oral Maxillofacial Surgery, Dental Practice Management, and Orthodontics.

This text offers an updated, comprehensive study manual that closely emulates the style and format of the Dental Assisting National Board. The review questions have been developed to broaden the student's knowledge in all aspects of dental auxiliary skills. In addition, an in-depth explanation of answers has been provided to reinforce the information.

A unique feature of this review text is that it includes a section in each chapter on Infection Control. In Chapter 1, disease transmission is covered through the interrelated areas of microbiology and sterilization. Aseptic techniques are discussed as they pertain to the practice of dentistry. Chairside assisting techniques provide the student with an overview of four-handed dentistry as it relates to the identification of instruments and their respective sequencing and subsequent tray set-ups. Questions are designed to enable the student to integrate effectively the theory of dental assisting with the practical application of various procedures. In addition, a charting exercise is included and related questions are presented to test the student's ability in this important area. Additionally, ethics and jurisprudence as it relates to dentistry will be discussed.

Chapter 2 presents a review of dental materials utilized in the office and laboratory. A highlight of this section includes the manipulation, properties, and usage of various materials such as esthetics, preventives, alloys, cements, impression materials, model and die materials, waxes, and prosthetics. Other content areas include questions pertaining to hazardous substances and infection control protocol in the dental laboratory.

Chapter 3 focuses on the theoretical as well as the practical aspects of dental radiography. Questions are designed to broaden the student's knowledge in the areas of radiation health and safety. In addition, methods for establishing quality control in radiology techniques are identified. A film-mounting exercise is provided to test student's skills in identifying anatomical landmarks, recognizing the various dental materials, and interpreting process and exposure errors.

The valuable information which is obtained from the patient's medical and dental history is emphasized for the prevention of medical emergencies which are covered in Chapter 4.

A distinctive feature of this text is that it offers an in-depth review of OSHA or the Occupational Safety and Health Administration's regulations that pertain to dental personnel. It provides information with regard to legal issues regarding the Bloodborne Pathogens Standard that was issued by OSHA in December of 1991. Chapter 5 is designed in a question and answer-type format to enhance the student's knowledge in this area.

Chapter 6 focuses on dental education and oral physiotherapy. Specific topics such as pre- and post-operative instruction, dental home care—which includes brushing and flossing techniques—hydrotherapy, and assorted oral hygiene aids are covered in this section. In addition, nutrition as it relates to oral health as well as preventive fluoride are discussed.

The practical aspects of dental office management are discussed in Chapter 7. A wide variety of questions have been presented to broaden the student's knowledge in such areas as communication and reception protocol, business records, bookkeeping and accounts receivable, inventory control, dental insurance, and managing patient records.

A comprehensive review of record keeping and clinical data in the dental office is highlighted in Chapter 8. The preliminary oral examination, diagnostic aids, and vital signs documentation is presented.

Dental Assisting Test Preparation provides the student with a complete overview of all aspects of dental assisting. It is our sincere hope that this text will enhance your understanding of dental auxiliary theory and applied tasks relating to assisting skills.

Dental Assisting Test Preparation has been designed to assist you in preparing for the Dental Assisting National Board Examination. This study manual offers the student a relevant perspective on dental assisting auxiliary skills that are required for a Certified Dental Assistant. There are more than 12,000 multiple choice and matching type questions included in this resource.

The book is divided into eight (8) chapters that closely correspond with the content area of the Dental Assisting National Board Examination. The chapters are:

1. Chairside Assisting
2. Dental Materials and Dental Laboratory Procedures
3. Dental Radiology
4. Medical Emergencies in the Dental Office
5. Occupational Safety
6. Dental Education and Oral Physiotherapy
7. Dental Office Management
8. Comprehensive Diagnosis and Treatment Planning

TEST QUESTION FORMAT

There are four basic types of multiple choice questions on DANB Certification Examinations: One Best Answer, Negative Format, Matching, and k-Type (Complex Multiple Choice). Here are some suggestions on how to best answer each question type.

One Best Answer

In these questions, the item stem is followed by several responses, including one that is the only absolutely correct answer, or the best or most correct of the choices offered.

Hints:
1. Attempt to select the correct answer directly. If this is not possible, attempt to determine the answer by eliminating the distractors.
2. Select the best answer of those provided, even though you may believe that there is another answer just as good or better, that is not included.
3. Read the question carefully. Do not add to or delete information provided. Do not read into items information that is not there, or construct situations that do not exist in the question as stated.

DIRECTIONS: In each of the following questions, select the one choice that answers the question or completes the sentence best.

1. If the dentist moves from the 9:00 o'clock to the 11:00 o'clock position to improve access and visibility, the dental assistant should
   A. change from the 11:00 to the 9:00 position
   B. remain in the 6:00 position
   C. change from the 3:00 position to the 6:00 position
   D. remain in the 3:00 position

Negative Format

These questions are used when several correct answers exist for a given question, but the exception (i.e., what is NOT true) is important to know. The stem of the question is followed by several correct responses, and one response that is not correct, or is the exception to the rule. The examinee should select this exception.

Hints:

1. Pay attention to words in the stem that are underlined, capitalized, or italicized.
2. Remember all the while that you are looking for the *exception,* not the correct answer. Sometimes it is difficult to keep this "reverse logic" in mind in a testing situation!

DIRECTIONS: In the following questions select the one choice that is not correct or is the exception to the rule.

2. All of the following will result in the sterilization of an instrument EXCEPT
   A. autoclave
   B. dry heat
   C. Chemiclave
   D. isopropyl alcohol

Matching

In these questions, the examinee is asked to match an item in Column A with its function or verbal or pictorial description in Column B. As this is a type of "One Best Answer" question, the hints in that section apply here as well.

DIRECTIONS: Match each instrument in Column A with its primary use in Column B.

Column A	**Column B**
3. Rongeur forceps	A. Used to place medication into root sockets

4. Periosteal elevator	B. Used to smooth alveolar process to promote healing
5. Bone file	C. Used to lift and raise mucous membrane and underlying tissue covering bone
	D. Used to remove small bone particles and bone processes after extraction
	E. Used to remove pathologic tissue and spicules of bone

DIRECTIONS: Match the orthodontic devices in Column A with their functions in Column B.

Column A	Column B
6. Archwire	A. Stabilizes treated teeth
7. Ligature wire	B. Secures archwire to molars
	C. Directs tooth movement
	D. Secures headgear to archwire
	E. Ties archwire to teeth

k-Type (Complex Multiple Choice)

In these items, the question stem is followed by four responses, at least one of which is correct. The examinee is directed to fill in only ONE circle on the answer sheet, as follows:

Choose A if only 1, 2, and 3 are correct.
          B if only 1 and 3 are correct.
          C if only 2 and 4 are correct.
          D if only 4 is correct.
          E if all are correct.

DIRECTIONS: For each of the questions or incomplete statements, ONE or MORE of the answers or completions given is correct. On the answer sheet fill in the circle that corresponds to the choices listed below.

          A if only 1, 2, and 3 are correct.
          B if only 1 and 3 are correct.
          C if only 2 and 4 are correct.
          D if only 4 is correct.
          E if all are correct.

FILL IN ONLY ONE CIRCLE ON YOUR ANSWER SHEET
FOR EACH QUESTION.

DIRECTIONS SUMMARIZED

A	B	C	D	E
1,2,3 Only	1,3 Only	2,4 Only	4 Only	All are correct

These questions are printed together in a separate section of the exam, with separate directions. The summarized directions appear at the top of each exam page that contains k-type questions, so you do not have to memorize the combinations.

Hints:

1. Familiarizing yourself with this item type response pattern before you sit for the examination will help you to deal with these items primarily on the basis of their content rather than the answer patterns allowed. It might be helpful to mark each option as "true" (+), "false" (-), or "unsure" (0) in your question booklet. Once you have looked at each option, the answer pattern should become apparent.
2. The process of elimination can be helpful in narrowing the field of response options. That is, only pay attention to the answer combinations that contain a response you think is correct.
3. Only fill in ONE circle on your answer sheet for each required response!

Note that the majority of questions on DANB Certification Exams are "One Best Answer" format. Negative variety and k-type questions are limited.

8. Limitations of radiographs in the detection of dental caries include
    1. inability to locate incipient pit and fissure caries
    2. difficult differentiation of buccal and lingual caries
    3. shadows at cemento-enamel junction
    4. lack of interproximal caries visibility

9. Following gingival surgery, which of the following can slow the rate of healing of the tissues?
    1. The use of alcohol and tobacco
    2. Physical and emotional stress
    3. Dietary deficiencies
    4. Diabetes mellitus

Answer Key

1. D
2. D
3. D
4. C
5. B
6. C
7. E
8. A
9. E

EXPLANATION OF THE TEXT
QUESTION AND ANSWER FORMAT

This book presents the question and answer type format which enables the student to select the correct answer. It would be beneficial for the student to review the detailed explanation that corresponds to the question to reinforce the correct information, data, and facts. In addition, the candidate may want to refer to the Dental Assisting National Board Examination application for a listing of reference materials.

HELPFUL HINTS FOR TEXT UTILIZATION

It is imperative that the student follow the directions that are given within the respective chapter for each of the content areas. Some sections will include a variety of question and answer types. (See earlier discussion of Test Question Format.)

Remember, you may use *Dental Assisting Test Preparation* as a mock exam review and/or as a study guide in preparation for the Dental Assisting National Board Examination.

We, the authors, wish you success in your professional career as a dental auxiliary.

ADDITIONAL INFORMATION

Requests for additional information or questions pertaining to the Dental Assisting National Board may be addressed to:

Dental Assisting National Board, Inc.
216 East Ontario Street
Chicago, Illinois 60611.

1

Chairside Assisting

CHAPTER OUTLINE

DIRECTIONS (Questions 1 through 42): In each of the following questions, select the one choice that answers the question or completes the sentence best.

I. Application of four- and six-handed dentistry techniques

1. The most common movements that are utilized by the operator and auxiliary involve:
   A. Movements of only the fingers
   B. Movements of the fingers and wrist
   C. Movements of the fingers, wrist, and elbow
   D. All of the above
   E. Only A and B

2. The functions of the dental mouth mirror include:
   A. Absorption of light
   B. Reflection of light
   C. Retraction of the cheeks and lips
   D. Retraction and control of the tongue
   E. All of the above

3. When the operator is seated at the ten o'clock position, the auxiliary can work most efficiently when seated at the _____ o'clock position.
   A. 1 to 3
   B. 2 to 3
   C. 1 to 4
   D. 2 to 4

4. What are the first two instruments that the auxiliary passes to the operator once the patient has been seated, bibbed, and positioned in the dental chair?
   A. Mouth mirror and explorer
   B. Explorer and cotton forceps
   C. Mouth mirror and cotton forceps
   D. Explorer and periodontal probe

5. The basic tray setup for all operative procedures includes:
   A. Mouth mirror

B. Explorer
C. Cotton pliers or cotton forceps
D. All of the above

6. When the chairside auxiliary prepares a tray setup, he or she places instruments:
   A. In the order of their use
   B. According to the dental assistant's preference
   C. In relation to their size
   D. In random sequence

7. A randomly prepared tray setup presents the following problems:
   A. Instruments for the procedure may be missing
   B. Instruments need to be located
   C. Instruments appear to be in disorder on the tray
   D. All of the above

8. The auxiliary's hands should be well groomed. Professional appearance of the nails requires that they be:
   A. Short, clean, and manicured
   B. Polished with red nail lacquer
   C. Preferably not polished
   D. Only A and B
   E. Only A and C

9. Six-handed dentistry requires the utilization of a:
   A. Chairside assistant
   B. Business assistant
   C. Laboratory assistant
   D. Coordinating assistant

10. During the treatment of a patient, if it is necessary to retrieve an item from a cabinet drawer, what precautionary measures should be followed to prevent cross-contamination?
    A. Plastic overglove may be worn
    B. Sterile gauze square may be utilized to open a drawer
    C. A cotton glove may be worn
    D. Only A and B
    E. All of the above

11. The foot and backrest controls are adjusted:
    A. After donning gloves, prior to performing the procedure
    B. Before donning gloves
    C. After washing hands and before performing the procedure
    D. None of the above

12. When the operator is seated correctly, he or she should:
    A. Have the shoulders parallel to the floor
    B. Be seated so the knees are a little above hip level
    C. Be able to focus at a distance of approximately 4 inches from his or her eyes to the patient's mouth
    D. Be positioned so his or her back is straight
    E. All of the above

13. When the auxiliary is seated correctly, he or she should:
    A. Be in a comfortable position, at least 4 to 5 inches higher than the operator
    B. Adjust the stool so that the back and buttocks are supported
    C. Maintain his or her feet firmly on the circular platform at the base of the stool
    D. Swing the arch extension from the back of the stool to the front to provide support in the abdomen
    E. All of the above

14. The methods utilized by the dentist to cool the tooth when using the high-speed handpiece during operative procedures include:
    A. Air
    B. Water
    C. Combined slurry of air and water
    D. All of the above
    E. Only A and B

15. How far away from the patient's oral cavity should the light be positioned?
    A. 12 inches

B. 24 inches
C. 36 inches
D. 48 inches

16. The lens of the operating light should be cared for by:
    A. Wiping it free of smudges after completion of dental procedures
    B. Cleansing with a mild detergent and a soft cloth
    C. Washing only when the lens is cool
    D. Only A and B
    E. All of the above

17. The fourth and little fingers rest on a tooth surface to maintain stability and enable the operator to utilize the instrument so as to avoid injury to the patient. This support is known as a:
    A. Guide
    B. Guard
    C. Fulcrum
    D. None of the above

18. The instrument to be delivered is positioned _____ to the instrument being returned.
    A. Parallel
    B. Above
    C. Below
    D. Beside

19. The auxiliary delivers and retrieves instruments with the _____ hand when assisting the right-handed operator.
    A. Right
    B. Left
    C. Right or left
    D. All of the above

20. When assisting a left-handed operator, the auxiliary delivers and retrieves instruments with the _____ hand.
    A. Left
    B. Right
    C. Right or left
    D. None of the above

21. When utilizing four-handed dentistry with the right-handed operator, the

auxiliary should be seated at the _____ o'clock position.

A. 12 to 2
B. 7 to 12
C. 4 to 7
D. 2 to 3

22. The exchange of an instrument from the auxiliary to the operator is completed by utilizing the:

A. Thumb and four fingers
B. Thumb, index, and third fingers
C. Thumb and index finger
D. Entire hand

23. The operator is able to convey to the auxiliary that he or she wishes to initiate an instrument transfer by maintaining a fulcrum and rotating the hand away from the patient's oral cavity.

A. True
B. False

24. The oral evacuation tip is held by utilizing the "modified pen" grasp and the:

A. Pen grasp
B. Reverse palm-thumb grasp
C. Reverse pen grasp
D. None of the above

25. If the operator is restoring the mandibular right first molar, the auxiliary should position the tip of the aspirator on the:

A. Buccal surface in front of the tooth to be prepared
B. Palatal surface behind the tooth to be prepared
C. Lingual surface of the mandibular right quadrant
D. Opposing arch

26. If the operator is restoring the maxillary left second molar, the auxiliary positions the high-volume evacuation tip toward the:

A. Facial surface of the maxillary left second molar
B. Lingual surface of the maxillary left second molar
C. Facial surface of the mandibular left second molar
D. Lingual surface of the mandibular left second molar

27. When working in the posterior area of the oral cavity, the auxiliary positions the high-volume evacuation tip:

A. At the gingival third of the tooth being prepared
B. At the occlusal third of the tooth being prepared
C. Parallel to the buccal or lingual surface of the tooth being prepared
D. Near the tooth that is being prepared
E. Only B, C, and D

28. When suction is required in the maxillary right molar area, the auxiliary positions the high-volume evacuation tip toward the:

A. Palatal surface of the maxillary right molar area
B. Facial surface of the maxillary right molar area
C. Facial surface of the maxillary central incisors
D. Lingual surface of the mandibular central incisors

29. Which instrument is not utilized in the placement of a Class II amalgam restoration?

A. Amalgam carrier
B. Amalgam condenser
C. Spoon excavator
D. Matrix band and retainer

30. When placing a Class II restoration, the missing wall will be replaced by the use of a _____ and a _____.

A. Space maintainer
B. Wooden wedge
C. Matrix band
D. Rubber dam
E. Only B and C

31. The function of hand-cutting instruments in operative dentistry is:
    A. Removing carious material from the cavity preparation
    B. Refining cavity preparations
    C. Trimming excess material from the restoration
    D. All of the above

II. Selection and organization of armamentarium

32. The design of the handle of the hand-cutting instrument is _____ to give stabilization for grip and leverage to the operator.
    A. Octagonal
    B. Hexagonal
    C. Pentagonal
    D. Tetragonal

33. Instruments that are classified as hand-cutting instruments include the:
    A. Mirror, explorer, and chisel
    B. Mirror, explorer, spoon excavator, and Vehe
    C. Hatchet, hoe, spoon excavator, gingival margin trimmer, and explorer
    D. Hatchet, hoe, spoon excavator, discoid/cleoid, gingival margin trimmer, and chisel

34. Carving instruments are classified as:
    A. Discoid/cleoid, gingival margin trimmer, and chisel
    B. Discoid/cleoid, Frahm, Vehe, Ward, and Hollenback
    C. Discoid/cleoid, Ward, Frahm, and spoon excavator
    D. Discoid/cleoid, Vehe, Frahm, and hatchet

35. The _____ is utilized to remove carious dentin in the cavity preparation.
    A. Discoid/cleoid
    B. Spoon excavator
    C. Gingival margin trimmer
    D. Angle former

36. The _____ reduces excess amalgam from the interproximal area.
    A. Hoe
    B. Explorer
    C. Chisel
    D. Amalgam file

37. The _____-angled handpiece is utilized to polish restorations.
    A. Contra
    B. Straight
    C. Ultraspeed
    D. Right

38. A round bur is identified by the numbers:
    A. 700 to 708
    B. 556 to 564
    C. 33½ to 37
    D. ½ to 9

39. Which numbers designate an inverted cone bur?
    A. ½ to 9
    B. 33½ to 37
    C. 556 to 558
    D. 700 to 701

40. The _____ places pressure on undermined enamel. It is utilized with a "push" motion.
    A. Hoe
    B. Hatchet
    C. Chisel
    D. Gingival margin trimmer

41. The Wedelstaedt chisel is designed with:
    A. Slight curve in the shank
    B. Straight shank
    C. Two angles in the shank
    D. Contra-angled shank

42. The hand instrument utilized to carve occlusal surface anatomy on an amalgam restoration is the:
    A. Spoon excavator
    B. Hollenback carver
    C. Discoid/cleoid
    D. Both B and C

DIRECTIONS (Questions 43-77): Match the instrument in Column A with its respective function in Column B:

Column A

43. ___ Matrix band

44. ___ Gingival margin trimmer

45. ___ Amalgam condenser

46. ___ Discoid/cleoid carver

47. ___ Amalgam carrier

Column B

A. Places amalgam in the cavity preparation

B. Compresses amalgam into the cavity preparation

C. Removes undermined enamel

D. Limits the filling material to the confines of the tooth

E. Shapes the amalgam restoration

Column A

48. ___ Celluloid matrix strip

49. ___ Articulating paper

50. ___ Hollenback carver

51. ___ Mouth mirror

52. ___ Wooden wedge

Column B

A. Utilized with the matrix band to prevent gingival overhangs

B. Used to determine high spots when a restoration has been placed in the oral cavity

C. Limits the filling materials to the confines of the tooth

D. Shapes an amalgam restoration and restores original anatomy to the tooth surface

E. Used to reflect light and to magnify objects in the oral cavity

Column A

53. ___ Burnisher

54. ___ Spoon excavator

55. ___ Plastic instrument

56. ___ College pliers or forceps

57. ___ Chisel

Column B

A. Removes carious material

B. Adapts margins of restorations

C. Utilized to insert composite filling material

D. Removes undermined enamel

E. Holds medicated cotton pledgets

Column A

58. ___ Broach

59. ___ Reamer

60. ___ File

61. ___ Paper points

62. ___ Luer-lok syringe

Column B

A. Enlarges the canal

B. Extirpates the vital pulp

C. Carries irrigating solution to the canal

D. Enlarges, shapes, and smooths the root canal

E. Absorbs moisture in the root canal

Column A

63. ___ Periodontal pocket marker

64. ___ Sickle scaler

65. ___ Jaquette scaler

66. ___ Hoe scaler

67. ___ File scaler

Column B

A. Removes calculus from either the lingual or facial surfaces of the posterior teeth

B. Smooths the tooth surfaces at the cemento-enamel junction

C. Scales supragingival calculus from the anterior teeth

D. Removes supra- and subgingival calculus from the posterior teeth

E. Measures the depth of the sulcus

Column A

68. ___ T-band

69. ___ Mouthguard

70. ___ Space maintainer

71. ___ Bite plane
72. ___ Splint

Column B

A. Retains traumatized teeth in an approximation of their normal position

B. Maintains a space until the normal eruption of a permanent tooth occurs

C. Custom matrix band that is adaptable to a child's prepared tooth

D. Protects the teeth from accidental injury

E. Encourages a lingual verted tooth into correct normal alignment

Column A

73. ___ Extraoral headgear
74. ___ Elastic bands

75. ___ Retainer

76. ___ Palatal bow
77. ___ Cervical strap

Column B

A. Form of simple anchorage

B. Maintains the position of the teeth after orthodontic treatment is completed

C. Used for anteriorly positioned first maxillary molars along with a rapidly growing maxilla

D. Form of extraoral anchorage

E. Form of intraoral anchorage

DIRECTIONS (Questions 78 through 105): In each of the following questions, select the one choice that answers the question or completes the sentence best.

78. A cavity preparation on the gingival third of the lingual surface of a maxillary left second molar is an example of a _____ cavity preparation.
   A. Class III
   B. Class IV
   C. Class V
   D. Class VI

79. A cavity preparation that includes the mesial incisal angle of the maxillary right central incisor is classified as a _____ cavity preparation.
   A. Class I
   B. Class II
   C. Class III
   D. Class IV

80. A cavity preparation that involves the mesial surface of the mandibular left central incisor is classified as a _____ cavity preparation.
   A. Class I
   B. Class II

   C. Class III
   D. Class IV

81. A restoration that involves the lingual surface of the maxillary right central incisor is classified as a _____ cavity preparation.
   A. Class I
   B. Class II
   C. Class IV
   D. Class V

82. An occlusal restoration on the mandibular left second premolar is classified as a _____ restoration.
   A. Class V
   B. Class III
   C. Class II
   D. Class I

83. An occlusal lingual restoration that is located on the maxillary right second molar is classified as a _____ restoration.
   A. Class I
   B. Class II
   C. Class IV
   D. Class V

84. A mesial occlusal cavity preparation on the maxillary right first molar is an example of a _____ cavity preparation.
   A. Class I
   B. Class II
   C. Class III
   D. Class IV

85. Which of the following explains the use of the Tofflemire matrix placed on a posterior tooth having a Class II, two- or three-surface cavity preparation?
   1. Provides for the contact area of amalgam restoration with adjacent teeth
   2. Provides a form for placing, condensing, and carving amalgam
   3. Adapts restorative materials to cavity preparations
   4. Provides a configuration for amalgam restoration at the junction of the tooth preparation and the restorative material
   A. 1, 2, and 3
   B. 1, 2, 3, and 4
   C. 2 and 3
   D. 3 and 4

86. A mesial-occlusal-distal amalgam restoration has been placed in the mandibular left second molar. This is an example of a _____ restoration.
   A. Class I
   B. Class II
   C. Class III
   D. Class IV

87. _____ is the trade name of the vasoconstrictor that may be added to certain types of local anesthetics that are administered to the dental patient prior to operative procedures.
   A. Benzocaine
   B. Epinephrine
   C. Metaphen
   D. Benedryl

88. Common topical anesthetic compounds include:
   A. Xylocaine, 5%
   B. Pontocaine, 1 to 2%
   C. Ethyl chloride
   D. Benzocaine
   E. All of the above

89. Toxicity is the adverse effect of anesthesia.
   A. True
   B. False

90. _____ anesthesia is a compound that is applied to the oral mucosa and, when absorbed, gives temporary anesthesia to peripheral nerve endings in the surface of the tissue.
   A. Local
   B. Topical
   C. General
   D. None of the above

91. The action of a local anesthetic will continue until the concentration is carried away by the bloodstream. The organ that dissipates the anesthesia is the _____.
   A. Kidney
   B. Liver
   C. Small intestine
   D. Large intestine

92. The hub is the bulbous portion of the needle. It provides a stop to hold the needle in the syringe during the expelling of the anesthetic solution.
   A. True
   B. False

93. The shorter needle length (1 inch) is usually used for _____ or _____ injections, and the longer length is utilized for _____ injections.
   A. Posterior/block/infiltration
   B. Posterior/infiltration/block
   C. Anterior/infiltration/block
   D. Anterior/block/infiltration

94. A vasoconstrictor is a substance that is

placed in an anesthetic compound to:
A. Retain the action of the anesthesia
B. Reduce the tendency for bleeding
C. Reduce the danger of systemic toxicity
D. All of the above
E. Only B and C

95. The red color-coded stopper on the carpule of anesthesia indicates that the epinephrine ratio is _____, which is utilized for the majority of routine dental treatments.
A. 1:50,000
B. 1:100,000
C. 1:150,000
D. 1:125,000

96. The hypodermic needle is made of _____ or _____:
A. Stainless steel/platinum
B. Stainless steel/titanium
C. Platinum/titanium
D. Tungsten carbide/platinum

97. The aspirating syringe differs from the nonaspirating syringe in that it has a:
A. Metal thumb ring
B. Hub
C. Harpoon
D. Only A and B

98. The most anxiety-producing procedure in dentistry is:
A. Removal of the Tofflemire retainer and matrix band
B. Placement of the rubber dam
C. Use of the high-speed evacuator
D. Administration of local anesthesia

99. Preparation of the anesthetic syringe by the auxiliary includes (1) engaging the harpoon, (2) placement of the carpule, (3) placing the anesthetic in the carpule, (4) placement of the topical anesthetic, (5) loosening of the cap covering the needle.
A. 1, 2, and 3
B. 1, 2, and 5

C. 2, 4, and 5
D. 3, 4, and 5

100. When administering a block injection to the patient in the mandibular arch, which nerve does the dentist want to anesthetize?
A. Optic nerve
B. Vagus nerve
C. Trigeminal nerve
D. Inferior alveolar nerve

101. During the administration of local anesthesia, aspiration of the dental syringe by the operator will:
A. Damage the mandibular artery
B. Be extremely painful
C. Determine if the lumen of the needle is in a blood vessel
D. Insure profound anesthesia

102. Local anesthetics that contain a vaso constrictor are contraindicated for those patients who have the following systemic conditions:
A. Hyperthyroidism
B. Hypertension
C. History of heart disease
D. Asthma
E. All of the above

103. Local anesthetics that do not contain a vasoconstrictor include:
A. Xylocaine
B. Carbocaine
C. Benzocaine
D. Only A and B

104. The most effective procedure for handling sharps is a:
A. One-handed recapping technique
B. Device for protecting the hand
C. Sterile gauze covering
D. All of the above
E. Only A and B

105. The patient may experience a toxic reaction to a local anesthetic. These reactions include:
A. Contact dermatitis

B. Asthma

C. Anaphylaxis

D. Only A and B

E. All of the above

DIRECTIONS (Questions 106-109): Match the lettered illustrations on page 11 with the respective questions.

III. General and specialty instruments

106. The basic instruments for any examination of a dental patient are:

    A. b, a, and f

    B. a, b, and j

    C. a, b, and d

    D. c, f, and k

107. Aside from the basic instruments, identify the other instruments used on an adult patient during prophylaxis to polish the teeth.

    A. a, b, and j

    B. k, c, and g

    C. g, c, and b

    D. h, i, and j

108. Identify the dappen dish, periodontal probe, and cotton pellets.

    A. b, l, and c

    B. h, d, and i

    C. f, j, and k

    D. f, c, and g

109. Identify the prophylaxis scaler, dental floss, and right-angle handpiece.

    A. m, h, and d

    B. n, b, and a

    C. l, i, and a

    D. k, e, and j

DIRECTIONS (Questions 110-115): Match the lettered illustrations on page 12 with the respective questions.

110. Identify the Frahm carver, straight chisel, and cement spatula.

    A. b, l, and g

    B. i, b, and d

    C. f, k, and m

    D. e, i, and j

111. Identify the instrument used to trim temporary crowns.

    A. e

    B. f

    C. h

    D. i

112. Identify the amalgam carrier, amalgam condenser, and spoon excavator.

    A. c, e, and n

    B. c, e, and i

    C. h, b, and d

    D. o, k, and i

113. Identify the crown scissors, discoid/cleoid, and enamel hatchet:

    A. a, d, and f

    B. p, f, and k

    C. p, d, and f

    D. h, f, and k

114. Identify the Tofflemire matrix band, Tofflemire matrix retainer, and plastic instrument.

    A. n, o, and d

    B. n, o, and b

    C. n, j, and c

    D. a, o, and n

115. Identify the ward carver, wedelstaet chisel, and straight chisel.

    A. m, h, and q

    B. m, p, and l

    C. m, b, and q

    D. m, c, and d

DIRECTIONS (Questions 116-121): Match the lettered illustrations on page 13 with the respective questions.

116. Which of the following instruments would be included in the tray setup for the removal of a maxillary cuspid?

    A. i, a, l, and e

    B. m, f, d, and e

    C. k, d, e, and a

    D. n, d, e, and a

117. Which of the following instruments would be included in the tray setup

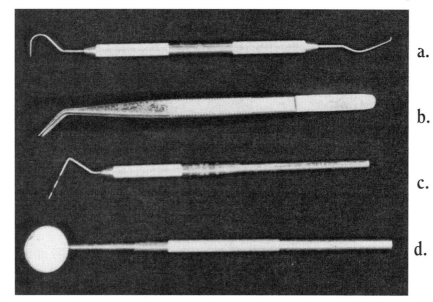

a.

b.

c.

d.

e.

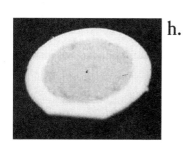

h.

f.   g.

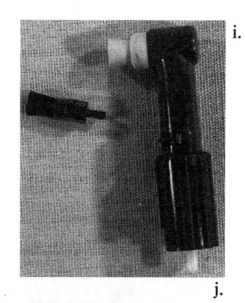

i.

j.

k.

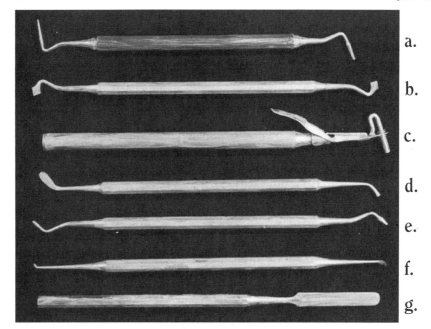

a.

b.

c.

d.

e.

f.

g.

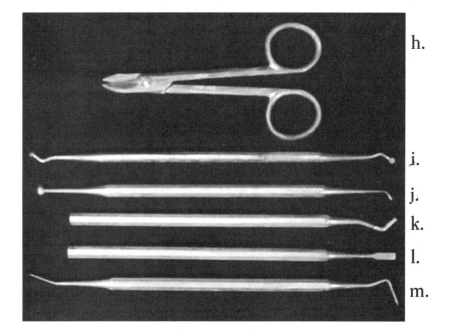

h.

i.

j.

k.

l.

m.

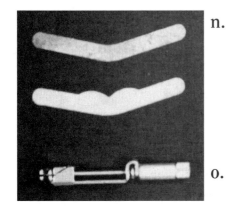

n.

o.

p.

q.

Chapter 1   **Chairside Assisting**

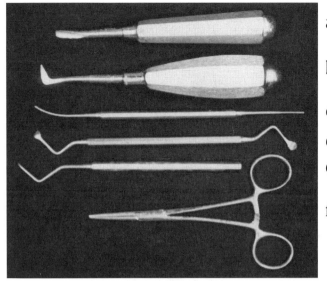

a.

b.

c.

d.

e.

f.

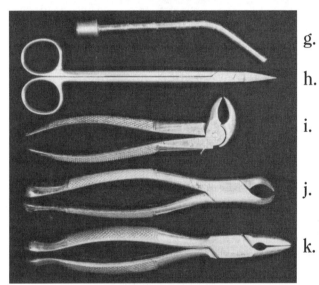

g.

h.

i.

j.

k.

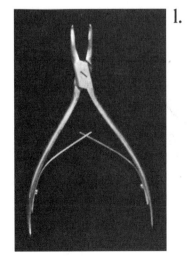

l.

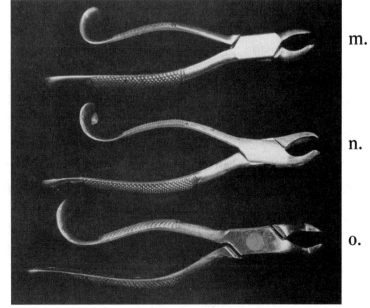

m.

n.

o.

for a simple extraction of a mandibular molar?

A. j, b, c, and l
B. n, e, c, and a
C. m, b, c, and l
D. i, d, e, and b

118. Identify the surgical curette and a Cryer root elevator.

A. a and e
B. b and f
C. d and b
D. a and f

119. Identify the straight elevator, hemostat, and gauze packer.

A. b, f, and c
B. a, g, and c
C. b, f, and h
D. a, f, and c

120. Identify the instrument that would be utilized to extract the maxillary third molar.

A. n
B. o
C. m
D. k

121. Identify the instrument that would be utilized to cut bone during surgical procedures.

A. d
B. c
C. f
D. o
E. l

DIRECTIONS (Questions 122-131): Match the lettered illustrations on page 15 with the respective questions.

122. Select a latch-type contra-angle handpiece and its corresponding bur.

A. c and d
B. a and o
C. a and b
D. c and t

123. Identify an ultraspeed handpiece and its corresponding bur.

A. a and b
B. a and d
C. c and d
D. c and b

124. Identify a round bur, an inverted cone bur, and a straight fissure plain cut bur.

A. e, g, and m
B. e, g, and k
C. e, k, and h
D. e, f, and g

125. Identify a cross-cut tapered bur, a round diamond bur, and a mandrel:

A. h, r, and v
B. l, r, and v
C. k, r, and v
D. f, o, and v

126. Identify a cross-cut tapered bur.

A. g
B. f
C. j
D. h
E. i

127. Identify a round bur.

A. h
B. j
C. i
D. m
E. e

128. Identify an inverted cone bur.

A. e
B. g
C. f
D. h
E. j

129. Identify a wheel bur.

A. k
B. m
C. l
D. j
E. f

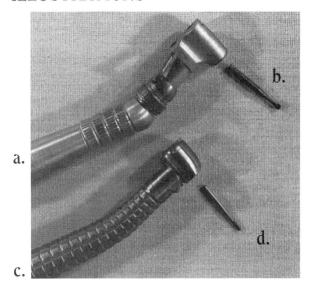

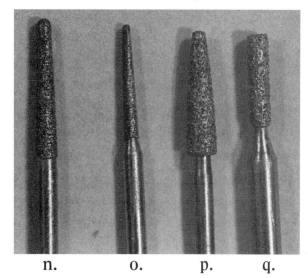

n.   o.   p.   q.

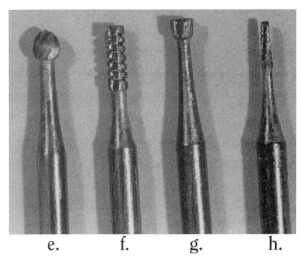

e.   f.   g.   h.

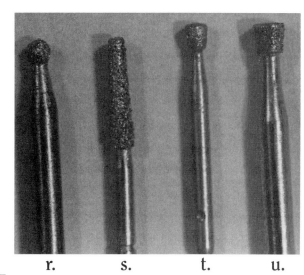

r.   s.   t.   u.

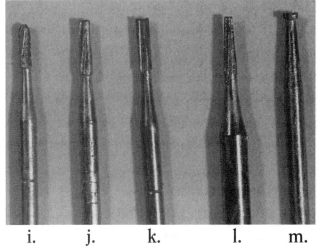

i.   j.   k.   l.   m.

v.

130. Identify a fine-cut tapered fissure bur.
A. l
B. j
C. h
D. f
E. k

131. Identify a round nose cross-cut fissure bur.
A. g
B. m
C. h
D. e
E. i

DIRECTIONS (Questions 132-139): Match the lettered illustrations on page 17 with the respective questions.

132. Identify a file, a reamer, and a Kentucky spreader.
A. g, f, and a
B. f, a, and g
C. f, g, and a
D. g, a, and f

133. Identify a rubber dam punch, a rubber dam forceps, and a rubber dam frame.
A. i, j, and h
B. i, k, and h
C. j, i, and h
D. i, a, and h

134. Identify a maxillary molar clamp and a universal clamp for the labial surfaces of the anterior teeth.
A. b and c
B. b and d
C. d and e
D. e and a

135. Identify a local anesthetic syringe.
A. k
B. h
C. j
D. i
E. a

136. Identify a winged rubber dam clamp that would be utilized for the maxillary and mandibular bicuspid.
A. d
B. b
C. e
D. c

137. Identify the universal clamp that is utilized for labial surfaces of anterior teeth.
A. c
B. e
C. b
D. d

138. Identify a rubber dam punch.
A. i
B. j
C. h
D. a

139. Identify a Kentucky spreader.
A. f
B. a
C. g
D. j

DIRECTIONS (Questions 140 through 234): In each of the following questions, select the one choice that answers the question or completes the sentence best.

140. Antibiotics may be prescribed prior to endodontic treatment if the patient has:
A. Moderate swelling
B. An elevated temperature
C. Nodular involvement
D. Poor drainage
E. All of the above

141. The pulp chamber and canals may be irrigated with:
A. Sodium hypochlorite
B. Hydrogen peroxide (3%)
C. Glutaraldehyde
D. Only A and B
E. Only B and C

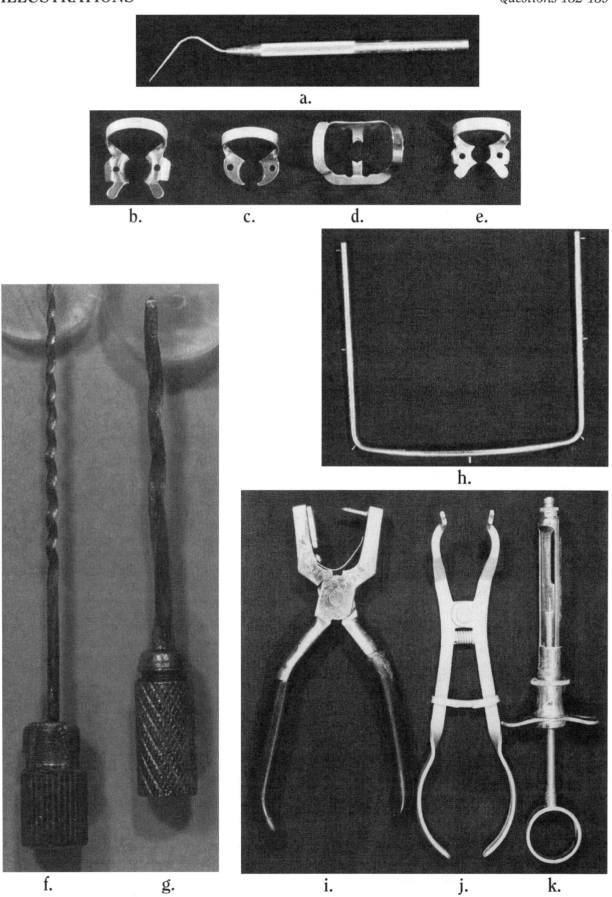

a.

b.   c.   d.   e.

h.

f.   g.   i.   j.   k.

142. The time-temperature ratio for steril izing instruments with the glass bead sterilizer is:
   A. 250°F for 5 to 10 seconds
   B. 450°F for 10 to 12 seconds
   C. 320°F for 8 to 10 seconds
   D. 360°F for 6 to 8 seconds

143. Gates-Glidden drills are rotary cutting instruments that attach to:
   A. Slow-speed contra-angled hand pieces
   B. Friction-grip straight handpieces
   C. High-speed contra-angled hand pieces
   D. Only A and B

144. The transillumination fiberoptic light may be placed on the lingual of the anterior tooth so the operator may view:
   A. Size of the roots
   B. Difference in the degree of translucency from one tooth to another
   C. Fractures
   D. Depth of alveolar bone
   E. Only B and C

145. When the auxiliary exposes a radiograph for endodontic diagnosis, the resulting picture should:
   A. Provide an accurate representation of the periapical area
   B. Be dimensionally accurate
   C. Be free of cone cuts
   D. All of the above

146. Subjective symptoms that may be felt by the endodontic patient may include:
   A. Pain
   B. Pressure
   C. Nausea
   D. All of the above
   E. Only A and C

147. By utilizing percussion, the operator can:
   A. Gently tap the tooth and sur-rounding teeth with a firm object
   B. Arrive at a diagnosis because inflamed tissues will provide discomfort for the patient
   C. Fracture a tooth root
   D. Only A and B
   E. Only A and C

148. If the operator places a piece of ice on a tooth and the patient states the pain is relieved, then usually the diagnosis is:
   A. Acute pulpalgia
   B. Exposed dentin
   C. Fractured tooth
   D. Pericoronal abscess

149. If the vitalometer registers 10 and the patient has not reacted to the electrical stimulus, then it would appear that the pulp is:
   A. Hyperactive
   B. Hypoactive
   C. Necrotic
   D. Only A and C

150. When a piece of ice is applied to the tooth surface and immediately followed by a stimulus of heat, and the patient perceives pain, then it would appear that the pulp is:
   A. Abscessed
   B. Normal
   C. Both A and B
   D. Only A

151. Pulpectomy is the:
   A. Surgical removal of the vital pulp from a tooth
   B. Partial excision of the dental pulp
   C. Surgical removal of the apex of the tooth
   D. None of the above

152. During an apicoectomy, the apex is retrofilled with:
   A. Composite resin
   B. Amalgam
   C. Gold
   D. Acrylic

153. At the final filling appointment, a cement is placed on the canal walls and on the apical third of the master cone.
    A. True
    B. False

154. When the assistant is exposing radiographs on the periodontal patient, it is extremely important that each film represents a true periapical projection of the teeth and the alveolus.
    A. True
    B. False

155. A periodontal probe is utilized to measure the depth of the sulcus. A normal sulcus reading is:
    A. 0 to 3 mm
    B. 4 to 6 mm
    C. 6 to 8 mm
    D. 8 to 10 mm

156. Suprabony pockets involve the:
    A. Alveolar bone as one wall of the pocket area
    B. Coronal portion above the level of the alveolar bone
    C. Lamina dura
    D. Only A and B

157. Treatment of periodontal pockets includes:
    A. Removing calculus, plaque, and bacteria with the use of instruments
    B. Cleaning an area or a pocket and removing the necrotic tissue in the area
    C. Smoothing and slightly contouring the root surface to remove the necrotic material found in the pocket
    D. All of the above
    E. Only A and B

158. After a gingivectomy, medication may be prescribed for the patient that includes:
    A. Analgesics
    B. Antibiotics

C. Both A and B
D. None of the above

159. Alcohol consumption is contraindicated after periodontal surgery.
    A. True
    B. False

160. Alveoplasty involves:
    A. Surgical reshaping of the gingivae and papillae
    B. Surgical reshaping of the alveolar bone
    C. Stabilizing periodontally involved teeth for additional support
    D. All of the above
    E. Only A and B

161. Pericoronitis is a condition caused by inflammation and infection of the gingival tissues surrounding the crown of the tooth. The teeth most commonly affected are:
    A. Mandibular central incisors
    B. Maxillary central incisors
    C. Mandibular third molars
    D. Maxillary third molars

162. Periodontal dressings may be purchased:
    A. With eugenol
    B. Without eugenol
    C. Both A and B
    D. None of the above

163. Acute necrotizing ulcerative gingivitis is a:
    A. Painful, progressive viral infection
    B. Painful, progressive bacterial infection
    C. Painful, progressive fungal infection
    D. None of the above

164. Osseous surgery may be:
    A. Additive
    B. Directive
    C. Subtractive
    D. Only A and C
    E. Only B and C

165. A periodontal abscess usually:
    A. Drains into a pocket area through a necrotic break in the tissue
    B. Involves the mandibular third molars
    C. Affects the apex of the tooth
    D. Involves periapical surgery

166. The postsurgical periodontal patient usually requires a strict oral hygiene regime that includes recall appointments scheduled every:
    A. 1 to 2 months
    B. 2 to 3 months
    C. 3 to 4 months
    D. 4 to 6 months

167. Drinking cold fluids for the first 24 hours will help keep a periodontal dressing firm.
    A. True
    B. False

168. In order to alleviate sensitivity for the periodontal patient, the dentist may prescribe a:
    A. Commercial desensitizing dentifrice
    B. 2% solution of sodium fluoride for brushing
    C. Mild saline rinse
    D. Only A and B
    E. Only B and C

169. The pediatric patient may be rewarded for good behavior after a dental appointment.
    A. True
    B. False

170. A medical history of the child patient includes:
    A. Parental information
    B. Prenatal and natal histories
    C. Postnatal and infancy histories
    D. All of the above

171. Pit and fissure sealants are indicated when:
    A. Deep pits and narrow fissures are present
    B. Fossae are wide and easy to clean
    C. Teeth are prone to caries
    D. Teeth are not prone to caries
    E. Only A and C

172. A radiographic survey for the pedodontic patient includes:
    A. Two bitewing films
    B. Two anterior periapical films
    C. Four posterior periapical films
    D. Two occlusal films
    E. All of the above

173. Barbiturates must be administered to the child _____ prior to dental treatment in order to be effective.
    A. 10 to 20 minutes
    B. 30 to 45 minutes
    C. 12 hours
    D. 24 hours

174. At the conclusion of dental treatment that involves an injection of local anesthesia, it is very important to make the child understand that:
    A. Cheek and tongue can be severely traumatized if bitten
    B. Cheek and tongue can be bitten with no resulting pain because they are anesthetized
    C. Local anesthetic affects the sensory nerves
    D. None of the above

175. Tranquilizers must be administered to the child _____ prior to dental treatment to be effective.
    A. 10 to 20 minutes
    B. 30 to 45 minutes
    C. 12 hours
    D. 24 hours

176. Prior to the application of a sealant, the tooth is cleared of debris and polished with a:
    A. Fluoridated dentrifice
    B. Fluoride-free abrasive
    C. None of the above

177. Anatomically, primary teeth differ from permanent teeth because:
    A. Enamel plate is thinner
    B. There are broad molar contacts
    C. Pulp chambers are larger and pulp horns are higher
    D. All of the above
    E. Only B and C

178. Matrices for the pedodontic patient include:
    A. T-band
    B. Ivory
    C. Tofflemire
    D. All of the above
    E. Only A and B

179. A tooth that is evulsed has been:
    A. Fractured
    B. Knocked free from the oral cavity
    C. Sealed with a sealant
    D. Restored with amalgam

180. Direct pulp capping encourages the formation of secondary dentin over the exposed pulp.
    A. True
    B. False

181. Various types of commercially pre-formed temporary crowns include:
    A. Tin-silver alloy
    B. Anodized aluminum
    C. Polycarbonate resin
    D. All of the above
    E. Only B and C

182. A vital pulpotomy involves:
    A. Placing a palliative dressing over sensitive or minutely exposed pulp
    B. Mechanical, radical removal of the vital portion of the tooth pulp
    C. Total surgical removal of an infected or traumatized pulp
    D. Only B and C
    E. None of the above

183. A bite plane encourages a lingual positioned tooth into normal facial alignment.
    A. True
    B. False

184. Librium and Ultran are:
    A. Sedatives
    B. Synthetic opiates
    C. Tranquilizers
    D. Only A and B
    E. Only B and C

185. The patient's role during orthodontic treatment includes:
    A. Keeping regular appointments
    B. Maintaining proper nutrition
    C. Practicing good oral hygiene
    D. Placing and removing elastics and headgear as directed by the dentist
    E. All of the above

186. Oral habits that may affect the dentition include:
    A. Tongue thrust swallowing
    B. Thumb and finger sucking
    C. Mouth breathing
    D. All of the above
    E. Only A and C

187. Malposed teeth and an unattractive smile may cause difficulty in psychological and social adjustments as a child matures.
    A. True
    B. False

188. Preventive orthodontic treatments involve:
    A. Taking steps to prevent or correct problems as they are developing
    B. Recognizing and eliminating irregularities and malpositions of the developing dentofacial complex
    C. Applying mechanical devices to restore the dentition
    D. Only A and C
    E. Only B and C

189. Orthodontic study casts may be taken with _____ impression material.
    A. Polysulfide
    B. Elastomeric

C. Hydrocolloid

D. Alginate

190. The material that is utilized to cement metal orthodontic bands is:
A. Zinc oxide-eugenol
B. Zinc phosphate
C. Polycarboxylate
D. None of the above

191. Extraoral anchorage is provided if the patient wears a:
A. Chin strap
B. Cervical strap
C. Only A or B
D. None of the above

192. Reciprocal force is the reaction that is produced by anchorage.
A. True
B. False

193. A patient's profile may exhibit a prominent mandible when the individual is classified as having a _____ occlusion.
A. Class I
B. Class II
C. Class III
D. None of the above

194. Resorption:
A. Is caused by compression of the periodontal ligament
B. Results in the development and deposition of new bone cells
C. Involves the stimulation of the osteoclast
D. Only A and C
E. Only B and C

195. In _____, the mesiobuccal cusp of the maxillary first permanent molar occludes in the buccal groove of the mandibular first molar.
A. Distoclusion
B. Neutroclusion
C. Mesioclusion
D. None of the above

196. Brackets may be bonded directly onto the facial surfaces of the teeth by utilization of an acid-etch technique to prepare the teeth.
A. True
B. False

197. _____ orthodontic treatment involves a full evaluation of the patient with the possibility of applying mechanical appliances to restore the dentition.
A. Interceptive
B. Preventive
C. Corrective
D. None of the above

198. A patient's profile may exhibit a prominent maxilla when the individual is classified as having _____.
A. Mesioclusion
B. Neutroclusion
C. Distoclusion
D. None of the above

199. _____ radiographs measure growth patterns of the cranial bones.
A. Periapical
B. Occlusal
C. Panoramic
D. Cephalometric

200. Antibiotics are often prescribed by the dentist either prior to and/or after oral surgery to control infection. Some common antibiotics of choice may include:
A. Penicillin
B. Erythromycin
C. Tetracycline
D. All of the above
E. Only A and B

201. Medication to control a patient's postoperative pain may include:
A. Codeine
B. Codeine and Tylenol
C. Tylenol
D. All of the above

202. After the first 24 hours, the patient may be instructed to rinse with a warm saline solution every 2 hours. The saline solution may be mixed at a ratio of:
    A. 1 teaspoon of salt to 8 ounces of warm water
    B. 1 tablespoon of salt to 4 ounces of warm water
    C. ½ teaspoon of salt to 8 ounces of warm water
    D. ½ tablespoon of salt to 4 ounces of warm water

203. To control swelling and promote slow circulation, a cold pack may be applied to the postsurgical patient's face for the first 24 hours in a cycle of:
    A. 10 minutes on and 10 minutes off
    B. 20 minutes on and 20 minutes off
    C. 20 minutes on and 10 minutes off
    D. 10 minutes on and 20 minutes off

204. A gauze pressure pack is placed over the socket for _____ minutes to control bleeding and encourage clot formation.
    A. 10
    B. 15
    C. 20
    D. 30

205. The postsurgical dental patient should be encouraged to drink large quantities of:
    A. Water
    B. Fruit juice
    C. Alcoholic beverages
    D. Carbonated beverages
    E. Only A and B

206. Alveolitis is the medical term for the condition known as:
    A. Surgical reshaping of the alveolus
    B. Dry socket
    C. Surgical reduction of the alveolar ridge
    D. None of the above

207. When performing the excision method to obtain a biopsy:
    A. Entire lesion is excised along with adjacent tissue
    B. Adjacent normal tissue and abnormal tissue are taken for comparison, and surgery is indicated if the tissue is malignant
    C. Deep-seated tumors are examined by exploring and taking a specimen through deep-seated surgical excision. The excision is closed, and the patient is informed if further surgery is required
    D. None of the above
    E. Only A and C

208. Pre- and postsurgical vitamin therapy for the patient may include:
    A. Vitamin C
    B. Vitamin E
    C. B-complex vitamins
    D. Only A and C

209. Signs and symptoms of a dry socket may include:
    A. Absence of a blood clot in an open bony socket
    B. Absence of granulation tissue
    C. Severe pain
    D. Grayish-colored tissue
    E. All of the above

210. An external heat pack applied after the first 24 hours _____ post-surgical healing:
    A. Increases
    B. Decreases

211. A frenectomy is a surgical procedure designed to:
    A. Cut bone
    B. Remove a lingual or labial frenum that is not attached correctly
    C. Enlarge a bony socket
    D. Reduce the alveolar ridge

212. An alveolectomy involves the surgical reduction and reshaping of the alveolar ridge.

A. True

B. False

213. Sedation may be administered by:

A. Intravenous injection

B. Intramuscular injection

C. Inhalation

D. All of the above

E. Only A and B

214. Preoperative instructions to the surgical patient who is scheduled to have general anesthesia include no food or water for _____ hours prior to arrival at the dental office.

A. 2 to 4

B. 4 to 6

C. 6 to 8

D. 14 to 16

215. Prior to constructing a removable dental prosthesis, the following intraoral factor must be considered:

A. Muscle attachment and tone

B. Salivary glands

C. Alveolar ridge

D. All of the above

E. Only A and C

216. The framework for a removable partial denture:

A. Provides support for the saddle and connectors

B. Relieves the abutment teeth from excessive occlusal load and stress

C. Retains the artificial teeth

D. Controls the "seating" of a prosthesis

217. Porcelain teeth:

A. Do not produce a clicking sound

B. Produce a clicking sound

C. Wear under occlusion

D. Only B and C

218. When selecting the shade and mold of an artificial tooth, the dentist considers the:

A. Age and body size of the patient

B. Lip length of the patient

C. Space to be occupied by the artificial tooth

D. All of the above

219. The components of a removable partial denture include the:

A. Bar

B. Saddle

C. Clasps

D. All of the above

E. Only A and B

220. _____ are utilized to support and provide stability to the removable partial prosthesis. They are designed for resiliency and flexibility.

A. Rests

B. Clasps

C. Precision attachments

D. None of the above

221. Rests are metal projections on or near the clasps of a partial denture. They control the "seating" of the prosthesis as well as:

A. Provide support for the saddle and connectors

B. Relieve the abutment teeth from the excessive loads and stresses

C. Prevent the appliance from moving gingivally

D. Retain the artificial teeth

E. Only B and C

222. Teeth that are most commonly utilized as abutment teeth when constructing a removable partial denture are the:

A. Cuspids

B. Molars

C. Maxillary premolars

D. All of the above

E. Only A and B

223. A secondary impression for a removable partial denture is taken with:

A. Custom tray

B. Elastomeric material

C. Zinc-oxide impression material

D. Alginate

E. Only A, B, and C

224. During the appointment for the delivery of a removable partial denture, the dentist will:

A. Make final adjustments, if necessary

B. Polish the appliance

C. Scrub the appliance with soap and water, disinfect it, and rinse it prior to delivery

D. Give the patient instructions for removal, care, and placement of the appliance

E. All of the above

225. When the patient is scheduled for a wax setup/try-in appointment, the partial appliance includes the frame work and the artificial teeth set in wax. Any alterations in the appliance can be made during this time.

A. True

B. False

226. A secondary impression for a removable partial denture is utilized to construct a working cast. This working cast is used to make:

A. Baseplates

B. Bite rims

C. Wax setup

D. Finished partial denture

E. All of the above

227. At the case presentation appointment for the construction of a removable partial denture, the:

A. Auxiliary gathers and organizes all the diagnostic and the instrument aids

B. Dentist reviews the diagnosis, proposed treatment plan, and prognosis with the patient

C. Administrative assistant arranges a mutually convenient financial plan and makes the necessary appointments

D. All of the above

E. Only B and C

228. The preliminary impression for diagnostic study casts for a removable partial denture is taken with:

A. Alginate

B. Silicone

C. Polysiloxane

D. Only A and C

E. All of the above

229. The components of a removable complete denture include the:

A. Base, which includes the saddle and gingival area

B. Artificial teeth

C. Bar

D. Only A and B

E. Only B and C

230. At the preliminary appointment, impressions for removable complete dentures are taken with:

A. Silicone

B. Polysulfide

C. Alginate

D. Zinc-oxide impression paste

E. None of the above

231. Baseplates for removable complete dentures are fabricated of:

A. Shellac

B. Wax

C. Acrylic resin

D. All of the above

E. Only A and C

232. Bite rims are attached to the baseplate when constructing a removable complete denture. They provide the vertical dimension and the occlusal relationship of the maxillary and mandibular arches.

A. True

B. False

233. The final impression for a removable complete denture is taken with _____, which is loaded into the baseplate.

A. Zinc oxide-eugenol impression paste

B. Silicone

C. Polysulfide

D. Alginate

234. When giving home-care instructions to the individual who has just received a removable complete denture, the auxiliary should instruct the patient to:

A. Wash the denture over a basin filled with water

B. Use a denture brush and denture toothpaste

C. Soak the denture in water when it is not in the oral cavity

D. Remove the denture at night

E. All of the above

DIRECTIONS (Questions 235-244): Match the item in Column A with its respective function in Column B.

Column A

235. ___ Pontic

236. ___ Joint
237. ___ Abutment

238. ___ Sanitary pontic

239. ___ Units

Column B

A. Natural tooth that becomes the support for the replacement tooth and teeth

B. Single components of the fixed bridge

C. Part of the appliance that replaces the missing natural tooth

D. Provides the occlusal surface with a spacer between the pontic and the gingiva

E. Portion of the bridge that serves as the union between the pontic and the abutment

Column A

240. ___ Partial crown

241. ___ Dowel crown

242. ___ Three-quarter crown

243. ___ Full-veneer crown

244. ___ Full Crown

Column B

A. Usually gold colored, it covers the entire anatomic crown of the tooth

B. Covers three-fourths or more of the anatomic crown of the tooth. Usually the facial surface is the patient's natural tooth

C. Covers three or more, but not all surfaces of the tooth

D. May be cemented into the pulp canal space on a root canal tooth

E. Most of the surface of the crown is covered with a tooth-colored substance, either porcelain fused to gold or porcelain fused to metal

---

DIRECTIONS (Questions 245 through 247): In each of the following questions, select the one choice that answers the question or completes the sentence best.

245. Gingival retraction is utilized to temporarily displace the gingival sulcus to enable the operator to obtain an accurate impression of the tooth preparation slightly beyond the detached gingiva.

A. True

B. False

246. When utilizing the chemical method of tissue displacement, a gingival retraction cord is impregnated with an astringent chemical of:

A. Racemic epinephrine

B. Aluminum chloride

C. Zinc chloride 28%

D. Tannic acid 20%

E. All of the above

247. _____ impression material adapts well to retention pin holes.

A. Polysulfide

B. Silicone

C. Hydrocolloid

D. None of the above

....

DIRECTIONS (Questions 248-259): Match the item in Column A with its respective function in Column B.

Column A	Column B
248. ___ Zinc phosphate cement	A. This cement possesses a greater crushing strength
249. ___ Silicophosphate cement	B. Chemical bond is formed between the tooth surfaces and the cement during the setting process
250. ___ Zinc oxide-eugenol reinforced cement	C. Mixed on a cool, dry slab to a medium, syrupy consistency
251. ___ Polycarboxylate cement	D. Utilized if there is a question of recurrent caries

Column A	Column B
252. ___ Surgical knife	A. Utilizes a gingival retraction cord impregnated with aluminum chloride
253. ___ Chemical method	B. Removes excess tissue by burning it with an electric loop or wire tip that is heated to a high temperature
254. ___ Mechanical method	C. Electric knife detaches the excess tissue
255. ___ Electric cautery	D. Contoured stock aluminum crown is filled with guttapercha
256. ___ Electrosurgery	E. Operator cuts excess gingiva and detaches it from the area

Column A	Column B
257. ___ Hydrocolloid impression material	A. Is easy to handle. Used for copper band impressions of a single tooth or full arch preparation
258. ___ Polysulfide impression material	B. Adapts well to retention pin holes
259. ___ Silicone impression material	C. Is a reversible agar material

....

DIRECTIONS (Questions 245 through 247): In each of the following questions, select the one choice that answers the question or completes the sentence best.

260. When obtaining an opposing arch impression for a fixed prosthodontic appliance, a perforated stock or custom tray is filled with:

A. Silicone

B. Polysulfide

C. Alginate

D. Zinc oxide-eugenol

261. A paste impression that is utilized to obtain a bite registration for fixed prosthodontics includes zinc oxide-

eugenol, resin, and plasticizers.

A. True

B. False

262. A gingival retraction cord that is impregnated with racemic epinephrine is contraindicated for the _____ patient.

A. Cardiovascular

B. Epileptic

C. Diabetic

D. Hypothyroid

IV. Ethics and jurisprudence

263. In order to obtain national certification status, a dental assistant needs to:

A. Graduate from an accredited dental assisting program

B. Provide proof of employment in a dental office for the required number of hours

C. Pass a written examination that is developed by the Certifying Board of the ADAA

D. Acquire continuing education credits by attending approved continuing education courses, seminars, and/or programs

E. All of the above

264. In a legal suit, an employee's statements to the patient are just as incriminating as the dentist's statements.

A. True

B. False

265. If you, as the chairside assistant, are asked to perform a task that is not a legal expanded function in your state, you:

A. Are guilty of performing an unlawful act if you perform the task

B. May not be breaking the law if the dentist told you to act in this fashion and you perform the task

C. May refuse to perform the task

D. Only A and C

E. Only B and C

266. _____ allows the certified dental auxiliary to perform legal functions from one state to another without being re-examined in the respective state.

A. Jurisprudence

B. Reciprocity

C. Libel

D. Technical assault

E. Only B and D

267. As a loyal employee, the chairside assistant will confide in the patient and tell the patient that the dentist provides superb results and that the dentist's work will last forever.

A. True

B. False

268. Breech of contract charges against the dentist may be avoided if you, as the chairside assistant:

A. Maintain accurate and legible records

B. Document in the patient's chart instructions regarding home care, brushing, flossing, etc.

C. Do not tell the patient that this dental work will last for a lifetime

D. Only A and C

E. All of the above

269. Accurate updated records and diagnostically sound radiographs are the most important evidence that the dentist may utilize if he or she is involved in a malpractice suit.

A. True

B. False

270. The patient may sue both the dentist and the auxiliary if the patient is injured as a direct result of the auxiliary's actions.

A. True

B. False

271. If a patient's records and radiographs need to be sent to another dentist, the auxiliary should:

A. Send them by registered mail, return receipt requested

B. Send them by air mail

C. Insure them

D. Only A and C

E. All of the above

272. Once the patient is seated in the dental chair, the patient has given the dentist implied consent or permission to examine his or her oral cavity.

A. True

B. False

V. Dental charting

DIRECTIONS: Chart the following conditions on the anatomical chart provided below.

root canal and a mesio-occlusal amalgam restoration.

4. The maxillary right canine has a facial and a lingual carie.

5. The maxillary right central incisor has a mesio-incisal composite restoration with two pins in the incisal edge.

6. The maxillary left central incisor has an apical abscess.

7. The maxillary left lateral incisor has a lingual carie.

8. The maxillary left canine has a mesial carie and a distal composite restoration.

9. The maxillary left second molar has a mesio-occlusal-distal amalgam restoration.

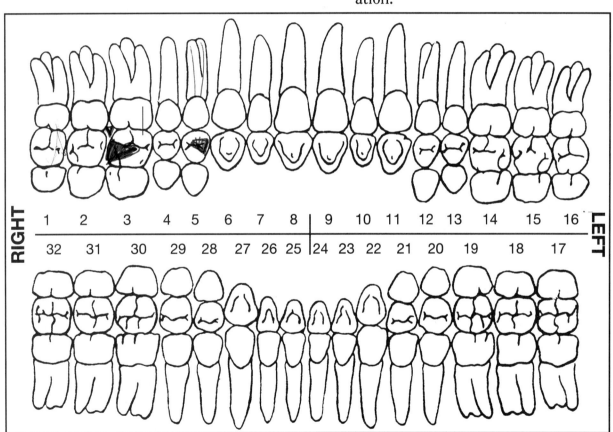

1. The maxillary right third molar is impacted and is drifting mesially.

2. The maxillary right first molar has a disto-occlusal amalgam restoration with an overhang on the distal surface.

3. The maxillary right first bicuspid has a

10. The maxillary left third molar is impacted and displays mesial drift.

11. The mandibular left third molar is missing.

12. The mandibular left first molar is missing.

13. The mandibular left second bicuspid has a mesio-occlusal-lingual amalgam restoration and a facial carie.

14. The mandibular left first bicuspid has a root canal.

15. The mandibular left canine has a root canal.

16. The mandibular left central incisor has a lingual composite restoration with recurrent caries.

17. The mandibular right central incisor has a gold veneer crown.

18. The mandibular right lateral incisor has a disto-incisal composite restoration.

19. The mandibular right canine has a lingual composite restoration and a facial carie.

20. There is a three-unit bridge from the mandibular right second premolar to the mandibular right second molar. The mandibular right first molar is missing. The mandibular right second premolar and the mandibular right second molar are the abutment teeth that are covered with full gold crowns.

21. The mandibular right third molar will be extracted.

DIRECTIONS (Questions 273-282): The following questions are to be answered on the basis of the charting you have just completed.

273. How many teeth indicate the presence of carious lesions on the maxillary arch?
A. One
B. Two
C. Three
D. Four

274. Which one of the following teeth has a faulty margin?
A. Maxillary left second molar
B. Mandibular left second molar
C. Maxillary right first molar
D. Maxillary right second molar

275. Which one of the following conditions exist on the maxillary left central incisor?
A. Lingual carie
B. Mesial-incisal composite restoration
C. Fractured root tip
D. Abscess

276. Which one of the following conditions exists on the maxillary left second molar?
A. Class I restoration
B. Class II restoration
C. Class III restoration
D. Class IV restoration

277. Which of the following teeth are charted as missing, (1) mandibular right third molar, (2) maxillary right third molar, (3) mandibular left third molar, (4) mandibular left first molar, and (5) mandibular right first molar?
A. 1, 3, and 4
B. 2, 3, and 4
C. 1, 4, and 5
D. 3, 4, and 5

278. Which one of the following conditions exists on the mandibular right central incisor?
A. Veneer crown
B. Composite restoration
C. Amalgam restoration with recurrent caries
D. Distal-incisal restoration

279. Which teeth of the fixed bridge are abutments, (1) mandibular right second pre-molar, (2) mandibular left first molar, (3) mandibular right second molar, (4) mandibular right first premolar, and (5) mandibular left second molar?
A. 1, 4, and 5
B. 2 and 3
C. 1 and 3
D. 2 and 4

280. How many tooth surfaces have been restored by amalgam?
    A. Seven
    B. Five
    C. Ten
    D. Eight

281. Which tooth is scheduled to be extracted?
    A. Maxillary right third molar
    B. Mandibular right third molar
    C. Maxillary left third molar
    D. Mandibular left third molar

282. How many teeth have been restored by utilizing a composite restoration material?
    A. Three
    B. Four
    C. Five
    D. Six

DIRECTIONS (Questions 283-297): Utilize the Universal System of tooth coding when answering the following questions.

283. The permanent maxillary right first molar is tooth number:
    A. 1
    B. 14
    C. 3
    D. 6

284. The permanent mandibular right second molar is tooth number:
    A. 31
    B. 18
    C. 15
    D. 3

285. The permanent third molars are classified as tooth numbers:
    A. 1, 16, 17, and 32
    B. 3, 6, 22, and 27
    C. 1, 18, 32, and 16
    D. 3, 14, 17, and 30

286. The permanent mandibular left second premolar is tooth number:
    A. 21
    B. 13

C. 28
D. 20

287. Tooth number 6 is the:
    A. Maxillary right cuspid
    B. Maxillary right first molar
    C. Mandibular left cuspid
    D. Mandibular right first molar

288. Tooth number 8 is the:
    A. Maxillary right cuspid
    B. Maxillary right lateral
    C. Maxillary right third molar
    D. Maxillary right central incisor

289. Tooth number 21 is the:
    A. Mandibular left second premolar
    B. Mandibular right first premolar
    C. Mandibular left first premolar
    D. Maxillary left first premolar

290. Tooth numbers 24 and 25:
    A. Contact on the distal surface
    B. Contact on the labial surface
    C. Contact on the mesial surface
    D. Are in different arches

291. The primary mandibular right cuspid is tooth letter:
    A. M
    B. C
    C. R
    D. Q

292. First premolars have _____ to the mesial aspect and _____ to the distal aspect.
    A. Laterals/second premolars
    B. Cuspids/first molars
    C. Cuspids/second premolars
    D. Laterals/first molars

293. The _____ have no opposing teeth toward the distal aspect.
    A. Central incisors
    B. Cuspids
    C. First molars
    D. Third molars

294. The permanent mandibular right cuspid is tooth number:

A. 27

B. 22

C. 11

D. 26

295. The permanent mandibular left second molar is tooth number _____. It is a _____ tooth.

 A. 15/posterior

 B. 18/posterior

 C. 31/posterior

 D. 19/posterior

296. The primary maxillary left second molar is tooth letter:

 A. A

 B. T

 C. K

 D. J

297. The primary mandibular left first molar is tooth letter:

 A. S

 B. L

 C. I

 D. B

VI. Infection control protocol

DIRECTIONS (Questions 298-303): In this section, the question stem is followed by four responses, at least one of which is correct. You should fill in only ONE circle on the answer sheet as follows:

A. If only 1, 2, and 3 are correct

B. If only 1 and 3 are correct

C. If only 2 and 4 are correct

D. If only 4 is correct

E. If all are correct

298. Sepsis is defined as the:

 1. Condition of being free from pathogenic microorganisms

 2. Process by which all forms of life are destroyed

 3. Process by which microbial life is destroyed, except for spore-forming organisms

 4. Presence of disease-producing microorganisms

299. Sterilization is the:

 1. Process by which the number of organisms on inanimate objects is reduced to safe level

 2. Condition of being free from pathogenic microorganisms

 3. Presence of disease-producing micro-organisms

 4. Process by which all forms of life are completely destroyed

300. _____ infection may result when infective microorganisms are present in the patient's oral cavity; however, they will not cause infection until they get into the patient's blood stream, e.g., through any type of dental surgery.

 1. Operator

 2. Indirect

 3. Droplet

 4. Self-

301. Disposable needles and scalpel blades are discarded by placing them in a:

 1. Wastepaper basket

 2. Rigid-sided container

 3. Wrapped plastic trash bag

 4. Puncture-proof container

302. Synthetic phenols display broad-spectrum disinfecting action. They are primarily used as a:

 1. Surface disinfectant

 2. Disinfectant for dental impressions

 3. Holding solution

 4. Liquid sterilant

303. Soap and water left on scrubbed instruments _____ the effectiveness of chemical disinfection/sterilization agents.

 1. Concentrate

 2. Dilute

 3. Increase

 4. Reduce

DIRECTIONS (Questions 304 through 329): In each of the following questions, select the one choice that answers the question or completes the sentence best.

304. At the end of each patient's dental treatment, the air-water syringe and the high-speed handpiece should be run for _____ to flush prior to sterilization.
A. 60 seconds
B. 30 minutes
C. 30 seconds
D. 3 minutes

305. Instruments should be left undisturbed and completely covered with the chemical or liquid disinfecting solution for _____ minutes in order for disinfection to occur.
A. 2 to 5
B. 30 to 60
C. 15 to 30
D. 5 to 15

306. How can you, as the chairside dental assistant, recognize a package of instruments that has been auto claved?
A. Temperature-sensitive tape will turn color
B. Instruments feel warm
C. Heat-sensitive autoclave bags will turn color
D. Autoclave bags are left open
E. Only A and C

307. Glutaraldehyde is capable of killing resistant spores if the item is immersed in the solution for at least _____.
A. 15 to 30 minutes
B. 10 to 20 minutes
C. 6 to 10 hours
D. 60 to 120 minutes

308. At 320°F, dry heat sterilization requires _____ minutes.
A. 60
B. 120
C. 150
D. 180

309. Autoclaving is considered to be the most reliable method of sterilization. Wrapped instruments are placed in the autoclave at 121°C or 250°F for at least _____ minutes.
A. 20 to 30
B. 5 to 15
C. 10 to 20
D. 60 to 120

310. The chemical sterilizer utilizes _____ in order to achieve sterilization.
A. Unsaturated chemical vapor
B. Moist heat which creates steam under pressure
C. Dry heat
D. None of the above

311. Sodium hypochlorite may be mixed in a 1:10 dilution to use as a disinfecting solution or a 1:100 dilution with water for surface disinfection. A 1:100 dilution translates to _____ cup(s) of bleach to _____ gallon(s) of water.
A. 2 to 1
B. 1½ to 2
C. 1½ to 1
D. ¼ to 1

312. Hands should be washed thoroughly with a liquid soap each time the chairside dental assistant comes to or returns to the dental chair. The best type of soap that can be utilized in the dental office is:
A. Iodine surgical scrub
B. Hexachlorophene soap
C. Chlorhexidine
D. Only A and B
E. All of the above

313. At 340°F, dry heat sterilization requires _____ minutes.
A. 30
B. 90
C. 120
D. 60

314. Disinfection is defined as the process

by which microbial life is destroyed, but spores or viruses are not.
A. True
B. False

315. Instruments are sterilized by chemical sterilization for _____ minutes at _____°F.
A. 10 to 20/250
B. 20 to 30/270
C. 30 to 60/340
D. 60 to 120/320

316. Endodontic instruments are usually sterilized at the dental chair during operative procedures with a glass bead or salt sterilizer that requires a temperature of _____°F for _____ seconds.
A. 250/10 to 20
B. 340/30 to 60
C. 450/10 to 12
D. 320/60 to 120

317. In the dental office, the best way the chairside assistant can reduce the risk of contracting a communicable disease is to:
A. Take a thorough medical history
B. Wear a face mask, sterile gloves, and protective eyewear
C. Practice aseptic techniques
D. Use disposable items
E. All of the above

318. The ultrasonic unit utilizes sound waves to cause cavitation that cleans debris from instruments and other dental objects. The ultrasonic solution is changed:
A. At the end of the day
B. Every other day
C. Every 14 to 21 days
D. Monthly

319. The chairside dental assistant's hands must be well-groomed. His or her nails should be clean and neatly trimmed.
A. True
B. False

320. Prior to heat sterilizing, the high-speed handpiece should be:
A. Placed in the ultrasonic unit to free it from excess debris
B. Wiped with a 2 times 2 alcohol gauze pad
C. Immersed in a cold disinfecting agent
D. Only A and B
E. None of the above

321. The high-speed and low-speed hand pieces should be sterilized:
A. After each use
B. At lunch time
C. At the end of the day
D. Once a week

322. The proper sequence for sterilizing the low-speed and high-speed handpieces is:
1. Scrub the handpieces with a detergent agent
2. Rinse the handpieces under a stream of clean tap water
3. Dry the handpieces thoroughly with a paper towel
4. Lubricate the handpieces according to the manufacturer's directions
5. Run the handpieces to expel excess lubricant
6. Bag and heat sterilize the handpieces
7. After sterilization lubricate the handpieces and run again to expel the excess lubricant
A. 1, 3, and 6
B. 1, 2, 3, and 6
C. 2, 1, 4, and 6
D. 2, 3, 4, 6, and 7
E. 1, 2, 3, 4, 5, 6, and 7

323. The fiberoptic light surface on the high-speed handpiece is cleaned with isopropyl alcohol and a swab:
A. Before heat sterilization
B. After heat sterilization and relubrication of the handpiece

C. Sterilization is not required with this type of handpiece

D. None of the above

324. The high-speed handpiece should be sterilized by:
A. Flash method of autoclaving
B. Dry heat sterilization
C. Chemical vapor sterilization
D. Only A and B
E. All of the above

325. The high-speed handpiece should be sterilized:
A. With the bur attached to the handpiece
B. Without the bur attached to the handpiece
C. By bagging handpiece and bur separately
D. Only B and C
E. None of the above

326. When lubricating the high-speed handpiece prior to and following sterilization:
A. Two separate cans of lubricant must be utilized in order to prevent contamination
B. One can of lubricant is sufficient for this procedure

C. Two separate cans of lubricant must be clearly labeled "before" and "after" in order to prevent contamination
D. None of the above

327. Phenolics and/or chlorine-based solutions should not be utilized for surface disinfection.
A. True
B. False

328. The high-speed and low-speed handpieces should be prepared for sterilization by:
A. Placing them directly onto the sterilization tray
B. Bagging them in a commercial autoclave pouch
C. Wrapping them in a paper towel
D. All of the above

329. Prior to sterilization, proper care of rotary instruments requires the chairside assistant to:
A. Presoak them for a brief period
B. Rinse and place them in a sterilizable bur block
C. Cleanse them in an ultrasonic unit
D. Only A and C
E. All of the above

DIRECTIONS (Questions 330-344): Match the item in Column A with its respective function in Column B.

Column A

330. ___ Chemiclave

331. ___ Dri-clave
332. ___ Steam autoclave
333. ___ Glass bead sterilizer
334. ___ Flash autoclaving

Column B

A. 8 minutes for a wrapped load at 132°C/250°F at 30 pounds pressure
B. 120 minutes at 320°F or 160°C
C. 450°F for 10 to 12 seconds
D. Utilizes deodorized alcohol formaldehyde
E. Utilizes moist heat to create steam under pressure

Column A

335. ___ Glutaraldehyde
336. ___ Ethylene oxide

Column B

A. Requires 8 to 10 hours for sterilization
B. Requires temperature of 450°F for 20 to 30 seconds to ensure metal instrument sterilization

337. ___ Glass bead sterilizer

338. ___ Steam autoclave

339. ___ Dri-heat sterilization

C. Items must be completely submerged and undisturbed for 6 to 10 hours for liquid sterilization

D. Cannot be used on plastic, paper, or cloth items

E. Requires distilled water

Column A

340. ___ Quaternary ammonium compounds

341. ___ Ethyl and isopropyl alcohol

342. ___ Iodophors

343. ___ Sodium hypochlorite

344. ___ Synthetic phenols

Column B

A. Not approved by the ADA for use in dentistry as surface disinfectants

B. Must be mixed using soft or distilled water

C. No longer accepted by the ADA for use in dentistry

D. May be utilized as a surface disinfectant in a ratio of 1:100 dilution with water

E. Must be mixed fresh daily at a ratio of 1:28 for use as a holding solution for instruments

DIRECTIONS (Questions 345 through 361): In each of the following questions, select the one choice that answers the question or completes the sentence best.

345. Disinfectant labels should:
    A. Be regulated by the EPA
    B. Display the EPA number on the label
    C. Be labeled as tuberculocidal, virucidal, and fungicidal
    D. All of the above
    E. Only A and B

346. Heat-sensitive tape:
    A. Informs the chairside assistant that sterilization has occurred
    B. Indicates that the sterilizer has reached the appropriate temperature
    C. Indicates that the instruments are not sterilized
    D. None of the above

347. Biological indicators containing one type of spore are specific and should be utilized with the respective sterilization method they are designed to monitor.
    A. True

    B. False

348. Biological indicators that are utilized to monitor the steam autoclave or chemical vapor sterilizers contain spores of:
    A. *Bacillus subtilis*
    B. *Bacillus stearothermophilus*

349. A positive sporicidal test indicates that:
    A. Sterilization did not occur
    B. Sterilization did occur

350. Biological indicators that are utilized to monitor dry heat or ethylene oxide contain spores of:
    A. *Bacillus subtilis*
    B. *Bacillus stearothermophilus*

351. A negative sporicidal test result indicates that:
    A. Sterilization did occur
    B. Sterilization did not occur

352. Chlorine dioxide may be utilized:
    A. For surface disinfection
    B. For instrument sterilization
    C. As a holding solution
    D. Only A and B

353. Adequate ventilation is required for _____ sterilization.
   A. Chemiclave
   B. Ethylene oxide
   C. Dri-clave
   D. Only A and B
   E. All of the above

354. Items that must be disinfected in the dental office are:
   A. Pens and pencils
   B. Shade guides
   C. Laboratory models
   D. Only A and B
   E. All of the above

355. A liquid soap utilized for hand scrubbing may include:
   A. Iodine surgical scrub
   B. Antimicrobial soap
   C. Chlorhexidine soap
   D. Hexachlorophene soap
   E. All of the above

356. To maintain aseptic technique, your hands should be thoroughly washed and dried each time you approach the dental chair. The following rules apply:
   A. Disposable paper towels should be utilized
   B. Terry cloth towels should be utilized by all dental personnel
   C. Paper towels may be utilized to turn off faucets if they are not controlled by a foot pedal
   D. Only A and B
   E. Only A and C

357. Latex gloves worn as a protective barrier technique:

   A. Provide the greatest protection in the first hour of patient contact
   B. Prevent contact with blood, saliva, and mucous membranes
   C. Can be exposed to disinfectants without causing a breakdown of the glove integrity
   D. Only A and B
   E. All of the above

358. Face masks are worn by dental personnel to:
   A. Reduce transmission of aerosol microorganisms
   B. Prevent contamination during splash procedures
   C. Eliminate offensive odors
   D. Only A and B
   E. All of the above

359. Utility gloves should be worn when handling:
   A. Synthetic phenols
   B. Iodophors
   C. Glutaraldehyde
   D. Only A and C
   E. All of the above

360. Ultrasonic cleaning is recommended for instruments prior to sterilization to:
   A. Prevent injury to the hands
   B. Eliminate hand scrubbing
   C. Reduce handling of instruments
   D. Only A and C
   E. All of the above

361. If a face shield is worn, it is not necessary to wear a face mask.
   A. True
   B. False

Answers

1. D. All the aforementioned movements are used by both the operator and auxiliary when they are utilizing four-handed dentistry.

2. E. The dental mouth mirror allows the operator to utilize indirect vision when examining the oral cavity. In addition, it is a valuable instrument that absorbs and

reflects light, retracts the lips, tongue, and cheeks, and controls movement of the tongue.

3. B. The clock positions in dentistry indicate that the chairside assistant has increased visibility when seated at the 2 to 3 o'clock position if assisting an operator who is working from the 10 o'clock position.

4. A. Every procedure necessitates viewing the patient's oral cavity. The mouth mirror and explorer are the two instruments that are needed to accomplish this task.

5. D. The basic tray setup includes the mouth mirror, explorer, and cotton pliers or cotton forceps.

6. A. Instruments on a prepared tray setup should be organized sequentially in the order of their use. This eliminates wasted time and motion by the operator and auxiliary during operative procedures.

7. D. All the aforementioned problems are likely to occur if instruments are not organized and arranged in the order of their use.

8. E. Preferably, nail polish should not be worn by dental personnel as it harbors microorganisms. In addition, it may chip and if it comes in contact with the patient's oral cavity, an infection may result. If worn, a clear or muted shade should be maintained.

9. D. Six-handed dentistry requires a third person, a coordinating assistant, to perform additional tasks in conjunction with the auxiliary.

10. D. In order to maintain the chain of asepsis, a plastic overglove may be donned or a sterile gauze square may be utilized to cover the drawer handle. Another sterile gauze square or sterile cotton forceps will enable the auxiliary to grasp the sterile instrument. Once treatment is initiated, the auxiliary's

gloves are contaminated and should be removed and discarded. Hands are washed prior to leaving the operatory.

11. B. After the patient has been seated and the chair is adjusted to the proper position, the auxiliary can wash his or her hands and don gloves.

12. E. If the operator is seated properly, all the aforementioned information is true.

13. E. All the aforementioned information is correct if the assistant is seated properly.

14. D. All the aforementioned methods are utilized by the operator to cool the tooth when the high-speed handpiece is used during operative procedures.

15. C. The dental light should be positioned approximately 3 feet from the patient's oval cavity. The auxiliary is responsible for adjusting the light during operative procedures.

16. E. The lens of the operating light is delicate and needs only a soft cloth and mild detergent to cleanse the area. The auxiliary should not attempt this task until the light has cooled since the heated lens could break if it comes in contact with a damp cloth.

17. C. The operator establishes a fulcrum when utilizing an instrument to stabilize the hand when working in the oral cavity.

18. A. During the exchange of the instruments from the auxiliary's hand to the operator's hand, the instruments must remain in a parallel relationship to avoid tangling.

19. B. The auxiliary delivers and retrieves instruments with the left hand when assisting the right-handed operator. This process is reversed if the operator is left-handed.

20. B. The auxiliary delivers and retrieves instruments with the right hand when assisting the left-handed operator. This process is reversed if the operator is right-handed.

21. D. Ideally, the auxiliary can work most efficiently at the 2 to 3 o'clock position when assisting the right-handed operator.

22. B. The thumb, index, and third fingers are utilized during the exchange of instruments.

23. A. This is the method that is utilized by the operator in order to alert the auxiliary that an instrument exchange is forthcoming.

24. B. The auxiliary utilizes the modified pen grasp when suctioning during shorter dental procedures and the reverse palm-thumb grasp when suctioning for longer procedures.

25. C. The tip of the aspirator is positioned on the lingual surface of the mandibular right quadrant when the operator is restoring the mandibular right premolar and molars.

26. A. The auxiliary positions the high-volume evacuation tip toward the facial surface of the maxillary left second molar when suction is required in this area.

27. E. Positions B, C, and D enable the auxiliary to place the high-volume evacuation tip in the correct manner when suction is needed in the posterior area of the oral cavity.

28. A. The auxiliary positions the high-volume evacuation tip toward the palatal surface of the maxillary right molar area when suction is required in this area.

29. C. A spoon excavator is a cutting instrument. It is utilized to remove soft debris when preparing the cavity preparation.

30. E. A matrix band is utilized to supply a missing wall when restoring a Class II restoration with amalgam. It attaches to the circumference of the tooth with a Tofflemire retainer. In addition, the wooden wedge ensures that the matrix band adheres tightly to the missing wall of the cavity preparation.

31. D. All the aforementioned are functions of hand-cutting instruments.

32. B. The hexagonal, or six-sided, shape enables the operator to stabilize the instrument and add leverage to the grip.

33. D. All these instruments are classified as hand-cutting and are utilized to obtain and refine the cavity preparation.

34. B. All these instruments are classified as carving and are utilized to restore the anatomical surface of the amalgam restoration.

35. B. The spoon excavator is designed to scoop out soft debris with its "spoon-like" shape.

36. D. The amalgam file is a cutting instrument that is designed to trim or take away an excess amount of amalgam from the mesial or distal surfaces of the restoration.

37. D. The right-angled handpiece is utilized to polish amalgam restorations. It attaches to the straight handpiece.

38. D. A round bur is identified and ordered by the sizes ½ to 9. The higher the number, the larger the head of the bur.

39. B. An inverted cone bur is utilized to remove a bulk amount of carious debris from a posterior tooth in addition to making retention grooves in the cavity preparation. It is designated by the numbers 33½ to 37.

40. C. The chisel is a small instrument which is utilized in a "push"

motion in order to place pressure on weakened enamel or dentin to fracture the carious debris. It is classified as a cutting instrument.

41. A. The Wedelstaedt chisel is designed with a slight curve in the shank. Chisels may also be straight in shape.

42. C. The discoid/cleoid can be designed as a double-ended instrument. It can be classified as both a cutting and a carving instrument. When utilized for carving, the discoid portion is used to restore the anatomy to the occlusal surface of an amalgam restoration.

43. D
44. C
45. B
46. E
47. A
48. C
49. B
50. D
51. E
52. A
53. B
54. A
55. C
56. E
57. D
58. B
59. A
60. D
61. E
62. C
63. E
64. C
65. A
66. D

67. B
68. C
69. D
70. B
71. E
72. A
73. C
74. E
75. B
76. A
77. D

78. C. Class V restorations are found on the gingival third of the facial or lingual surfaces of all teeth.

79. D. Class IV restorations occur on the mesial and distal surfaces of the anterior teeth and include the incisal edge.

80. C. Class III restorations occur on the mesial and distal surfaces of the anterior teeth and do not include the incisal edge.

81. A. Class I restorations include the lingual surfaces of the maxillary incisors.

82. D. Class I restorations occur on the occlusal surfaces of the posterior teeth.

83. A. Class I restorations are found on the occlusal two-thirds of the lingual surfaces of the maxillary molars.

84. B. Class II restorations are located on the posterior teeth and include the mesial and the distal surfaces in addition to the occlusal surfaces.

85. B. All the aforementioned are functions of the Tofflemire matrix band.

86. B. Class II restorations are located on the posterior teeth and include the mesial and distal surfaces as well as the occlusal surfaces.

87. B. Epinephrine is the vasoconstrictor that is added to some local anesthetics. It decreases the blood flow around the injection site, and delays the amount of systemic absorption, which, in turn, decreases the chances for an allergic reaction in addition to intensifying the effect of the anesthetic and prolonging the anesthesia.

88. E. All the aforementioned are examples of topical anesthetic compounds.

89. A. Toxic reactions may occur in those individuals who may be sensitive to anesthetics.

90. B. Topical anesthetic agents have the ability to be absorbed into the oral mucosa. They numb the peripheral nerve endings so the local anesthetic injection is not as painful for the patient.

91. B. The liver breaks down the local anesthetic, which is then excreted by the kidneys.

92. A. The hub screws into the threaded tip of the syringe. It prevents the needle from disengaging from the syringe during the expulsion of anesthetic.

93. C. The 1-inch shorter needle is usually utilized for infiltration injections, and the 1⅝-inch longer needle is used to administer block anesthesia.

94. D. All the aforementioned are functions of a vasoconstrictor.

95. B. The color coding on the rubber stopper that is located in the anesthetic cartridges quickly enables auxiliary personnel to identify the epinephrine ratio of the various local anesthetics. A red color-coded stopper indicates that the epinephrine ratio is 1:100,000, which would be utilized for routine dental treatment. For cases which require an anesthetic of longer duration, the green color-coded cartridge, which contains an epinephrine ratio of 1:50,000, is preferred.

96. A. Hypodermic needles are made of either stainless steel or platinum.

97. C. The harpoon is found on the aspirating syringe.

98. D. The administration of local anesthesia is the most anxiety producing procedure for the dental patient.

99. B. All these steps are followed when loading the aspirating syringe.

100. D. The inferior alveolar nerve originates from the nerve ganglion that is located in front of the ear and runs down the mandible to the central incisor. When this nerve is anesthetized, the patient is numb from the mandibular third molar to the mandibular central incisor. In addition, half the tongue is anesthetized.

101. C. When injecting with the aspirating syringe, the operator pulls back on the plunger to aspirate fluid into the cartridge. If blood appears in the cartridge, the operator must reposition it at the injection site.

102. E. All the aforementioned systemic diseases warrant the use of a local anesthetic that does not contain a vasoconstrictor.

103. D. Only Xylocaine and Carbocaine do not contain vasoconstrictors.

104. E. Health care workers are at the greatest risk for needle-stick injury when recapping a contaminated syringe after the operator has administered local anesthesia. A one-handed recapping technique or a device for protecting the hand should be utilized during this time.

105. E. All the aforementioned conditions may occur as a result of a patient's sensitivity to a local anesthetic.

106. C

107. D

108. D

109. D

110. A

111. C

112. B

113. D

114. A

115. B

116. C

117. A

118. C

119. D

120. B

121. E

122. C

123. C

124. B

125. A

126. D

127. E

128. B

129. B

130. A

131. E

132. C

133. A

134. B

135. A

136. C

137. D

138. A

139. B

140. E. An antibiotic would be prescribed if the patient exhibits all or any of these signs and symptoms of infection.

141. D. Sodium hypochlorite or bleach is utilized more often as an irrigating solution as it dissolves dead tissue in addition to disinfecting and bleaching the canal(s). Hydrogen peroxide (3%) may be used as an alternative to sodium hypochlorite. Peroxide is effervescent and it functions by bubbling out debris and disinfecting the canal.

142. B. Glass bead sterilization requires the nub of the instrument to be completely submerged in the unit for 10 to 12 seconds at a temperature of 450°F.

143. D. The Gates-Glidden drill is utilized with either the slow-speed contra-angled handpiece or the friction-grip straight handpiece to enlarge the canal(s).

144. E. Transillumination with the fiber-optic light is a valuable diagnostic tool as it allows the operator to compare the differences in the degree of translucency from one tooth to another. In addition, fractures may be viewed during this procedure.

145. D. All the aforementioned statements describe a radiograph that is acceptable for diagnosing endodontic conditions.

146. D. All the aforementioned subjective symptoms would be felt by the patient and are valuable clues to aid the operator when diagnosing endodontic disease.

147. D. The blunt end of a mouth mirror may be utilized to tap the tooth to determine sensitivity. Inflamed tissues will respond by causing the patient to feel pain.

148. A. When the patient has acute pulpalgia or pulpal pain, it is usually relieved momentarily when a cold stimulus, such as ice, is applied to the tooth in question.

149. C. A tooth with a necrotic pulp will not react at all to the electrical stimulus

supplied by the vitalometer.

150. A. An abscessed tooth will react this way when the stimulus of hot and cold is applied to the area.

151. A. The surgical removal of the vital pulp from the tooth is known as pulpectomy.

152. B. Amalgam is utilized to retrofill the apex of the root canal. Zinc-free amalgam is the material of choice since it does not react with any moisture that may be found in the root canal.

153. A. The canal walls and the apical third of the master cone are coated with a cementing medium prior to being placed into the canal.

154. A. An accurate radiograph that shows a nondistorted image of the periapical area is needed by the operator in order to properly diagnose periodontal conditions.

155. A. A normal sulcus reading is no deeper than 3 mm.

156. B. Suprabony pockets involve the coronal portion of the gingiva above the level of the alveolar bone.

157. D. All the aforementioned treatments are effective ways to treat and eliminate the periodontal pocket.

158. C. Both analgesics, to relieve pain, and antibiotics, to prevent infection, may be prescribed by the dentist for the patient who has had a gingivectomy.

159. A. The patient should be instructed not to consume alcoholic beverages after periodontal surgery.

160. B. Surgical reshaping of the alveolar bone is known as alveoplasty. This process is performed to remove defects and to restore normal contour to the bone.

161. C. The mandibular third molars are usually affected as they are difficult to cleanse and often accumulate food debris.

162. C. Eugenol and non-eugenol periodontal dressings may be purchased; however, the non-eugenol dressing may be preferred by the dentist as it is less irritating to painful tissues.

163. B. Acute necrotizing ulcerative gingivitis or Vincent's infection is a bacterial infection. Typically, the patient may feel tired, have a foul odor to the breath, and exhibit grayish or yellowish-gray ulcers that are scattered throughout the oral cavity. In addition, a white pseudomembrane forms over the ulcers; however, it may be wiped off.

164. D. Additive osseous surgery attempts to restore the alveolar bone to a normal level by utilizing autoosseous implants to stimulate bone cell formation. Subtractive osseous surgery resects, reshapes, and recontours the bone by surgical means.

165. A. A periodontal abscess forms in the gingival tissue. It usually does not involve the pulpal tissue or the apex.

166. A. Recall appointments for the postsurgical periodontal patient should be scheduled every 1 to 2 months.

167. A. Drinking any type of cold fluid such as water or soda will allow the periodontal dressing to set.

168. D. The dentist may advise the postsurgical periodontal patient to use a commercial desensitizing dentifrice or a 2% solution of sodium fluoride and water to brush with in order to decrease the patient's sensitivity.

169. A. If the pediatric patient has demonstrated "good behavior," he or she may be offered a reward or gift after the dental appointment is completed.

170. D. All the aforementioned information is included as part of the child's medical history.

171. E. When the dentist observes deep pits and narrow fissures in the child's dentition, as well as teeth that are prone to caries, he or she may recommend that the areas in question be sealed.

172. E. All the aforementioned radiographs are included in a full-mouth series for the pedodontic patient.

173. B. The child is usually given barbiturates 30 to 45 minutes prior to the scheduled appointment.

174. A. Children must be advised not to bite the cheeks, lips, or tongue after an injection of local anesthesia as severe trauma to the area may result. Parents should closely monitor their children until the anesthetic wears off.

175. D. In order for tranquilizers to relax and calm the fearful child, they should be administered 24 hours prior to the dental appointment.

176. B. A fluoride-free abrasive such as pumice is usually utilized to cleanse the tooth surface prior to the application of a sealant. Fluoride neutralizes the etching liquid; therefore, it does not allow the sealant to adhere to the enamel surface.

177. D. All the aforementioned qualities are anatomical differences between the primary and permanent teeth.

178. D. All the aforementioned types are examples of matrices that are utilized in pediatric dentistry.

179. B. An evulsed tooth has been knocked free from the oral cavity. This is an emergency situation that requires immediate attention.

180. A. Direct pulp capping is performed to stimulate the formation of a dentinal bridge or secondary dentin over the exposed pulp.

181. D. All the aforementioned types are examples of the crowns that can be utilized in pediatric dentistry.

182. A. A vital pulpotomy usually includes the pulp horns. Sterile technique is extremely important as contamination by blood and/or saliva may cause the procedure to fail.

183. A. The bite plane is comprised of cold-cure acrylic. It functions to move a tooth that is positioned lingually into facial alignment.

184. C. Librium and Ultran are categorized as tranquilizers.

185. E. All the aforementioned are responsibilities that the orthodontic patient assumes when undergoing treatment.

186. D. Oral habits, such as those listed, may affect the dentition and must be corrected and/or eliminated prior to orthodontic treatment.

187. A. Psychological and social development may be impaired if the child feels inferior due to malocclusion.

188. B. This category of orthodontic treatment allows the dentist to discover genetic and congenital problems and, if needed, begin to formulate a long-range treatment plan.

189. D. Alginate may be utilized when obtaining impressions to produce study and working casts.

190. B. Zinc phosphate cement is utilized to cement metal orthodontic bands.

191. B. Extraoral anchorage is worn when the patient's maxillary first molars are anteriorly positioned and the maxilla is growing too rapidly. The vertical and the oblique or high-pull headgear utilize a cervical strap to provide traction.

192. A. During orthodontic treatment, the resistance of one or more teeth is

utilized when moving a single or several opposing groups of teeth.

193. C. Class III or mesioclusion is evident when the mesiobuccal cusp of the maxillary first molar occludes in the interdental space between the distal cusp of the mandibular first molar and the mesial cusp of the mandibular second molar. The patient's profile shows that the mandible is protruding and appears to be mesial to the maxilla.

194. D. The process of resorption occurs readily with 48 to 72 hours of the activation of orthodontic appliances. Resorption is responsible for compressing the periodontal ligament which, in turn, stimulates the osteoclasts to break down bone in the direction of tooth movement.

195. B. Class I or neutroclusion is evident if the occlusion occurs when the patient is in centric occlusion. This is considered to be normal occlusion.

196. A. The orthodontic brackets may be bonded to the facial surfaces of the teeth by utilizing the acid-etch technique.

197. C. This orthodontic treatment is utilized when there is a possibility of applying mechanical appliances to correct malocclusion.

198. C. Class II or distoclusion is evident when the mesiobuccal cusp of the maxillary first molar occludes in the interdental space between the mandibular second premolar and the mesial cusp of the mandibular first molar. The patient's profile shows that the maxilla is protruding or that the mandible is distal to the maxilla.

199. D. A cephalometric radiograph is required by the orthodontist to measure growth patterns of the cranial bones as well as any pathology that may be observed in the skull.

200. E. Both penicillin and erythromycin are effective against gram-positive microbes and may be prescribed either pre- or postoperatively to control infection.

201. D. All the aforementioned analgesics may be prescribed by the dentist to control the patient's post-operative pain.

202. A. The patient may rinse with a saline solution that may be mixed by adding 1 teaspoon of salt to eight ounces of warm water.

203. B. The postsurgical patient may apply a cold pack for the first 24 hours in a cycle of 20 minutes on and 20 minutes off to control swelling. An ice bag is utilized for this purpose.

204. D. The gauze pressure pack is applied directly over the socket for 30 minutes to control bleeding and ensure the formation of a clot.

205. E. The postsurgical dental patient is encouraged to drink a lot of water and fruit juices. Alcoholic and carbonated beverages should be avoided.

206. B. If the patient should experience a dry socket following surgery, the clot has been lost and there is an absence of healthy granulation tissue. This is a painful postoperative condition.

207. A. The excision biopsy is obtained by removing the lesion as well as the adjacent and underlying normal tissue for comparison.

208. D. To aid in wound healing, vitamin C and B-complex vitamins may be prescribed postsurgically to supplement the patient's nutrient intake.

209. E. All the aforementioned signs and symptoms are characteristics of a dry socket.

210. A. An external heat pack that is applied to the wound area after the first 24 hours increases circulation

which, in turn, aids in healing the surgical site.

211. B. A lingual frenum located under the tongue or a labial frenum found in the midline mucobuccal fold of the maxillary or mandibular arch may be cut to either remove, loosen, or reposition it in the oral cavity.

212. A. An alveolectomy is performed in order to reduce and reshape the alveolar ridge, usually after teeth have been extracted or prior to the construction of a full or a partial denture.

213. D. All the aforementioned are routes by which sedation may be administered to the patient.

214. C. The surgical patient should be instructed not to eat or drink anything for 6 to 8 hours prior to general anesthesia.

215. D. All the aforementioned intraoral factors must be considered when constructing a removable dental prosthesis.

216. A. The framework is composed of gold alloy or chromium and provides a metal skeleton that functions as a support for the saddle and connectors.

217. B. Porcelain teeth do produce a clicking sound when chewing; however, acrylic teeth tend to wear under the force of mastication. Therefore, the dentist may choose to utilize a combination of both acrylic and porcelain teeth when constructing a removable prosthesis.

218. D. All the aforementioned factors are taken into consideration when selecting artificial teeth for the patient's prosthesis.

219. D. The bar, saddle, and clasps are components of a removable partial denture.

220. B. Clasps aid in providing support and stability to the removable partial denture. In addition, they are resilient and flexible to allow the patient to remove and replace the prosthesis in the oral cavity.

221. E. Rests are designed to relieve the abutment teeth from excessive load and stress so as to evenly distribute the force during mastication. In addition, rests prevent the prosthesis from moving gingivally when chewing.

222. D. All the aforementioned teeth are utilized as abutments when constructing a removable partial denture.

223. E. Alginate is not utilized to take a secondary impression for a removable partial denture.

224. E. All the aforementioned steps are necessary prior to delivering a removable partial denture to the patient.

225. A. The removable prosthesis is designed in wax to allow the patient and the dentist to make any necessary changes during this appointment.

226. E. All the aforementioned components are made from the working cast.

227. D. All the aforementioned are responsibilities of the auxiliary, the dentist, and the administrative assistant during the case presentation appointment for the construction of a removable partial denture.

228. A. The preliminary impression for a diagnostic cast is taken with alginate when constructing a removable partial denture.

229. D. A removable complete denture has two components: the base and the artificial teeth.

230. C. Alginate impression material is utilized to take a preliminary impression for a removable complete denture.

231. D. All the aforementioned dental materials may be utilized in order to construct baseplates for a removable complete denture.

232. A. Bite rims are constructed of baseplate wax, which is utilized to determine vertical dimension. In addition, the patient's occlusal relationship is determined by the bite rim.

233. A. Zinc oxide-eugenol impression paste is loaded into the baseplates for an accurate final impression when constructing a removable complete denture.

234. E. All the aforementioned home-care instructions should be given by the auxiliary to the individual who has just received a complete removable denture.

235. C

236. E

237. A

238. D

239. B

240. C

241. D

242. B

243. E

244. A

245. A. Gingival retraction is utilized in dentistry to temporarily displace the gingival sulcus in order to obtain an accurate impression of the tooth preparation slightly below the detached gingiva. This ensures that the fixed crown will contour and adapt to the tooth preparation.

246. E. All the aforementioned astringents may be employed when utilizing the chemical method of tissue displacement.

247. B. Silicone-base elastomeric materials are especially suitable as impression materials when constructing a fixed crown or bridge prosthesis.

248. C

249. D

250. A

251. B

252. E

253. A

254. D

255. B

256. C

257. C

258. A

259. B

260. C. Alginate impression material is utilized with either a perforated stock or a custom tray when obtaining an opposing arch impression for a fixed prosthesis.

261. A. Zinc oxide-eugenol, resin, and plasticizers are utilized to obtain a bite registration for fixed prosthodontics.

262. A. Epinephrine is a vasoconstrictor which may cause problems in the cardiovascular patient as it has the potential to stress the heart.

263. E. All the aforementioned conditions must be present in order for the dental assistant to obtain national certification status.

264. A. As an employee, you should project a trustworthy image; however, you need to be professional and choose your words wisely as your statements are damaging and could be as incriminating as those of the dentist.

265. D. If you, as the auxiliary, perform a task that is not legal within your state, your are guilty of performing an illegal or an "unlawful" act. In addition, you may also refuse to

perform this task in the dental office.

266. B. Reciprocity is an agreement by two or more states that allows auxiliaries to perform legal functions in the respective states.

267. B. The dental auxiliary should never tell the patient that the dentist's dental work will last forever.

268. E. All the aforementioned information should be adhered to if the dentist wishes to avoid a charge of breech of contract.

269. A. All this evidence is useful and is necessary if the dentist should be involved in a malpractice suit.

270. A. The patient may choose to sue both the auxiliary and the dentist if the patient is injured as a direct result of the auxiliary's actions; however, most of the time the patient sues the dentist because he or she has more assets.

271. A. The patient's record and radiographs are sent by registered mail, with a return receipt requested.

272. A. Once the patient is seated in the dental chair, the patient is expressing implied consent or permission to have the dentist examine his or her oral cavity. Consent can also be expressed in an oral manner or documented in written form.

273. C

274. C

275. D

276. B

277. D

278. A

279. C

280. C

281. B

282. C

283. C

284. A

285. A

286. D

287. A

288. D

289. C

290. C

291. C

292. C

293. D

294. A

295. B

296. D

297. B

298. D. Sepsis is defined as the presence of disease-producing microorganisms.

299. D. All forms of life are completely destroyed during the sterilization process.

300. D. When self-infection occurs, the patient infects her or himself when microorganisms invade the bloodstream through any type of dental procedure that causes a break in the oral tissues.

301. C. A puncture-proof, rigid-sided container is employed in the dental office to discard sharps such as disposable needles and scalpel blades.

302. A. When phenols are utilized as disinfectants, they are mixed in a 1:32 ratio. In addition, phenolic solutions are recommended for disinfection of polysulfide, silicone, and polyether impressions. If the auxiliary intends to utilize phenol as a holding solution for instruments, the ratio is 1:28.

303. C. Soap and water reduce and dilute the efficiency of chemical disinfection or sterilization agents.

304. C. The high-speed handpiece and the

air-water syringe should be flushed for 30 seconds before beginning the sterilization process.

305. C. Instruments must be completely submerged and left undisturbed for 15 to 30 minutes in order for chemical or liquid disinfection to occur.

306. E. Instruments should be placed in a clear-view pouch that is impregnated with heat-sensitive markings that turn color once it is heated. In addition, heat-sensitive tape may be utilized to seal autoclave bags. The tape also turns color when exposed to heat.

307. C. Sterilization can be achieved when using glutaraldehyde if instruments are left undisturbed and completely submerged for 6 to 10 hours.

308. B. Dry heat sterilization requires 120 minutes if the temperature is 320°F.

309. A. Wrapped instruments require 20 to 30 minutes of sterilization if the autoclave achieves a temperature of 121°C or 250°F.

310. A. Deodorized alcohol formaldehyde or unsaturated chemical vapor is utilized.

311. D. Sodium hypochlorite or bleach may be diluted with water to prepare a surface disinfectant. One-quarter cup of bleach is mixed with 1 gallon of water to achieve a 1:100 ratio. If a disinfecting solution is required, 1½ cups of bleach may be added to one gallon of water to achieve a 1:10 ratio.

312. E. All the aforementioned liquid soaps may be utilized for hand scrubbing in the dental office.

313. D. Dry heat sterilization requires 60 minutes if the temperature is 340°F.

314. A. Disinfection is the process by which microbial life is destroyed; however, it does not kill spores or viruses.

315. B. Sterilization in the Chemiclave requires the instruments to be exposed to 270°F for 20 to 30 minutes.

316. C. Sterilization with the glass bead or salt sterilizer requires the endodontic instruments to be exposed to a temperature of 450°F for 10 to 12 seconds.

317. E. All the aforementioned techniques may be utilized by the chairside assistant to reduce the risk of contracting a communicable disease in the dental office.

318. A. The ultrasonic solution is changed at the end of each day. Ultrasonic cleaning of instruments is preferred over hand scrubbing as it reduces the risk of injury.

319. A. The chairside assistant's hands must be free of open wounds and/or sores. Nails should be clean and neatly trimmed.

320. E. None of the aforementioned statements are correct.

321. A. At the conclusion of each patient's treatment, both the high-speed and low-speed handpieces are sterilized.

322. E. This is the proper sequencing that is followed when sterilizing the low-speed and high-speed handpieces.

323. B. After heat sterilization and relubrication the fiberoptic light surface of the high-speed handpiece can be cleaned with isopropyl alcohol and a cotton swab.

324. E. Chemical vapor sterilization and autoclaving at 250°F for 15 to 30 minutes at 15 pounds of pressure are the methods utilized to sterilize the high-speed handpiece. In addition, the new dry heat steriliz-

ers can be utilized to sterilize certain handpieces.

325. D. The high-speed handpiece is sterilized by bagging it without the bur attached. Burs should be bagged and sterilized separately.

326. C. In order to prevent contamination, two separate cans of lubricant labeled "before" and "after" must be utilized when lubricating the high-speed handpiece.

327. B. Phenolics and/or chlorine-based solutions can be utilized as surface disinfectants.

328. B. The low-speed and high-speed handpieces need to be bagged in a commercial autoclave pouch prior to sterilization.

329. E. All the aforementioned steps should be taken when rotary instruments are being prepared for sterilization.

330. D

331. B

332. E

333. C

334. A

335. C

336. A

337. B

338. E

339. D

340. C

341. A

342. B

343. D

344. E

345. D. All the aforementioned information should be included on disinfectant labels.

346. B. Heat-sensitive tape indicates that the sterilizer has reached the appropriate temperature; however, it does not indicate that sterilization has occurred.

347. A. Biological indicators are specific and should be utilized with the respective sterilization method they are designed to monitor.

348. B. Biological indicators that contain *Bacillus stearothermophilus* are utilized to monitor steam autoclaves or chemical vapor sterilizers.

349. A. A positive sporicidal test indicates that sterilization did not occur.

350. A. Dry heat and ethylene oxide sterilizers are monitored by utilizing a biological indicator that contains spores of *Bacillus subtilis*.

351. A. A negative sporicidal test indicates that sterilization has occurred.

352. D. Chlorine dioxide may be utilized for surface disinfection as well as instrument sterilization. Surfaces that are to be disinfected need to be thoroughly cleaned prior to spraying with chlorine dioxide. A 1- to 3-minute contact time is sufficient for disinfection purposes. Instruments must be completely submerged and undisturbed for 6 hours in order for liquid sterilization to occur.

353. D. The Chemiclave utilizes deodorized alcohol formaldehyde for clinical vapor sterilization. Ethylene oxide, which is a gas, is the medium that is used with this sterilization method. Both of these sterilizers require adequate ventilation to disperse the toxic fumes.

354. E. All the aforementioned items must be disinfected at the end of each patient's treatment.

355. E. All the aforementioned soaps may be utilized in the dental office for hand scrubbing.

356. E. Ideally, each sink in the dental office should be controlled by foot pedals for infection control purposes. In addition, disposable paper towels should be available at each sink station to prevent cross-contamination.

357. D. Latex gloves offer barrier protection from blood, saliva, and mucous for about 1 hour of patient contact.

358. D. Dental personnel wear face masks to reduce the risk of inhaling aerosol microorganisms and to prevent contamination from blood and saliva during splash procedures.

359. E. Dental personnel should wear utility gloves when handling synthetic phenols, iodophors, and glutaraldehyde.

360. E. Ultrasonic cleaning prevents injury to the hands, eliminates the need for hand scrubbing, and reduces handling of the instruments.

361. B. If a face shield is worn, a face mask is also required to prevent the inhalation of fluid aerosols and particles of dust.

2

Dental Materials and Dental Laboratory Procedures

CHAPTER OUTLINE

I. Selection of armamentarium and application and fabrication of:
   A. Gypsum products
   B. Irreversible and reversible hydrocolloids
   C. Impression compound
   D. Custom tray materials
   E. Elastomeric/rubber-base impression materials
      1. Polysulfide
      2. Silicone
         a. Condensation type
         b. Addition type
      3. Polyether
   F. Cements
      1. Zinc phosphate
      2. Polyacrylate
      3. Zinc oxide and eugenol
      4. Periodontal dressing and gingival pack
      5. Calcium hydroxide
      6. Varnishes and liners
      7. Resin cements
      8. Glass ionomers
   G. Amalgam
   H. Composites
   I. Waxes
   J. Preventive materials
      1. Sealants
      2. Fluoride
      3. Mouthguards
   K. Dentures
   L. Crowns
   M. Bleaching
   N. Enamel and dentin bonding
   O. Handling hazardous substances in the dental office
   P. Infection control protocol

DIRECTIONS (Questions 1 through 232): In each of the following questions, select the one choice that answers the question or completes the sentence best.

I. Selection of armamentarium and application and fabrication of:

A. Gypsum products

1. Which of the following materials are used primarily for making positive reproductions of the oral cavity?
   A. Colloids
   B. Waxes
   C. Alginates
   D. Model plaster

2. A gypsum replica of hard and soft tissues that is used for observation is known as a(n):
   A. Rubber mold
   B. Custom acrylic tray
   C. Stone model
   D. Alginate impression

3. Dental plaster is primarily used to fabricate a:
   A. Working cast
   B. Model for articulation
   C. Study model
   D. None of the above

4. A replica of a single tooth is referred to as a:
   A. Model
   B. Die
   C. Cast
   D. Plastic

5. Model plaster and dental stone are examples of:
   A. Resin products
   B. Electroplated products
   C. Gypsum products
   D. Investment products

6. The process in which the mineral gypsum is heated and converted into a powdered form is known as:
   A. Dydration
   B. Interlocking
   C. Calcination
   D. Dyhydrating

7. When fabricating dies for crowns, bridges, and inlays, alternatives to high-strength stone may include:
   A. Epoxy dies
   B. Silver-plated dies
   C. Copper-plated dies
   D. Only A and B
   E. All of the above

8. Which material undergoes an exothermic reaction upon setting?
   A. Amalgam
   B. Composite
   C. Gypsum
   D. Gold

9. W/P is an expression for:
   A. Plaster and stone ratio
   B. Liquid and powder ratio
   C. Water and powder ratio
   D. Water and stone ratio

10. The strength of the gypsum product is determined by the:
    A. W/P ratio
    B. Amount of powder
    C. Final setting
    D. Amount of water

11. Armamentarium utilized to measure the gram weight of gypsum powder is a:
    A. Vibrator
    B. Graduated cylinder
    C. Gram scale
    D. Flexible rubber bowl

12. When spatulating a gypsum product, the water is placed into a:
    A. Paper cup
    B. Plastic container
    C. Flexible rubber bowl
    D. Ceramic bowl

13. When mixing gypsum products, the correct method of adding materials is:
   A. Add water to the powder
   B. Add powder to the water
   C. Add powder and water at the same time
   D. Sequence of adding either product does not matter

14. The mixing time for gypsum products is _____ seconds.
   A. 15 to 30
   B. 30 to 60
   C. 60 to 90
   D. 90 to 120

15. The motion that is used to mix gypsum is:
   A. Stirring
   B. Pressing
   C. Wiping
   D. Chopping

16. In order to prevent air bubbles in the final gypsum model, the following measure may be employed:
   A. High water/powder ratio
   B. Boxing technique
   C. Mechanical vibrator
   D. Low water/powder ratio

17. If air is incorporated into a gypsum mix, the result may be:
   A. Smooth surface
   B. Added strength
   C. Surface inaccuracies
   D. None of the above

18. Higher water temperatures used to mix gypsum products will have the following effect:
   A. Lengthen setting rate
   B. Decrease expansion rate
   C. Shorten setting time and increase expansion rate
   D. Have no effect

19. It is clinically correct to add water to a previously mixed gypsum material that is too thick.
   A. True
   B. False

20. A dry and crumbly mix of a gypsum product will result when there is _____ the minimum amount of water employed.
   A. More than
   B. Less than
   C. Equal amounts of
   D. None of the above

21. If you increase the water/powder ratio of a gypsum product it will result in a _____ model.
   A. Strong
   B. Weak
   C. Thermoplastic
   D. None of the above

22. Chemical additives utilized with gypsum products will result in:
   A. Lengthening the setting time and expansion rate
   B. Increasing the expansion rate
   C. Shortening the setting time and expansion rate
   D. No effect

23. _____ are chemicals that will increase the rate of reaction so that the setting time of gypsum products is reduced by several minutes.
   A. Retarders
   B. Hardening solutions
   C. Accelerators
   D. Modifiers

24. Examples of retarders that will affect the setting reaction of stone casts are:
   A. Food
   B. Blood
   C. Saliva
   D. All of the above
   E. A and B only

25. The time required to mix and pour a gypsum product should be approximately:

A. 1 minute

B. 3 minutes

C. 5 minutes

D. 10 minutes

26. When pouring the mixed gypsum product into the alginate impression, the small increment of the mix is placed first in the:

A. Posterior molar area

B. Central anterior area

C. Right canine area

D. Left premolar area

27. A lower water/powder ratio, which reflects more powder and less water, results in:

A. Reduced strength

B. Decreased setting expansion

C. Increased setting expansion and strength

D. Reduced hardness of the product

28. Hygroscopic setting expansion occurs in gypsum products when they are immersed in water.

A. True

B. False

29. Final setting of a gypsum product takes approximately:

A. 1 hour

B. 30 minutes

C. 24 hours

D. 2 days

30. The finished gypsum model is comprised of two portions that replicate the tissues of the teeth and the base. They include the following:

A. Anatomic

B. Art

C. Angle

D. Only A and B

E. Only B and C

31. Ideally, to ease the task of trimming the gypsum models, they should be submerged in:

A. Cool water for 5 minutes

B. Warm water for 1 hour

C. Tepid water for 20 seconds

D. Warm water for 5 minutes

32. Bite registration wax is utilized when trimming the gypsum model because it:

A. Assists in establishing the symmetrical relationship of the arches

B. Avoids the fracturing of teeth during the trimming of the maxillary and mandibular base

C. Allows for the articulation of the maxillary and mandibular arch

D. Only A and C

E. All of the above

33. Gypsum products should be properly stored in a(n):

A. Warm, humid room

B. Cool, dry air-tight container

C. Dark, moist area

D. Open container

34. A finished gypsum model should be properly identified for storage, detailing:

A. Patient's name

B. Patient's age

C. Date

D. Only A and C

E. All of the above

B. Irreversible and reversible hydrocolloids

35. An impression is considered to be a _____ reproduction of the oral tissues.

A. Negative

B. Positive

C. Permanent

D. None of the above

36. An accurate dental impression provides the operator with a _____ reproduction of the dentition, quadrant, or tooth.

A. Positive

B. Permanent

C. Negative

D. None of the above

37. To obtain an accurate alginate impression of the dental arch and maintain patient comfort during the process, the following technique(s) may be employed:

A. Including all the dentition in the impression

B. Adapting utility wax on the periphery of the tray

C. Covering the area beyond the attached gingiva with the material

D. Only A and B

E. All of the above

38. Which tray is best suited for taking an alginate impression?

A. Water-cooled tray

B. Rim-lock tray

C. Perforated tray

D. Only A and B

E. Only B and C

39. The ideal temperature of water when mixing alginate should be:

A. Hot

B. Cold

C. Room temperature

D. None of the above

40. If the temperature of the water is increased when mixing alginate, the setting time will be:

A. Lengthened

B. Shortened

C. Not affected

D. None of the above

41. When mixing alginate impression material, the water is measured and dispensed in a:

A. Cup

B. Glass

C. Graduated cylinder

D. Plastic water measurer

42. If excess water is mixed with the alginate powder, the final set impression will be:

A. Strengthened

B. Weakened

C. Not affected

D. More solid

43. Alginate should be mixed for:

A. 30 seconds

B. 45 seconds

C. 1 minute

D. One and one-half minutes

44. The correct mixing procedure for alginate impression material requires the following:

A. Incorporate powder and water in a gentle manner until completely moistened

B. Hold the bowl in the right or left hand while spatulating the mix with a wiping motion

C. Spatulate the mix into a creamy homogenous consistency

D. Only B and C

E. All of the above

45. Many difficulties can occur when manipulating irreversible hydrocolloid materials. They include:

A. Tearing alginate from the stone model

B. Voids in the surface of the impression

C. Premature separation of the impression and cast

D. Only A and B

E. All of the above

46. Undermixing alginate impression material will result in:

A. Grainy mix and a model with poor detail

B. Increased tear strength

C. Increased setting time

D. Finer surface detail

47. When loading a perforated or a rim-lock tray for an alginate impression:

A. Material is added to the anterior portion first

B. Material is added to the posterior portion of the tray and pushed toward the center first

C. More material is used in the posterior portion

D. It is loaded very slowly

48. Which factor can cause the deterioration of alginate impression materials?
A. Lowered temperatures
B. Air conditioning/dry air
C. Elevated temperatures and moisture
D. All of the above

49. An impression material capable of changing from a gel to a sol and back to a gel is known as:
A. Alginate
B. Reversible hydrocolloid
C. Compound
D. Silicone

50. Agar-hydrocolloid material is heated until it flows and is cooled. It changes from a:
A. Gel to a sol to a gel
B. Sol to a gel
C. Gel to a sol
D. Sol to a gel to a sol

51. The loss of solution from a hydrocolloid impression is known as:
A. Hysteresis
B. Syneresis
C. Imbibition
D. Preservation

52. The appropriate tray that is utilized for obtaining a hydrocolloid impression is referred to as a(n) _____ tray.
A. Alginate
B. Custom
C. Water-cooled
D. Rim-lock

53. Which material should be tempered prior to taking an impression?
A. Alginate
B. Impression plaster

C. Reversible hydrocolloid
D. Silicone

54. The tempered material is placed into a hydrocolloid tray for impression taking; the next steps include:
A. Attaching the water tubing and the connector to the dental unit cold water supply
B. Removal of a retraction cord from the patient's sulcus
C. Removal of the loaded syringe from the hydrocolloid storage bath. The excess moisture is removed and the material is extruded around the sulcus and the prepared tooth surfaces.
D. Only B and C
E. All of the above

C. Impression compound

55. A characteristic of impression compound is that it returns to a rigid state when it is cooled.
A. True
B. False

56. The impression material utilized with impression compound to record edentulous arches is known as:
A. Addition silicone
B. Tray compound
C. Impression plaster
D. Zinc oxide-eugenol

57. A custom tray is used as a:
A. Secondary impression for an edentulous impression
B. Preliminary impression for an edentulous impression
C. Wash impression
D. Reproduction of fine detail of the dentition

58. The first step prior to fabricating a custom tray is:
A. Preparing a gypsum cast for custom tray placement
B. Dispensing the powder and measuring the resin

C. Measuring the resin liquid only

D. Kneading the doughy resin and powder resin

D. Custom tray materials

59. What procedure should be followed when constructing a custom acrylic impression tray?
    A. Mix the tray resin to a doughy-like consistency
    B. Shape the resin mix into a tray form on a model or cast
    C. Extend an anterior handle when shaping the tray resin material on the maxillary or mandibular arch
    D. Only A and B
    E. All of the above

60. The procedure for finishing an acrylic custom tray is accomplished by utilizing:
    A. Acrylic bur
    B. Straight handpiece
    C. Laboratory bench lathe
    D. All of the above
    E. None of the above

61. A vacuum molding unit can be effectively utilized to form a custom acrylic impression tray. The procedure requires a sequence of steps during the formation process which includes:
    A. Selection of the correct acrylic sheet thickness according to the manufacturer's specification
    B. Setting the heating controls on the vacuum former unit in preparation for molding the tray
    C. Heating the acrylic sheet and applying pressure during the placement over the model or case
    D. Only B and C
    E. All of the above

E. Elastomeric/rubber base impression materials

62. A secondary impression:
    A. Reproduces fine detail

B. Is produced in an alginate tray
C. Provides a preliminary impression
D. Sets slowly

63. Rubber-base impression material is used with which one of the following?
    A. Custom trays
    B. Copper bands
    C. Alginate trays
    D. Aluminum trays

64. The armamentarium utilized during the preparation of rubber-base impression material is:
    A. Tapered spatula
    B. Paper mixing pad
    C. Catalyst and base
    D. Only A and B
    E. All of the above

1. Polysulfide

65. Polysulfide impression material is mixed with a:
    A. Straight spatula
    B. Tapered stiff spatula
    C. Tongue depressor
    D. Cement spatula

66. When taking a polysulfide rubber-base impression _____ is utilized as the medium to ensure the retention of the rubber-base impression material onto the custom tray.
    A. Putty
    B. Cement
    C. Adhesive
    D. Wax

67. A polysulfide rubber impression material is mixed for:
    A. 4 minutes
    B. 1 minute
    C. 45 seconds
    D. 30 seconds

68. A regular-bodied polysulfide impression material is placed in a(n) ___ for a final impression.
    A. Aluminum tray
    B. Perforated metal tray

C. Compound tray

D. Custom tray

69. When mixing polysulfide rubber-base impression material, the end product should be:

A. Tempered before use

B. Homogeneous

C. In a liquid state

D. Putty-like

70. The substance in the catalyst that stains clothing is found in polysulfide and is known as:

A. Plasticizer

B. Mercaptan

C. Calcium sulfate

D. Lead dioxide

71. The recommended cleanup procedure for a regular-bodied polysulfide impression material is to:

A. Clean the spatula with a 2 by 2 gauze pad

B. Peel the set material from the spatula blade

C. Remove the used sheet of the mixing pad and appropriately dispose of it

D. Tightly recap the impression materials

E. All of the above

2. Silicone

72. A light-bodied impression material is placed into the cavity preparation using a:

A. Needle

B. Tube

C. Syringe

D. Spatula

73. Types of silicone rubber impression materials utilized in dentistry are:

A. Condensation

B. Addition

C. Polyether

D. Only A and B

E. All of the above

74. Silicone rubber impression material is sensitive to:

A. Moisture

B. Heat

C. Light

D. Only A and B

E. All of the above

75. Silicone rubber impression materials are available in the following consistency:

A. Light

B. Regular

C. Heavy

D. Only A and B

E. All of the above

76. When compared with polysulfide rubber impression materials, silicone rubber materials:

A. Are more viscous

B. Have less viscosity

C. Are harder to mix

D. Are easier to mix

E. Only B and D

77. Condensation silicone rubber impression material has a shorter setting and working time if there is an increase in the following:

A. Heat

B. Moisture

C. Acid

D. Only A and B

E. All of the above

78. Addition vinyl silicone material undergoes a _____ dimensional change during setting.

A. High

B. Low

C. Large

D. None of the above

79. An addition silicone impression material causes less tissue reaction than a condensation silicone impression material.

A. True

B. False

80. Preparation of a putty addition silicone material for a two-step procedure requires the following necessary steps:
    A. Selection of the armamentarium, which includes the stock tray, mixing pad, and light-bodied and heavy-bodied impression materials
    B. Proportioning a scoop of putty material and catalyst onto a mixing pad
    C. Spatulating the base and catalyst material and donning plastic or vinyl overgloves
    D. Kneading the mixture for the specified time
    E. All of the above

81. Polysiloxane impression materials, commonly known as addition silicone materials, are available in an automatic dispensing unit which includes:
    A. Extruder gun
    B. Cartridge containing the impression material catalyst and base
    C. Mixing tip
    D. Only A and B
    E. All of the above

82. The proper assembly of an extruder gun requires two or more steps in the proper order:
    A. Place the cartridges into the extruder gun
    B. Properly engage the plunger and remove the cartridge cap
    C. Place a mixing tip on the end of the cartridge and turn it to a locked position
    D. Only A and C
    E. All of the above

83. When handling elastomeric materials, special precautions can be followed to prevent problems during impression manipulation. They include:
    A. Not placing the caps on the opposite tubes of the accelerator or base impression materials
    B. Draping the patient with ample protection during the impression placement process in order to avoid staining of the patient's clothes
    C. Mixing the catalyst and base from other packaged systems
    D. Only A and B
    E. All of the above

3. Polyether

84. A polyether impression can be silver-plated and produced into a die.
    A. True
    B. False

85. A polyether is _____ to mix as compared to polysulfide impression material.
    A. Easier
    B. More difficult
    C. About the same
    D. None of the above

86. Polyether rubber impression material is mixed on a:
    A. Glass slab
    B. Paper mixing pad

87. Polyether rubber impression material can irritate the tissue. This is avoided by:
    A. Shorter mixing time
    B. Longer mixing time
    C. Mixing thoroughly
    D. None of the above

88. A polyether is slower setting than a polysulfide material.
    A. True
    B. False

89. A polyether impression material is removed from the oral cavity with a _____ stroke.
    A. Fast, single
    B. Slow, single

F. Cements

1. Zinc phosphate

90. When mixing zinc phosphate, the mixing time is:
    A. 1 minute
    B. 2 minutes
    C. 3 minutes
    D. 1½ minutes

91. When mixing zinc phosphate cement, the powder and liquid are mixed over a large area with a _____ motion.
    A. Chopping
    B. Short sweeping
    C. Tapping
    D. Figure-eight rotary

92. Excess zinc phosphate cement powder left on the mixing slab is always:
    A. Returned to the bottle
    B. Placed under the cement base in the cavity preparation
    C. Placed over the cement base in the cavity preparation
    D. Discarded

93. A factor that will lengthen the setting time of zinc phosphate is:
    A. High temperature
    B. Low temperature, below 65°F
    C. Thick mix
    D. Moisture

94. The _____ reaction is initiated during the manipulation of zinc phosphate.
    A. Interlocking
    B. Tensile
    C. Exothermic
    D. Buffered

95. The lengthened setting time of zinc phosphate is affected by the following:
    A. Increased powder/liquid ratio
    B. Decreased powder/liquid ratio
    C. None of the above

96. Zinc phosphate powder is properly prepared by _____ the bottle.
    A. Shaking
    B. Swirling
    C. Both A and B
    D. None of the above

97. Zinc phosphate is mixed by utilizing _____ strokes with a cement spatula.
    A. Short
    B. Long
    C. Broad
    D. None of the above

98. The frozen slab method is ideally utilized when preparing zinc phosphate for:
    A. Cementing orthodontic bands
    B. Cementing bridges
    C. Prolonging work time
    D. All of the above
    E. Only A and B

99. Zinc phosphate mixed as a luting agent should elongate approximately _____ inch(es) above the slab when the operator places it on the edge of the cement spatula.
    A. 2
    B. 1
    C. ½
    D. ¾

100. The cement that is mixed on a glass slab to minimize the temperature rise (exothermic) from the heat given off is:
    A. Zinc oxide-eugenol
    B. Zinc polyacrylate
    C. Zinc phosphate
    D. Composite resin

2. Polyacrylate

101. A polyacrylate or polycarboxylate cement should be mixed for approximately _____ seconds in order to allow time for seating of the fixed prosthesis.
    A. 15

B. 30

C. 45

D. 50

102. A polyacrylate cement is _____ to the pulp than zinc phosphate cement.

A. More irritating

B. Less irritating

C. More harmful

D. None of the above

103. A polyacrylate cement is utilized for:

A. Final cementation of crowns and bridge

B. High-strength base

C. Temporary filling

D. Only B and C

E. All of the above

3. Zinc oxide and eugenol

104. The cement that has a sedative effect on the pulp is known as:

A. Zinc phosphate

B. Zinc polyacrylate

C. Composite resin

D. Zinc oxide-eugenol (ZOE)

105. Reinforced zinc oxide - eugenol cements are utilized for:

A. Sedative restorations

B. Cementation of stainless crowns

C. Luting agents

D. Only A and B

E. All of the above

106. Zinc oxide-eugenol cements are considered the cement of choice for temporary restorations because they are:

A. Palliative to the pulp

B. Insulating bases

C. Protective against thermal shock to the pulp

D. Only A and B

E. All of the above

107. Intermediate restorations provide extended periods of clinical observation for a tooth with a questionable prognosis. Materials of choice include:

A. Reinforced ZOE cements

B. Zinc silicon phosphate

C. Zinc phosphate

D. Only A and B

E. All of the above

108. If a patient should experience alveolitis (dry socket), the dental auxiliary-may make a paste of zinc oxide and eugenol. The operator would place this dressing in the socket to provide temporary relief from this painful condition.

A. True

B. False

109. Reinforced ZOE cements provide _____ usage as a restorative material.

A. Permanent

B. Extended

C. Temporary

D. None of the above

110. Root canal sealers are formulated from:

A. Zinc phosphate

B. Zinc oxide-eugenol

C. Composite resins

D. Glass ionomers

111. Zinc oxide and eugenol are mixed on a:

A. Glass slab

B. Paper pad

C. Both A and B

D. None of the above

112. _____ will accelerate the setting time of zinc oxide and eugenol.

A. Moisture

B. Oil

C. Heat

D. None of the above

113. What is the consistency of zinc oxide-eugenol cement when used as a temporary restoration?

A. Fluid

B. Firm and brittle

C. Putty-like

D. None of the above

4. Periodontal dressing and gingival pack

114. Periodontal dressing is utilized to dress the surgical gingival tissue. The type of cement used is:
    A. Composite resin
    B. Zinc phosphate
    C. Calcium hydroxide
    D. Zinc oxide-eugenol

115. A periodontal dressing is mixed with a _____ spatula.
    A. Stiff
    B. Flexible
    C. Disposable
    D. Only A and B
    E. Only A and C

116. Gingival tissue pack is utilized for:
    A. Surgical dressing
    B. Displacement of tissue
    C. Cementing orthodontic bands
    D. Root canal sealing

5. Varnishes and liners

117. Varnishes and liners are used for:
    A. Prevention of irritation from metal restorations
    B. Coating the pulp and dentin
    C. Barrier protection
    D. Only A and B
    E. All of the above

118. A cavity varnish is effectively used during cavity preparation primarily because it:
    A. Creates leakage around the margins and walls of the cavity preparation
    B. Reduces leakage around the margins and walls of the cavity preparation
    C. Promotes secondary dentin formation
    D. None of the above

119. Varnish is delivered to the operator utilizing:
    A. Cotton pellet and cotton pliers
    B. Cotton roll and cotton pliers
    C. Cotton applicator
    D. 2 by 2 gauze square

6. Calcium hydroxide

120. Calcium hydroxide cement is utilized for:
    A. Direct pulp capping
    B. Indirect pulp capping
    C. Protective barrier under composites
    D. Only A and B
    E. All of the above

121. Calcium hydroxide cement has the following property:
    A. High thermal conductivity
    B. High mechanical strength
    C. Long setting time
    D. Stimulates formation of reparative dentition

122. Most calcium hydroxide cement systems are supplied as a:
    A. Powder and liquid
    B. Two-paste component
    C. Single paste
    D. None of the above

123. The instrument used to mix and dispense calcium hydroxide is the:
    A. Disposable wooden spatula
    B. Stiff spatula
    C. Ball-pointed insertion instrument
    D. Agate spatula

7. Resin cements

124. Resin cements are utilized for:
    A. Bonding Maryland bridges
    B. Bonding orthodontic brackets
    C. Temporary fillings
    D. Only A and B
    E. All of the above

125. Direct bonding of orthodontic brackets is accomplished with:
    A. Zinc oxide-eugenol cements
    B. Zinc phosphate cements

C. Composite resin cements

D. Calcium hydroxide

8. Glass ionomers

126. High-strength-base glass ionomer cements provide:
    A. Insulating protection
    B. Low solubility
    C. Prevention against decay
    D. Only A and B
    E. All of the above

127. Glass ionomer cements are supplied in various formulations that are utilized for:
    A. Class V caries
    B. Protective bases
    C. Cervically eroded areas
    D. Only A and C
    E. All of the above

128. Glass ionomers have beneficial features, including:
    A. Fluoride-releasing base
    B. Chemical bonding to enamel and dentin
    C. Radiopacity
    D. Only A and C
    E. All of the above

G. Amalgam

129. The most common silver alloy used as a restorative is a _____ type.
    A. Low-copper
    B. High-copper

130. Amalgam is primarily utilized in stress-bearing posterior teeth.
    A. True
    B. False

131. Mercury is a(n):
    A. Alloy
    B. Metal
    C. Dense solid
    D. Dense liquid metal

132. Mercury is dispensed by:
    A. Weight

B. Volume

C. Both A and B

D. None of the above

133. Improper manipulation of amalgam can lead to:
    A. Tooth sensitivity
    B. Marginal leakage
    C. Protruded restoration
    D. Only A and B
    E. All of the above

134. Trituration is a process defined as:
    A. Contamination of the amalgam
    B. Mixing of mercury with silver alloy
    C. Leakage of mercury from a worn capsule
    D. None of the above

135. The auxiliary prepares to triturate amalgam by:
    A. Setting the timer
    B. Filling the capsule with mercury and alloy
    C. Activating the amalgamator
    D. Opening the capsule

136. Mulling the amalgam results in the mix being:
    A. Uniform
    B. Grainy
    C. Separated
    D. Bonded

137. A pestle is a small rod comprised of metal or plastic that is utilized to:
    A. Extend mixing time
    B. Mix powdered alloy
    C. Shorten mixing time
    D. None of the above

138. A properly mixed mass of amalgam should appear:
    A. Black
    B. Silver black
    C. Silver grey
    D. Silver

139. An undermixed mass of amalgam is:
    A. Shiny
    B. Soupy
    C. Dull
    D. Crumbly
    E. Only C and D

140. An overworked mass of amalgam would appear:
    A. Soupy
    B. Shiny
    C. Dull
    D. Crumbly

141. Condensation of amalgam affects the following:
    A. Reduction of excess mercury
    B. Compaction of a uniform mass
    C. Adaptation of a mass to the cavity walls
    D. Only B and C
    E. All of the above

142. The amount of force applied to a hand condenser when placing the amalgam into the cavity preparation is:
    A. 5 to 6 pounds
    B. 7 to 8 pounds
    C. 8 to 10 pounds
    D. 10 to 12 pounds

143. The excessive expansion of an amalgam restoration after insertion will result in:
    A. Sensitivity of the tooth
    B. Leakage of the restoration
    C. Tarnishing of the restoration
    D. Corrosion of the restoration

144. A discoloration caused by the deposit of a surface film on an amalgam restoration is known as:
    A. Tarnishing
    B. Corrosion
    C. Disintegration
    D. None of the above

145. When are spherical high-copper alloys usually finished and polished?
    A. 24 hours after carving

B. At the same appointment
    C. 3 hours after carving
    D. None of the above

146. A polishing abrasive utilized for finishing amalgam is known as:
    A. Tin oxide
    B. Hydrogen peroxide
    C. Silver oxide
    D. Carbon dioxide

147. The dry polishing of amalgam results in:
    A. Shiny appearance
    B. Smooth surface
    C. Vaporization of mercury
    D. None of the above
    E. All of the above

148. Precautions for safe handling of mercury are:
    A. Automatic ultrasonic condensers
    B. No-touch technique
    C. Premeasured capsules
    D. All of the above
    E. Only B and C

149. A health hazard of handling mercury is:
    A. Inhalation of mercury vapor
    B. Skin absorption of mercury
    C. Inhalation of airborne particles
    D. Only A and B
    E. All of the above

150. Systemic absorption of mercury occurs through:
    A. Airborne particles
    B. Vapor
    C. Inhalation
    D. Skin

151. The American Dental Association recommends utilizing premeasured capsules of mercury and alloy as a preventive measure for safe handling of mercury.
    A. True
    B. False

152. Amalgam scrap is considered to be hazardous waste and should be disposed of in a:
   A. Plastic jar
   B. Wooden box
   C. Capped unbreakable jar
   D. Plastic bag

153. Mercury intoxication may be encountered by dental personnel from:
   A. Direct absorption from exposed surfaces
   B. Excessive trituration
   C. Premeasured capsules of mercury and alloy
   D. None of the above

H. Composites

154. Composite restorative materials consist of:
   A. Silicate materials
   B. Acrylic unfilled polymer fillers
   C. Dimethacrylate polymer and inorganic reinforcing agents
   D. Acidulated fluoride materials

155. The trend to utilize hybrid composite restoratives in dentistry today provides the following:
   A. Higher concentration of fine filler material
   B. Polishing of a smoother surface
   C. Blend of fine and microfine filler particles
   D. Only A and B
   E. All of the above

156. What is the purpose of acid etching a tooth when using a composite restorative?
   A. Formation of tags on the etched tooth surface
   B. Formation of a bond on the buccal surface of the tooth
   C. Sealing of the dentinal tubules
   D. Penetration into the pulp of the tooth

157. Composite materials are utilized for

_____ restoratives:
   A. Class V
   B. Class IV
   C. Class III
   D. Class I
   E. All of the above

158. Polymerization of direct esthetic restoratives is initiated by:
   A. Autocure
   B. Visible light
   C. Both A and B
   D. None of the above

159. A single-paste system of packaging composites is polymerized by:
   A. Visible light
   B. Autocuring

160. The presence of moisture during polymerization of a composite restorative will:
   A. Inhibit and lengthen the setting time
   B. Accelerate and shorten the setting time
   C. Have no effect on the setting time
   D. Produce an excellent product

161. Most often the type of spatula used to mix a composite restorative material is:
   A. Stainless steel
   B. Plastic
   C. Metal
   D. None of the above

162. The average curing time for a single-paste composite material ranges from:
   A. 1 to 2 minutes
   B. 1 to 2 seconds
   C. 3 to 5 seconds
   D. 20 to 60 seconds

163. Looking directly at the light beam of the visible light can cause retinal damage; therefore, protection must be practiced by utilizing:
   A. Protective eyewear

B. Shields, both attached and hand-held

C. Curved shields

D. Only A and B

E. All of the above

164. Repeated exposure to the curing light can cause damage to the:
A. Fingers
B. Face
C. Retina
D. Nose

I. Waxes

165. The major uses of dental waxes are:
A. Patterns, processing, and impressions
B. Construction of models, dies, and casts
C. Preliminary impressions and final impressions
D. None of the above

166. The three general classifications of waxes include: (1) inlay wax, (2) processing wax, (3) paraffin wax, (4) impression wax, (5) beeswax, and (6) pattern wax.
A. 1, 3, and 4
B. 1, 3, and 5
C. 2, 4, and 6
D. 1, 2, and 3

167. Which wax is not used intraorally?
A. Baseplate wax
B. Sticky wax
C. Utility wax
D. Pattern wax

168. The primary use for utility wax is to:
A. Place on a gypsum model
B. Hold impression compound in place
C. Wrap around the periphery of an alginate tray
D. Construct a bit wax rim

169. The function of sticky wax is to:
A. Rebuild cusps on models

B. Take bite registrations

C. Take tooth impressions

D. Hold fractured denture parts together

170. Casting wax is utilized for:
A. Replacing inlay wax
B. Pattern for partial framework
C. Retaining wax in castings
D. Holding dies in position

171. Corrective impression wax is clinically used for:
A. Articulation of models
B. Registration of soft tissue detail
C. Assembling a fractured denture
D. Only A and C
E. None of the above

172. The wax used to make a rim around an impression that contains gypsum material is called:
A. Boxing wax
B. Utility wax
C. Periphery wax
D. Blue wax

173. The type of wax commonly used for registering a patient's occlusion is known as:
A. Pattern wax
B. Utility wax
C. Boxing wax
D. Bite registration wax

J. Preventive materials

1. Sealants

174. The material suitable for preventing occlusal caries is:
A. Amalgam
B. Glass ionomer
C. Composite
D. Sealant

175. Prior to applying the pit and fissure sealant material the teeth should be cleansed with a(n):
A. Toothbrush

B. Pumice and prophylaxis cup or brush

C. Polishing agent

D. Antiseptic solution

176. _____ improves the retention of a sealant.

A. Elastic modulus

B. Acid etching

C. Knoop hardness

D. Bonding

177. The purpose of a bonding agent when utilizing sealant material is to:

A. Prevent microleakage

B. Form tags for retention

C. Improve wettability of enamel

D. Supply a space for the sealant

178. Pit and fissure sealants require polymerization by utilizing:

A. A self-cured, two-component system light cured

B. A light cured single syringe system

C. Occlusal polishing with an oil-based abrasive material

D. Only A and B

179. A single-component pit and fissure system requires _____ for polymerization.

A. Visible white light application

B. Mixing of the base and the catalyst

2. Fluoride

180. During the application of a topical fluoride treatment the correct sequence of procedures should be followed:

Match the procedures with the sequenced steps:

A. Suction the excess saliva with the ejector or high-speed evacuation

B. Apply a ribbon of fluoride into a mandibular and maxillary tray

C. Place the fluoride tray onto the mandibular and then maxillary arches for the specified time

D. Dry the teeth with the air syringe

E. Complete a prophylaxis

Step 1. _____

Step 2. _____

Step 3. _____

Step 4. _____

Step 5. _____

181. When applying a fluoride gel to the teeth, the teeth should be dried free of saliva.

A. True

B. False

182. Following a fluoride treatment, the patient is instructed not to eat for:

A. 1 minute

B. 5 minutes

C. 30 minutes

D. 1 hour

3. Mouthguards

183. A custom-made athletic mouth protector is fabricated by using a:

A. Model trimmer

B. Hanau heater

C. Bunsen burner

D. Vacuum former

184. An athletic mouth protector is used to prevent:

A. Injuries

B. Infection

C. Caries

D. Periodontal disease

185. The method of proper care for an athletic mouth guard is to:

A. Brush with a toothbrush and toothpaste

B. Rinse with warm water and soap

C. Rinse with cool water and soap

D. Rinse with an antiseptic

K. Dentures

186. The most widely used prosthetic material utilized for a denture base is:

A. Vinyl plastic

B. Acrylic plastic

C. Polymer plastic

D. Ethylene plastic

187. During the processing of acrylic denture base materials, the denture cast is invested in a:

A. Container

B. Flask

C. Water

D. Jar

188. The curing of the resin when processing the denture requires:

A. Lathe

B. Dry heat

C. Moist heat under pressure

D. Cool water

189. Patients who have denture sores or have a problem retaining a denture may require a:

A. Hard liner

B. Soft liner

C. Base plate wax

D. Corrective wax

E. Utility wax

190. Most partial frameworks are fabricated from:

A. Palladium

B. Cobalt-chromium

C. Silver

D. Gold alloy

191. When grinding or polishing dental models or appliances:

A. Rag wheel should not be sterilized

B. Working surface should not be covered with a barrier

C. Masks, gloves, and glasses should be worn

D. Rag wheel is reused

192. What methods are utilized to remove unsightly stains and calculus deposits on dentures?

A. Professional polishing

B. Soaking in a denture cleansing product

C. Brushing the denture with a den-

ture toothpaste

D. All of the above

193. Dentures should be rinsed in _____ water.

A. Cool

B. Hot

C. Tepid

D. None of the above

L. Crowns

194. Crowns that provide temporary coverage are fabricated of:

A. Custom-made acrylic

B. Preformed acrylic

C. Preformed aluminum

D. Polycarbonate

E. All of the above

195. When seating the temporary crown, excess height may be removed by utilizing a(n):

A. Acrylic trimming bur

B. Garnet disc

C. Amalgam file

D. Only A and B

E. All of the above

196. Once the temporary crown is seated, it may be polished with:

A. Green stone with a fine grit polishing agent

B. Tin oxide paste and a prophylaxis cup

C. Pumice and water and a prophylaxis brush

D. Only A and B

E. All of the above

197. Temporary crowns are cemented with:

A. Zinc oxide-eugenol (ZOE)

B. Intermediate restorative material (IRM)

C. Zinc phosphate

D. Only A and B

E. All of the above

198. During the cementation of a temporary crown the following step(s)

should be completed:

A. Excess cement removed with an explorer or a scaler

B. Contact areas checked with dental floss

C. Crowns checked for a secure fit

D. Occlusion checked with articulating paper

E. All of the above

M. Bleaching

199. The types of bleaching techniques utilized in the dental office are:

A. Heat

B. Light

C. Gels and microabrasions

D. Only B and C

E. All of the above

200. A bleaching procedure would be performed in the dental office on a patient who had the following condition:

A. Dental fluorosis

B. Tetracycline stain

C. Acquired superficial surface discolorations or blemishes

D. Only A and B

E. All of the above

201. Bleaching agents will not harm teeth restored with:

A. Gold alloy

B. Amalgam

C. Microfilled composite and porcelain

D. All of the above

N. Enamel and dentin bonding

202. Enamel bonding applications may be utilized to:

A. Correct a diastema

B. Cover surfaces that have been chipped, fractured, or worn

C. Cover teeth that have been discolored or stained

D. Only A and B

E. All of the above

203. Dentin bonding systems require the following consideration during clinical use:

A. Pretreatment with acid etching

B. May be subject to microleakage

C. May be light-cured or self-cured

D. Only A and C

E. All of the above

O. Handling hazardous substances in the dental office

204. The Occupational Safety and Health Administration (OSHA) provides guidelines and regulations for employees that pertain to:

A. Dangers with hazardous chemicals

B. Maintenance of a hazard communication program

C. Employee training

D. Only B and C

E. All of the above

205. Hazardous dental products utilized by employees in the dental office setting require:

A. Label identification

B. Hazardous warnings on the product

C. Cost-effective measures

D. Only A and B

E. All of the above

206. Material Safety Data Sheets (MSDS) contain information that pertains to:

A. Precautions concerning the product

B. Safe handling of the product

C. Cost of the product

D. Only A and B

E. All of the above

207. How may the dentist provide proper training for employees in the workplace regarding the handling of hazardous products in the dental office?

A. Staff meetings

B. Continuing education courses

C. Self-learning

D. Only A and B

E. All of the above

208. Proper precautionary handling of hazardous dental products in the office includes:

A. Tightly sealing all bottle chemical products

B. Using protective OSHA-approved eyewear and masks

C. Disposal of all products following the MSDS guidelines

D. Only B and C

E. All of the above

209. When handling acid-etch solutions and gels, precautionary measures should be followed, and they include:

A. Proper protection with gloves

B. Utilization of a commercial clean-up kit

C. Copious rinsing with the emergency eye wash fountain in case of eye exposure

D. Only A and C

E. All of the above

210. The handling of asbestos during the fabrication of a casting ring requires the following precaution:

A. Eyewear

B. Gloves

C. NIOSH-approved mask

D. Only A and B

E. All of the above

211. When handling flammable liquids such as acetone and alcohol, precautions should include:

A. Access to a fire extinguisher

B. Proper ventilation

C. A scavenging system

D. Only A and B

E. All of the above

212. When mixing gypsum products, the employee should practice safe-handling precautions such as:

A. Wearing eyewear and gloves

B. Utilizing an exhaust system

C. Wearing a NIOSH-approved mask

D. Only B and C

E. All of the above

213. The safe handling of mercury entails the following precautions:

A. Avoiding skin contact with the mercury product

B. Proper storage avoiding extreme heat

C. Submerging scrap amalgam in an old fixer solution or a commercial photographic product

D. Commercial cleanup kit

E. All of the above

214. Gloves, eyewear, and NIOSH-approved masks are required when handling:

A. Alloys and metals

B. Gypsum

C. Asbestos

D. Only B and C

E. All of the above

215. A scavenging system and adequate ventilation in the dental operatory is appropriate when using the following:

A. Asbestos

B. Acetone

C. Nitrous oxide

D. Mercury

E. All of the above

216. Methyl methacrylate and dimethylacrylate require the following precaution during handling:

A. Avoidance of inhalation of the vapors and contact with skin

B. Properly ventilated work area

C. Commercial flammable solvent cleanup kit

D. Utilization of forceps or gloves

E. All of the above

217. Radiographic processing chemicals require the following precautionary

handling:

A. Protective eyewear

B. Utility gloves

C. Proper disposal and hazardous labeling of used fixer solution

D. Only B and C

E. All of the above

218. Safety goggles, utility gloves, and a commercial acid spill cleanup kit should be employed when handling:

A. Gypsum products

B. Mercury

C. Pickling solutions

D. Nitrous oxide

219. The proper protection for employees working with the visible light in the dental office requires:

A. Avoidance of direct visible light exposure

B. Protective eye shields

C. Protective visible light eyewear

D. Only B and C

E. All of the above

P. Infection control protocol

220. The purpose of rinsing an impression with cool water and spraying it with disinfectant is to:

A. Remove saliva and blood

B. Remove food and debris

C. Eliminate microorganisms

D. All of the above

221. Polyether can be adversely affected by immersion in a disinfectant. Which disinfectant can be utilized for immersion and for how long?

A. Chlorine compound for 2 to 3 minutes

B. Phenolic for 1 minute

C. Iodophor for 2 to 3 minutes

D. Glutaraldehyde for 1 to 3 minutes

222. The proper procedure for disinfecting alginate impressions is:

A. Rinsing under cool, running water

B. Spraying with a disinfectant

C. Sealing in a plastic bag

D. Only B and C

E. All of the above

223. Elastomeric impressions that include polysulfide rubber, polyether, and addition silicone materials are disinfected by:

A. Soaking, rinsing, and drying for 10 minutes in an acceptable EPA disinfectant

B. Autoclaving

C. Wiping with ethyl alcohol

D. Immersing for 1-hour in an acceptable disinfectant

E. Wiping with quaternary ammonium compounds

224. The receiving area of the dental laboratory can be appropriately disinfected with a(n):

A. Iodophor

B. Chlorine compound

C. Synthetic phenolics

D. Only A and C

E. All of the above

225. Ragwheels should be properly cared for in the laboratory setting by:

A. Washing

B. Autoclaving

C. Reusing

D. Only A and B

E. Only A and C

226. Incoming and outgoing laboratory cases should always be:

A. Disinfected

B. Sterilized utilizing steam heat

C. Submerged in isopropyl alcohol

D. Chemiclaved

227. The disinfection of reusable hydro-colloid impressions includes:

A. Iodophor solution

B. Glutaraldehyde

C. 10-minute spray/rinse/pour

D. Only B and C

E. Only A and C

228. During laboratory polishing, pumice is:
   A. Dispensed in small disposable increments
   B. Disposed of after each use
   C. Never reused for the next case
   D. Only A and C
   E. All of the above

229. Ultrasonic cleansing of dentures and removable appliances requires the assistant to:
   A. Place the appliances into a small plastic bag
   B. Fill the plastic bag with an ultrasonic solution
   C. Place the plastic bag and appliance directly into the glass beaker
   D. Only A and B
   E. All of the above

230. The correct disinfection procedure for a prosthesis includes:
   A. Rinsing the patient's prosthesis under running water to remove excess saliva and blood
   B. Soaking the prosthesis in an EPA-registered disinfectant for the manufacturer's specified time
   C. Soaking a nonmetallic prosthesis for 10 minutes in diluted bleach (¼ cup of bleach to 1 gallon of water) that is mixed fresh each day
   D. Only A and B
   E. All of the above

231. Protective eyewear, masks, and gloves should be worn when trimming, grading, or polishing laboratory impressions, prostheses and casts.
   A. True
   B. False

232. The shade guide should be cared for by:
   A. Washing with an antimicrobial soap
   B. Disinfecting
   C. Autoclaving
   D. Only A and B
   E. All of the above

Answers

1. D. Gypsum products such as model plaster produce a positive replication of the patient's oral cavity.

2. C. The gypsum stone model provides the dentist with a permanent replication of the patient's dentition and oral structures.

3. C. Ideally, dental plaster is utilized for study models that provide a permanent record of the patient's oral cavity.

4. B. A die is defined as a replication of a single tooth.

5. C. Gypsum products include model plaster, dental high-strength stone, and investment materials.

6. C. Calcination is defined as the process of converting the mineral gypsum into a laboratory gypsum product. The heating process causes the conversion of the mineral product to a fine powder.

7. E. All the aforementioned materials are utilized as alternatives to high-strength stone when fabricating dies.

8. C. Gypsum products undergo an exothermic reaction, which is the giving off of heat during the initial setting time of the chemical reaction.

9. C. W/P describes the water/powder ratio that is utilized when mixing the gypsum powder with the prescribed amount of water.

10. A. The water/powder ratio determines the strength and hardness of the gypsum.

11. C. The gram scale enables the powder to be correctly weighed in gram increments.

12. C. A flexible rubber bowl and stiff plastic spatula are part of the armamentarium that is utilized when mixing a gypsum product.

13. B. The correct sequence for mixing gypsum requires the powder to be added to the water and allowed to settle for a short time of 30 seconds to eliminate trapped air.

14. B. The correct mixing time for gypsum products depends upon the manufacturer's recommendations, which usually require 30 to 60 seconds.

15. C. A vigorous wiping motion is utilized when spatulating gypsum material in a rubber bowl.

16. C. A mechanical vibrator prevents air from being incorporated into the mix.

17. C. Surface inaccuracies will result if too much air is incorporated into a gypsum mix. These markings will distort the gypsum model.

18. C. Higher water temperatures of 37°C will cause the setting time to be shortened and the expansion rate to be increased.

19. B. Once the water and gypsum powder has been mixed, a chemical reaction is initiated. Adding more water to the mix at this time will cause another chemical reaction to occur.

20. B. Using too little water will result in a dry, crumbly mixture of unusable gypsum.

21. B. Increasing the water/powder ratio results in a thin mix and, therefore, a weaker model.

22. C. Chemical additives such as table salt will shorten the setting time and decrease the expansion rate of a gypsum product.

23. C. Accelerators increase the setting time and expansion rate of the gypsum product.

24. D. Food, blood, and saliva are colloidal systems that can act as retarders and will alter the setting reaction of gypsum stone products.

25. C. The required time to mix and pour a gypsum product is usually 5 minutes.

26. A. Gypsum should be added to the alginate impression in small increments beginning at the posterior molar area.

27. C. A reduction in the water/powder ratio results in an increase in the expansion rate and a stronger gypsum product.

28. A. The hygroscopic expansion of gypsum products occurs when they are submerged under water and can be approximately twice the normal amount of setting expansion, which is determined by the thrust of the dehydrate crystals.

29. A. Usually it is advantageous to remove the gypsum model from the impression in 1 hour once the mix is initiated.

30. D. The finished gypsum model is made up of the anatomic portion, which replicates the teeth and tissues, and the art portion, which includes the formal base.

31. A. Cool water is used to submerge the gypsum models for approximately 5 minutes prior to trimming.

32. E. Bite registration wax performs all of the aforementioned functions during the trimming of gypsum models.

33. B. Gypsum products should be stored in a cool, dry area in a closed, airtight container.

34. E. As a complete patient record, the gypsum model should be stored in a box and include all the aforementioned data.

35. A. The operator obtains a negative reproduction of oral tissues when he takes an impression. An exact replica of the patient's oral cavity is produced once the impression is poured from the existing negative reproduction.

36. C. The impression material of choice provides the negative reproduction of the dentition, quadrant, or tooth.

37. E. In order to obtain an accurate impression, a sufficient amount of alginate material should cover the dentition and the area beyond the attached gingiva. The utility wax is added to the periphery of the tray for depth and/or length. In addition, it adds to the patient's comfort during the procedure.

38. E. A perforated tray or a rim-lock tray can be utilized when taking an alginate impression.

39. C. Water should be at room temperature when mixing an alginate.

40. B. Higher water temperatures result in an accelerated setting time and a shortened working time.

41. D. Water is measured and dispensed in a plastic water measurer when mixing alginate impression material.

42. B. Excessive water will result in weaker alginate impressions.

43. C. Ideally, alginate should be mixed for 1 minute for a normal setting time.

44. E. All the aforementioned steps are necessary when manipulating alginate impression material.

45. E. All the aforementioned are the most common difficulties that can occur during the manipulation of irreversible hydrocolloid.

46. A. If alginate material is not mixed well, the mixture will appear grainy and the model will exhibit poor detail.

47. A. The correct loading procedure is to have the operator first load the alginate impression material into the anterior portion of the tray to ensure an even distribution of the material.

48. C. High temperatures and moist conditions can alter the chemical composition of alginate impression materials.

49. B. Reversible hydrocolloid impression material can be converted from a solid to a liquid in a conditioning unit.

50. A. Agar-hydrocolloid material is heated in a hydrocolloid conditioner, which has three temperature-controlled water bath compartments. Agar gel is converted to a sol at 212°F for 10 to 15 minutes. The tube is then transferred to a second bath at 140° to 150°F, where it can remain in a fluid state. When the impression is to be made, the tube is then tempered in the third bath at 110°F to 115°F so that the oral tissues are not burned.

51. B. The storage of a hydrocolloid impression in 100% relative humidity can cause shrinkage from syneresis, or the loss of solution from the impression.

52. C. Reversible hydrocolloid requires the use of a water-cooled tray as part of the armamentarium for this type of impression material.

53. C. Reversible hydrocolloid material needs to be placed in the tempering bath to increase its flow prior to taking an impression.

54. E. All the steps sequenced in order are essential for the proper placement of tempered hydrocolloid impression material.

55. A. Impression compound characteristically is classified as a rigid dental impression material that can be softened upon heating.

56. D. Zinc oxide-eugenol impression material is utilized with tray compound, which is referred to as a secondary impression material.

57. B. A custom tray is ideally used to obtain a preliminary impression for an edentulous impression material.

58. A. A custom tray is fabricated by adapting the material to a dental stone cast.

59. E. All the aforementioned steps should be followed during the fabrication of a custom acrylic impression tray.

60. D. Finishing the acrylic impression tray will result in smooth edges and provide more comfort for the patient during impression placement. The procedure requires the utilization of an acrylic bur in a straight handpiece or a laboratory bench lathe.

61. E. All the steps mentioned are included during the vacuum-forming procedure of preparing an acrylic custom tray.

62. A. A secondary impression provides a detailed reproduction of the soft tissue/arch.

63. A. Custom trays are fabricated and utilized with rubber-base impression materials.

64. E. The armamentarium for rubber-base impression materials includes all the aforementioned items.

65. B. A tapered stiff spatula is recommended for the proper manipulation of polysulfide impression material.

66. C. Adhesive is required as a medium to hold the rubber-base impression material onto the custom tray when taking a polysulfide rubber-base impression.

67. C. The mixing procedure should be completed in approximately 45 seconds.

68. D. The regular-bodied impression material is placed into a custom acrylic tray.

69. B. If the rubber-base catalyst and base are mixed well, the mix should be streak-free.

70. D. The catalyst paste contains lead dioxide, which can permanently stain clothing.

71. E. All the cleanup steps mentioned are essential after working with a polysulfide impression material.

72. C. A syringe is utilized to inject and expel light-bodied impression material onto the preparation site.

73. D. Types of silicone impression materials include condensation and addition, which is also known as a vinyl silicone type.

74. D. Both moisture and heat will affect silicone rubber impression material.

75. E. Addition silicone materials are available in light - regular, or heavy-bodied consistencies.

76. B. Silicone materials have less viscosity and are, therefore, easier to mix than polysulfide materials.

77. D. Condensation silicone rubber impressions are sensitive to both heat and moisture, and an increase in both will result in shortened working and setting times.

78. B. The dimensional change of addition vinyl silicone material is significantly low and is estimated to be -0.1% in a 24-hour period.

79. A. Oral tissues are less sensitive to addition silicone impression materials.

80. E. All the aforementioned steps are required in the preparation of the putty material for a polysiloxane impression material.

81. E. The automatic dispensing unit utilized to manipulate polysiloxane

impression material is easy to operate and should be appropriately disinfected after use.

82. E. All the aforementioned steps are to be followed in order during the assembly of an extruder gun.

83. E. Special handling measures should be followed when working with elastomeric impression materials in order to avoid ruining the product and for patient protection. All the measures mentioned are important for proper handling.

84. A. True.

85. A. Polyether impression material is easier to mix than the polysulfide impression materials. In addition, it has a shorter working time, which increases the viscosity of the material during mixing.

86. B. Equal lengths of the catalyst and base are extruded on a paper mixing pad and mixed for approximately 30 to 45 seconds. The mix should be uniform and free of streaks.

87. C. The catalyst can be irritating to the skin. Thorough mixing of the catalyst and the base can prevent irritation of the oral tissues.

88. A. True.

89. B. It is important to break the seal by removing the polyether impression tray with a slow pulling motion utilizing a single stroke.

90. D. Zinc phosphate is mixed in increments for approximately 90 seconds.

91. D. A figure-eight rotary motion is utilized when incorporating zinc phosphate.

92. D. Excess cement powder is never returned to the bottle. It is discarded.

93. B. Cooler temperatures, especially those below 65°F, will retard or slow down the setting time of zinc phosphate cement.

94. C. Exothermic reaction is the process of giving off heat.

95. B. Decreased powder/liquid ratio.

96. A. Shake the powder bottle gently before dispensing the required amount.

97. C. Broad strokes are utilized when incorporating the powder and liquid on the glass slab.

98. D. All of the above.

99. B. Ideally, the operator handling the luting cement should be able to elongate it by directing it vertically with a cement spatula approximately 1 inch above the surface of the glass slab.

100. C. Zinc phosphate.

101. B. When prepared as luting agents, zinc polycarboxylate or polyacrylate cements are effectively utilized for the final cementation of crowns. In order to allow adequate time for seating the fixed prosthesis, these cements are mixed for approximately 30 seconds.

102. B. A polyacrylate cement is not as strong as zinc phosphate, but is less irritating to the pulp.

103. E. All the aforementioned are applicable regarding the utilization of a polyacrylate cement.

104. D. Zinc oxide-eugenol (ZOE) cements are known to have a sedative effect on the pulp.

105. E. Reinforced ZOE cements are especially effective as a sedative for the pulp and are utilized for luting and cementing temporary and permanent restorations.

106. E. All the aforementioned properties make ZOE an excellent choice when temporary restorations are required.

107. A. Reinforced ZOE provides a palliative effect as well as extended wear-

ing properties when there is a questionable prognosis for the involved tooth.

108. A. True. When mixed in a paste form, ZOE provides a palliative dressing for postsurgical wounds.

109. C. ZOE provides temporary protection as a restorative material.

110. B. Root canal sealers are filled with gutta-percha point and are comprised of zinc oxide and eugenol.

111. C. A glass slab or a paper pad may be utilized to mix ZOE.

112. A. Moisture will accelerate the setting time of ZOE. Also, a cotton roll saturated with cool water will hasten the setting time of this cement.

113. C. Putty-like consistency.

114. D. Zinc oxide-eugenol cement, which has palliative properties.

115. E. The mixing instruments utilized to prepare a periodontal dressing include a stiff blade or a wooden disposable spatula.

116. B. Gingival tissue pack is utilized to displace tissue temporarily when completing restorative procedures that require a packing placed around the gingival sulcus area for 2 to 7 days.

117. E. Cavity liners and varnishes provide a protection barrier to the dentin, prevent oral fluids from irritating the restoration tooth surface, and can be therapeutic.

118. B. Varnishes are known to be insoluble in oral fluids. They will effectively reduce leakage around the margins and walls of the cavity preparation.

119. A. Varnish is delivered to the operator utilizing a cotton pellet and cotton pliers.

120. E. Cavity liners such as calcium hydroxide are utilized as a protective barrier for the pulp from composites and cements. The liner is also placed over carious dentin to encourage the formation of reparative dentin; this is known as indirect pulp capping. The calcium hydroxide mix is effectively placed on exposed pulp; this is known as direct pulp capping.

121. D. Calcium hydroxide cement is effectively utilized to stimulate the formation of reparative dentin.

122. B. Most of the time calcium hydroxide is supplied as a two-paste system.

123. C. Calcium hydroxide is mixed and dispensed with a ball-pointed insertion instrument.

124. D. Ideally, resin cements are utilized for bonding brackets, cementing orthodontic bands, and cementing Maryland bridges.

125. C. Composite resin cements.

126. E. Glass ionomer cements are utilized as a protective insulating base and have good strength properties. The cement also contains fluoride and is effective in preventing recurrent decay.

127. D. Glass ionomers are used specifically for Class V caries and cervically eroded areas.

128. E. All the aforementioned features are beneficial to the dentist during clinical application of the ionomer material.

129. B. The high-copper alloy is considered to be the most common type utilized in dentistry.

130. A. True.

131. D. Mercury is a highly toxic dense liquid metal.

132. B. Mercury is dispensed by volume.

133. E. Improper manipulation of amalgam can cause marginal leakage as a result of excessive contraction, and tooth sensitivity and protrusion of the restoration because of

excessive expansion.

134. B. Silver alloy and mercury are mixed and the process is referred to as trituration. A mechanical amalgamator is the unit utilized to mix the alloy and mercury.

135. C. The amalgamator is the unit that mixes the mercury and the alloy together.

136. A. A uniform mix of amalgam is achieved by mulling.

137. C. A pestle is a small rod that will shorten the mixing time and improve the mixing process.

138. C. The appearance of amalgam when it is mixed is silver grey.

139. E. The undermixed mass appears dull and crumbly.

140. A. The overmixed mass appears soupy and will not have any form.

141. E. Condensation requires adequate force to adapt amalgam to the cavity wall, develop a uniform mass with few or no voids, and reduce excess mercury. Hand condensing instruments require the dentist to utilize a firm and even force to small increments or amounts of almagam.

142. C. The force is estimated to be approximately 8 to 10 pounds at the tip of the condensing instrument.

143. A. Excessive expansion of amalgam after insertion can lead to tooth sensitivity.

144. A. Tarnishing can be caused by amalgam restorations that are not adequately polished. The surface attracts the accumulation of calculus and plaque.

145. B. At the same appointment, because high-copper alloys achieve sufficient strength immediately after they are placed in the oral cavity.

146. A. Tin oxide may be utilized as a polishing agent.

147. C. Dry polishing is not recommended because it can cause mercury vapors to be released and will ultimately affect the strength of the amalgam.

148. E. Safe handling of mercury includes the use of premeasured capsules and the no-touch technique. Ultrasonic condensers should not be utilized because mercury vapors can be released.

149. E. Proper handling of mercury in the dental office is essential in order to prevent inhalation of mercury vapor, skin absorption of mercury, and inhalation of airborne particles.

150. D. Systemic absorption of liquid mercury occurs through the skin.

151. A. True. Premeasured capsules prevent the handling of mercury and eliminate possible spillage accidents.

152. C. Mercury and amalgam scrap should be disposed of in a capped unbreakable jar. The holding water should contain sulfur.

153. A. Mercury is absorbed directly into the skin by mishandling or poor mercury hygiene practices.

154. C. The dimethacrylate polymer and inorganic reinforcing agents comprise composite restorative materials.

155. E. Hybrid composites are a blend of both fine and micro-fine particles and have a higher filler concentration. The surface can be polished to a smooth result.

156. A. Acid etching provides mechanical retention by forming tags on the tooth surface being prepared for composite restorations.

157. E. Composites are utilized for Class I, III, IV, and V restorations, as well as a variety of other applications, such as core buildups, temporary

bridge construction, repair of porcelain, orthodontic bonding, and restoring cervical areas.

158. C. Polymerization of direct esthetic restoratives is initiated by the self-curing or autocuring process and by visible white light. Self-curing occurs when a direct esthetic material is combined by mixing the catalyst paste and the universal paste together for the directed time (30 to 45 seconds). The visible light cures or sets the direct esthetic material that is supplied in a single syringe. The material is expelled, placed, and light-cured for the required time.

159. A. Visible light.

160. A. Moisture will lengthen and inhibit setting time of composite restorative materials.

161. B. Composite materials require the utilization of a plastic spatula, as a metal one will discolor the restoration.

162. D. An average curing time for single-paste composite materials is 20 to 60 seconds, if the restoration depth is approximately 3 mm.

163. E. Many types of protection shields are available to ward off exposure from the visible light and provide protection to the retina of the eye.

164. C. Protective eyewear and shields offer adequate protection to the eye area during curing light utilization.

165. A. Waxes are primarily utilized clinically for obtaining impressions, taking bite registrations, boxing impressions, and bordering impression trays.

166. C. The general classifications of dental wax include processing, impression, and pattern wax.

167. B. Sticky wax is used to repair or hold together a broken or fractured den-

ture or partial until it is sent to the dental laboratory.

168. C. Utility wax provides a border or added contour on the impression tray.

169. D. Sticky wax is utilized for prosthetic repairs.

170. B. Casting wax provides the pattern for the fabrication of the metal framework of a partial denture.

171. B. Corrective impression wax registers the occlusal relationship of the dental arches and details of the soft tissue.

172. A. Boxing wax provides a method of containing gypsum material during the pouring and setting process.

173. D. Bite registration wax is utilized to obtain a wax bite of the patient's occlusion.

174. D. Pit and fissure sealants are applied to the occlusal surfaces of posterior teeth as a preventive measure for tooth decay.

175. B. A prophylaxis brush or cup and pumice are used to clean the occlusal surface prior to applying the pit and fissure material.

176. B. Acid etching is a procedure that prepares the enamel surface by cleansing and forming retention tags.

177. B. Bonding agents are applied to the enamel in order to provide mechanical retention to the acid-etched enamel surface.

178. D. The polymerization of the pit and fissure sealant occurs in two ways: self-curing, which is caused by a chemical reaction of the catalyst and the base material, or by a single-syringe dispensing system which is cured by the visible white light.

179. A. Visible white light application.

180. The fluoride application sequence is as follows:

Step 1. E.

Step 2. D.

Step 3. B.

Step 4. C.

Step 5. A.

181. A. True. The teeth should be dried and free of saliva for the uptake of fluoride into the enamel for caries prevention.

182. C. 30 minutes.

183. D. A vacuum former is a unit that allows the lab assistant to fabricate a customized mouth protector from a gypsum cast model.

184. A. An athletic mouth protector offers prevention from injury that may be caused by contact sports.

185. C. The proper care of a removable mouth protector requires the wearer to rinse with cool water and soap. The mouth protector should not be scrubbed with an abrasive dentifrice, nor should it be placed in warm water.

186. B. Acrylic plastic is the most universally used material for denture base fabrication.

187. B. A flask is a metal three-section container in which a denture is molded.

188. C. For heat curing denture resin, moist heat under pressure is utilized at a temperature of approximately 170°F, or 77°C.

189. B. A soft liner is usually the initial corrective protocol for relieving sore and tender areas of ill-fitting or immediate dentures. If this is not effective in relieving the problem, other alternate corrective measures may be undertaken.

190. B. Cobalt-chromium is the metal utilized to fabricate the framework of the partial denture.

191. C. When utilizing the model trimmer or the lathe, protective devices such as masks, gloves, and eyewear should be worn to protect the operator from microbial contamination.

192. D. All the aforementioned methods will clean and remove unsightly stains and deposits from a denture or partial.

193. A. Cool water should always be used for rinsing dentures. Hot water may distort the acrylic.

194. E. All the materials mentioned may be utilized to construct temporary coverage while the patient is having fixed prosthodontics constructed.

195. D. An acrylic trimming bur or a garnet disc may be used to reduce the excess height of a temporary crown.

196. A. A temporary crown is polished with a green stone and fine grit polishing material.

197. D. A temporary crown is cemented with either ZOE or IRM.

198. E. All the aforementioned steps should be followed when cementing a temporary crown.

199. E. All the aforementioned methods of bleaching are appropriately utilized in the dental office.

200. E. In an office, bleaching techniques are effective for patients afflicted with unsightly staining conditions such as dental fluorosis, tetracycline stains, and superficial discolorations.

201. D. Bleaching agents do not adversely affect these types of restorative materials. Side effects may occur and can include: hypersensitivity, soft tissue lesions, sloughing, nausea, Temporomandibular Joint syndrome, and sore throat caused by

swallowing the bleaching agent.

202. E. Enamel bonding is utilized for a wide variety of applications that include bonding a diastema, covering worn or fractured teeth, and covering stained teeth.

203. E. All the aforementioned considerations are important regarding the utilization of dentin bonding systems. Careful perusal of the manufacturer's directions is essential.

204. E. All the aforementioned are areas that are covered by OSHA.

205. D. Label identification and hazardous warnings are required for hazardous dental products.

206. D. MSDS provide precautionary and safe-handling information regarding hazardous dental products.

207. E. All the aforementioned are ways in which the dentist may properly train employees.

208. E. Proper precautionary handling of hazardous dental products requires all the aforementioned guidelines.

209. E. All the listed precautionary measures should be followed when handling acid-etch and gel solutions in the dental office.

210. E. All the aforementioned precautions need to be observed when handling asbestos.

211. D. Proper ventilation and easy accessibility to fire extinguishers are required when handling acetone and alcohol-based products.

212. E. All the aforementioned precautions should be observed by the employee when handling gypsum products.

213. E. Safe handling of mercury requires all the aforementioned precautions.

214. E. Gloves, eyewear, and NIOSH-approved masks are required when handling alloys, metals, gypsum, and asbestos.

215. C. When utilizing nitrous oxide gas, it is imperative to have adequate ventilation and a scavenging system that monitors leakage.

216. E. Methyl methacrylate and dimethylacrylate are odoriferous organic chemicals that require strict precautionary guidelines such as those listed.

217. E. Radiographic processing chemicals should be routinely handled utilizing all the aforementioned precautions.

218. C. Pickling solutions require the employee to utilize safety goggles, and utility gloves and have a commercial acid spill cleanup kit available in case of an accident.

219. E. In order to avoid retinal damage to the eye when using the visible light, the aforementioned protections should be employed by all members of the dental team.

220. D. Impression materials should be appropriately rinsed and disinfected to prevent the transmission of infectious diseases and cross-contamination.

221. A. In order to reduce or minimize any dimensional change of a polyether impression material, a chlorine compound product should be utilized for disinfection for 2 to 3 minutes. A disinfectant spray may also be used.

222. E. The recommended procedure for disinfecting alginate impression material is to rinse the saliva, blood, and debris with tap water and gently shake to remove water. The alginate impression surface is disinfected and then sealed in a plastic bag. Disinfection time should be followed appropriately. The alginate impression is then cast in stone.

223. A. Elastomeric impressions should be properly soaked, rinsed, and dried

for 10 minutes with an acceptable disinfectant in order to ensure that disinfection has occurred.

224. E. The receiving area of the dental laboratory should be separated from the production section. The area including the countertops and working surfaces should be disinfected with an iodophor, a synthetic phenolic, or a chlorine compound.

225. D. Ragwheels should be washed and autoclaved after use on each patient's prosthesis.

226. A. All patients' incoming and outgoing laboratory cases should be disinfected. It is important to communicate disinfection protocol between the laboratory and dental office.

227. E. Iodophor solution and a 10-minute spray/rinse/pour should be used when disinfecting reusable hydrocolloid materials.

228. E. Pumice should be discarded after each use during laboratory polishing. It is economical to dispense a small amount for use.

229. E. Dentures and removable appliances should be placed in a plastic bag, fully submerged in ultrasonic solution, placed in a glass beaker, and cleansed for a set time.

230. E. All the aforementioned procedures are approved as methods of cleaning and disinfecting dental prostheses.

231. A. True. The individual should don this protective equipment to ensure safe handling of the product.

232. D. Shade guides need to be washed with microbial soap, rinsed, and disinfected prior to returning them to the operatory.

3

Dental Radiology

QUESTIONS

DIRECTIONS (Questions 1-31): In each of the following questions, select the one choice that answers the question or completes the sentence best.

I. Characteristics of dental radiation

1. Professor Wilhelm Roentgen:
   A. Advocated radiology in the United States
   B. Exposed the first radiographs in the United States
   C. Discovered the X-ray
   D. Employed the first dental auxiliary in the United States

2. A dental imaging system known as xeroradiography involves:
   A. Exposures made on electrically charged plates
   B. Exposures made on an X-ray film
   C. Cross-sectional pictures of the human body
   D. Radioisotope scanner

3. A form of energy is:
   A. Heat
   B. Light
   C. Electricity
   D. X-radiation
   E. All of the above

4. Photons are described as:
   A. Bundles of energy
   B. Dental film mounts
   C. Electrically neutral particles
   D. Negatively charged atomic particles

5. Limited penetration long-wavelength radiation is known as:
   A. Short wavelengths
   B. Hard radiation
   C. Soft radiation
   D. Desirable wavelengths

6. Background radiation originates from:
   A. Environment
   B. Outer space
   C. Radionuclides
   D. Terrestrial radiation
   E. All of the above
   F. Only A and B

7. Ionizing radiation is produced when:
   A. Radiation passes through body tissues
   B. Ions compress into the atmosphere
   C. Isotopes flow freely on air
   D. None of the above

8. Common characteristics of radiation are:
   A. Wavelengths that determine the penetrating power of the energy
   B. Forms of electromagnetic radiation
   C. The giving off of electrical fields at right angles to the path of travel
   D. Straight lines that travel at 186,000 miles per second
   E. All of the above

9. Hard radiation is considered to be the:
   1. Short wavelengths with great penetrating power
   2. Long wavelengths with limited penetrating power
   3. Type of radiation that is most desirable and capable of penetrating oral structures
   4. Type of radiation that is unsuitable for exposing radiographs
   A. 1 and 2
   B. 2 and 3
   C. 1 and 3
   D. 2 and 4

10. An electron is known as:
    A. Anything that occupies space and has mass
    B. Electrically neutral tiny particle
    C. Center of the atom
    D. Negatively charged atomic particle

11. Penumbra is known as:
    A. Magnification of an object
    B. Diverging X-rays

C. Distortion of the shape of an image

D. Fuzzy outline of a radiographic image

12. The classification of X-rays according to their wave forms is:
    A. Gamma radiation
    B. Natural radiation
    C. Electronic circuits
    D. Electromagnetic spectrum

13. Ionizing types of radiation include:
    A. Gamma rays
    B. Cosmic rays
    C. X-rays
    D. Only A and B
    E. All of the above

14. X-rays are grouped according to:
    A. Milliliters
    B. Seconds
    C. Liters
    D. Wavelengths

15. The measurement of the number of oscillations per second of electromagnetic radiation is known as:
    A. Crest
    B. Wavelength
    C. Bremsstrahlung
    D. Frequency

16. X-rays characteristically:
    A. Travel in straight lines
    B. Are invisible
    C. Have no mass
    D. Only B and C
    E. All of the above

17. A unit measuring X-rays in the air is known as:
    A. Rad
    B. Rem
    C. Roentgen
    D. Angstrom

II. The X-ray machine and its components

18. A unit measuring the effect of X-rays on the tissues is defined as:
    A. Rad
    B. Rem
    C. Roentgen
    D. Angstrom

19. X-rays originate when components in the X-ray tube are heated and free electrons are propelled at high speeds toward the:
    A. Cathode
    B. Electrode
    C. Focusing cup
    D. Tungsten target

20. Dense structures such as bone and enamel:
    A. Absorb more X-rays
    B. Absorb less X-rays
    C. Appear radiopaque
    D. Appear radiolucent
    E. Only A and C
    F. Only B and D

21. Within the X-ray tube, converted energy produces:
    A. 50 percent heat and 50 percent X-rays
    B. 85 percent heat and 15 percent X-rays
    C. 90 percent heat and 10 percent X-rays
    D. 99 percent heat and 1 percent X-rays

22. The electrical circuits of the X-ray machine include the:
    A. Filament circuit (low voltage)
    B. Cathode-anode circuit (high voltage)
    C. Tuning circuit
    D. All of the above
    E. Only A and B

23. The electric current flows through the filament circuit and heats the:
    A. Tungsten target
    B. Cathode filament
    C. Coolidge tube
    D. Focal spot
    E. None of the above

24. The positive terminal or electrode in an electric circuit is the:
    A. Cathode
    B. Anode
    C. Yoke
    D. Timing device

25. Thermionic emission is created by a:
    A. Vacuum within the tube
    B. Filament wire heated to incandescence
    C. Stream of electrons
    D. High-voltage current

26. A tungsten button set into copper at a 20° angle is located in the _____ of the Coolidge tube.
    A. Definition
    B. Anode
    C. Cathode
    D. None of the above

27. The sharpness or definition of the radiograph is determined by the:
    A. Anode
    B. Cathode
    C. Electric circuit
    D. Focal spot

28. Within the X-ray machine the direction of electric current flows from the:
    A. Anode to the cathode
    B. Target of the anode to the filament of the wire
    C. Filament of the cathode to the target of the anode
    D. None of the above

29. The amperage control determines the:
    A. Number of free electrons at the cathode filament
    B. Speed of electrons toward the target
    C. Duration of exposure
    D. None of the above

30. When the amperage is increased on the master control unit, the amount of radiation produced will:
    A. Decrease
    B. Increase
    C. Remain the same

31. The highest voltage to which the current in the tube rises during an exposure is called:
    A. Kilovoltage peak
    B. Milliamperage
    C. Milliamperage seconds
    D. None of the above

DIRECTIONS (Questions 32-41): Match the items in Column A with their primary function in Column B.

COLUMN A

32. Transformer
33. Position indicating device

34. Filter

35. Collimator

36. Anode

COLUMN B

A. The positive pole in the Coolidge tube
B. A lead disk that limits the size of the X-ray beam to 2.75 inches
C. An electromagnetic device which initiates the electrical current for the production of X-rays
D. Utilized to screen out long wavelengths
   It is constructed of aluminum
E. An open-ended extension that is attached to the X-ray tubehead

COLUMN A

37. Primary beam
38. Aperture

COLUMN B

A. A round opening in the collimator
B. The middle portion of the useful beam

39. Cathode

40. Central beam

41. Tungsten target

C. The X-rays that are emitted from the position indicating device

D. Located on the anode. It is approximately 1 millimeter in size and it contains the focal spot

E. A negative pole in the Coolidge tube

· ·

DIRECTIONS (Questions 1-31): In each of the following questions, select the one choice that answers the question or completes the sentence best.

III. Technical aspects of dental radiation

42. What factor must be changed in order to maintain optimum film density when the target-film distance is increased?
    A. Exposure time
    B. Developing time
    C. Fixing time
    D. None of the above

43. When the target film distance is doubled and the film speed and the machine variables remains constant, the exposure time will:
    A. Increase by ninefold
    B. Decrease by ninefold
    C. Increase by fourfold
    D. Decrease by fourfold

44. The total radiation generated during dental radiographic exposure is determined by:
    A. Milliamperage
    B. Exposure time
    C. Kilovoltage
    D. Milliampere seconds (mAs)

45. A decrease in the milliamperage will lighten the density of the radiograph.
    A. True
    B. False

46. Long-scale contrast indicates that the density differences between areas on the processed radiograph will appear small.

A. True
B. False

47. Short-scale contrast indicates that differences in the density of the processed radiograph will appear to be small.
    A. True
    B. False

IV. Intraoral/extraoral radiographic procedures

48. Foreshortening of the film is due to _____ of the position indicating device.
    A. Too much vertical angulation
    B. Too little vertical angulation
    C. Too much horizontal angulation
    D. Too little horizontal angulation

49. Conecutting is due to the:
    A. Central ray not being aimed at the teeth of interest
    B. Central ray being aimed at the teeth of interest
    C. Film not being placed in a perpendicular position
    D. Film not being vertical to the occlusal plane

50. Overlapping is caused by an error of:
    A. Vertical angulation
    B. Vertical position
    C. Horizontal angulation
    D. Horizontal position

51. The type of film that shows the entire tooth and its structure around the root apex is the:
    A. Bitewing
    B. Occlusal

C. Periapical

D. Panorex

52. The correct position of the patient's occlusal plane during the bisecting technique is:

A. Perpendicular to the floor

B. Parallel to the midsagittal plane

C. Parallel to the floor

D. None of the above

53. When utilizing the paralleling technique, the vertical edge of the position indicating device should be parallel to the:

A. Occlusal plane

B. Long axis of the teeth

C. Biting portion of the film-holding device

D. Floor

E. All of the above

54. The correct film position that is required during the paralleling technique is:

A. ½ inch above the occlusal plane

B. Parallel to the long axis of the tooth

C. Horizontal to the long axis of the tooth

D. None of the above

55. An insufficient amount of vertical angulation will produce an image appearing:

A. Foreshortened

B. Elongated

C. Overlapped

D. Herringboned

56. Please refer to the accompanying illustration. If the operator bisects the angle formed by the long axis of the tooth and the film, then the following information will be true:

A. Central ray will be directed so it is perpendicular to the bisector line

B. Central ray will strike the bisector line at a 90° angle

C. The vertical edge of the position indicating device and the bisector line will be parallel to one another

D. All of the above

E. Only B and C

57. The advantage of utilizing the parallel technique is that it:

A. Prevents penumbra

B. Reduces superimposition of the zygomatic shadow

C. Provides reliability of the exposed radiograph

D. All of the above

E. Only A and B

58. Which position indicating device is considered to be most advantageous in the reduction of radiation exposure?

A. 8-inch, open-ended PID

B. 8-inch, plastic pointed cone

C. 16-inch, open-ended cone

D. Rectangular cone

59. The advantage of increasing the target-film distance for patient protection is that it serves to:

A. Increase scatter radiation

B. Reduce film speed

C. Decrease radiation intensity

D. None of the above

E. All of the above

60. The film-holding device utilized for the paralleling technique is the:

A. Patient's finger

B. Hemostat

C. Snap-a-ray

D. X-tension Cone Paralleling (XCP)

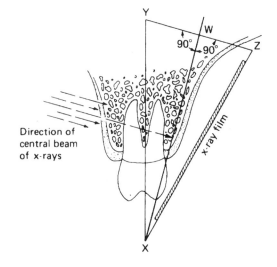

61. When the target-film distance is doubled when utilizing a 16-inch position indicating device the exposure time is:
    A. Multiplied by 2
    B. Multiplied by 8
    C. Multiplied by 4
    D. Divided by 2

62. Prior to exposing the patient to a bitewing or full mouth series, the mouth is examined for:
    A. Abnormal morphology
    B. Removable partials
    C. Variations in the palate
    D. All of the above
    E. Only A and B

63. When taking exposures on children, the operator should:
    A. Decrease exposure time
    B. Increase exposure time
    C. Decrease exposure time in the maxillary region
    D. Increase exposure time in the posterior region

64. The following number of films comprise a full mouth series:
    A. 18 to 20
    B. 10 to 15
    C. 20 to 25
    D. 8 to 10

65. The embossed dot on the film is positioned toward the _____ surface during exposure:
    A. Mesial
    B. Buccal
    C. Occlusal/incisal
    D. Apical

66. The pedodontic film survey should include the following:
    A. Smaller film size
    B. Shorter exposure times
    C. Slightly steeper vertical angulation when utilizing bisect-the-angle technique
    D. Only A and B
    E. All of the above

67. Radiographic technique for exposing the edentulous survey requires:
    A. Utilization of cotton rolls, styrofoam blocks, and XCPs
    B. Operator to substitute the alveolar ridge for the long axis of the missing tooth
    C. Approximately 25 percent less exposure time
    D. Only A and C
    E. All of the above

68. For a rapid survey of large areas of the maxilla and mandible use:
    A. Panoramic film
    B. Cephalometric film
    C. Occlusal film
    D. Interproximal film

69. The type of film utilized to record, measure, and compare changes in the growth of the bones and the teeth is:
    A. Panoramic film
    B. Interproximal bitewing
    C. Cephalometric film
    D. Occlusal film

70. A photographic image of teeth and surrounding structures requires a technique known as:
    A. Tomography
    B. Xeroradiography
    C. Extraoral radiography
    D. Electric imaging

71. Extraoral films are utilized for:
    A. Viewing the skull
    B. Detecting fractures
    C. Detecting anomalies
    D. Only A and B
    E. All of the above

72. A technique utilized to expose a radiographic image of a curved layer with a narrow beam of X-rays is known as:
    A. Periapical radiography
    B. Xeroradiography
    C. Nuclear magnetic resonance
    D. Rotational panoramic radiography

73. An area of dental anatomy that includes the dimensions of the dental arches and the sinuses is the:
   A. Center beam
   B. Center of rotation
   C. Focal trough
   D. Central plane

74. A panoramic film is loaded into a cassette under the following conditions:
   A. Under a safe light in the darkroom
   B. In the daylight in a clinical setting
   C. In the daylight loader/developer/ processor
   D. None of the above

75. The line that is utilized as a positioning guide during panoramic radiography is known as the _____ plane.
   A. Central
   B. Occlusal
   C. Sievert
   D. Frankfort

76. A clear area on the middle of a processed panoramic film indicates a:
   A. Smooth image
   B. Split image
   C. No image
   D. Continuous image

77. The advantage of panoramic film is that it provides information regarding:
   A. Interproximal decay
   B. Periodontal disease
   C. Entire dentition
   D. Periapical abnormalities

78. The disadvantage of panoramic radiography is:
   A. Loss of radiographic detail
   B. Inherent magnification and image distortion
   C. Both A and B
   D. None of the above

79. A common error in panoramic radiography is due to:

   A. Malpositioning of the head
   B. Exposure errors
   C. Both A and B
   D. None of the above

80. A panoramic radiograph is called a:
   A. Radiograph
   B. Tomograph
   C. Laminograph
   D. Cassette

81. A film-holding device for panoramic films is the:
   A. Free-standing holder
   B. Rare earth screen
   C. Cassette
   D. Intensifying screen

82. An intensifying screen located in the cassette _____ radiation for the patient:
   A. Reduces
   B. Increases
   C. Does not alter
   D. None of the above

83. Panoramic films should be marked with a(n):
   A. Indelible pen
   B. Pen and ink
   C. Felt-tip marker
   D. Lead marker

84. Panoramic film is sensitive to _____ fluorescent light.
   A. Violet
   B. Blue
   C. Green
   D. Only A and B
   E. All of the above

85. Panoramic film can only be developed with an automatic film processor.
   A. True
   B. False

86. The patient should be draped with th following during panoramic radiography:
   A. Lead apron

B. Thyroid collar

C. Both A and B

D. None of the above

87. The maxillary and mandibular incisors are held into position with a _____ during panoramic radiography.

A. X-tension cone paralleling (XCP)

B. Stabe

C. Bite block

D. Bite tab

88. The position of the back and the spine is _____ during panoramic radiography.

A. Erect

B. Tipped back

C. Forward

D. None of the above

89. When positioning the patient for a panoramic radiograph, the following item should be removed from the patient:

A. Eye wear

B. Metal wear

C. Partials and/or dentures

D. Only A and C

E. All of the above

90. Various factors that can influence the exposure setting include the:

A. Size of the patient

B. Patient that is edentulous

C. Size of the bone structure

D. Only B and C

E. All of the above

91. What devices are utilized to establish correct patient positioning during panoramic radiography?

A. Chin rests

B. Head-positioning devices

C. Thyroid collars and conventional lead aprons

D. Only A and B

E. All of the above

92. If the patient is positioned too far forward during panoramic radiography, the image will appear:

A. Unfocused in the maxillary and mandibular anterior arches

B. Overlapped in the premolar region

C. Narrowed in the anterior region

D. Only B and C

E. All of the above

93. A panoramic film that has a ghostlike appearance in which the mandible is wide and blurred is due to the patient being positioned:

A. Too far forward

B. Too far backward

C. Too far upward

D. In a slumped position

94. If only a portion of the panoramic radiographic image is blurred, the cause is likely due to:

A. Patient movement

B. Patient twisting head to one side

C. Slumped position of the patient

D. Lint on the film of the intensifying screen of the cassette

95. If a patient does not stand or sit erectly when having a panoramic film taken, the resulting image may appear:

A. Opaque and pyramid-shaped and located in the mid-portion of the panoramic film

B. Translucent and pyramid-shaped and located in the border area of the panoramic film

C. With irregular pyramid-shaped borders located near the ramus of the mandible

D. With black edging on the ends of the film

96. A dark area on the edge of a panoramic film is caused by:

A. Overexposure

B. Overdevelopment

C. Light leak

D. Incorrect mA setting

E. Incorrect kVp setting

97. If a panoramic film cassette is not closed completely during exposure, the resulting image can appear:
    A. Overexposed
    B. Fogged
    C. Lined
    D. Only A and C
    E. Only A and B

98. A solid opaque vertical line appearing on the radiographic panoramic processed film may be caused by:
    A. Cracked intensifying screen
    B. Releasing the exposure button for a moment
    C. Earrings
    D. Partials or dentures
    E. Patient movement

99. An extraoral projection is utilized for:
    A. Caries detection
    B. Handicapped person with Temporomandibular Joint syndrome
    C. A heart patient
    D. Root canal therapy

100. Extraoral films are contained in a metal carrier known as:
    A. Film loop
    B. XCP
    C. Canthus
    D. Cassette

101. The calcium tungstate crystals in the intensifying screen of an extraoral film functions to decrease exposure time.
    A. True
    B. False

102. The film projection used to survey the whole skull is known as the _____ and is commonly used by the orthodontist.
    A. Occlusal
    B. Panorex
    C. Transcranial
    D. Lateral skull

103. The projection that is used to survey one side of the mandible from the distal of the canine to the angle of the ramus, the condyle, and coronoid processes is the:
    A. Lateral skull
    B. Lateral oblique
    C. Transcranial
    D. Panorex

104. The posterior-anterior projection of the sinus is called the _____ view.
    A. Water's
    B. Edge's
    C. River's
    D. Lateral skull

105. When the central ray is directed at an angle of 90° to the film when taking an occlusal film, it is called the _____ projection.
    A. Cross-sectional
    B. Topographic
    C. Transcranial
    D. Obtuse angle

V. Quality control assurance standards for dental radiation

A. Dental X-ray film processing equipment and darkroom errors

106. Films are repeatedly rinsed in the water bath for _____ to remove the developing solution before fixing.
    A. 5 to 10 seconds
    B. 20 to 30 seconds
    C. 40 to 50 seconds
    D. 60 to 70 seconds

107. Stirring rods are utilized during darkroom processing for:
    A. Agitating the rinse water
    B. Mixing the developer and fixer
    C. Obtaining uniform concentration throughout the solutions
    D. Only A and B
    E. All of the above

108. Periodically, the darkroom is checked for light leaks. This is accomplished

by utilizing the:

A. Stir test

B. Badge test

C. Coin test

D. All of the above

109. A _____ watt bulb is used when developing dental films, and it is mounted _____ feet away from the working surface.

A. 6/3

B. 5/4

C. 7/3

D. 7.5/4

110. The developing and fixing tanks can be cleaned by utilizing:

A. Cleansing powder

B. Commercial acid solution and water

C. Detergent

D. Bleach and water

E. None of the above

111. An invisible image on an exposed radiograph that has not been processed is referred to as a:

A. Backscatter

B. Oral image

C. Latent image

D. Record image

112. Fixing solution should be disposed of by:

A. Pouring it down the drain

B. Pouring it into a suitable plastic container

C. Labeling and disposing of it as a hazardous waste product

D. None of the above

113. The purpose of the reducing agent in the developing solution (Hydroquinone and Elon) is to:

A. Build up density, contrast, and detail in the film

B. Soften the film emulsion

C. Prolong the life of the developer

D. Dilute the chemicals

114. Automatic processors require the following maintenance regime:

A. Check the solution temperatures and levels

B. Check for solution exhaustion

C. Routine cleaning and proper automation check

D. Only A and C

E. All of the above

115. Duplication of films is accomplished by:

A. Utilizing double film packets

B. Duplicating unit

C. Reexposing the patient to radiation

D. Only A and B

E. All of the above

116. When a maxillary occlusal film is taken utilizing the topographic projection, the central ray should be aimed at _____.

A. 40°

B. 20°

C. 90°

D. 65°

117. In order to localize objects and pathologic conditions in the buccal-lingual dimension, the _____ projection is used.

A. Panoramic

B. Periapical

C. Bitewing

D. Occlusal

118. The thermometer is placed in the:

A. Water bath

B. Fixer tank

C. Developing tank

D. Only A and B

119. The ideal developing time and temperature during the processing procedure for radiographic films are:

A. 5 minutes at 72°F

B. 6 minutes at 68°F

C. 5 minutes at 68°F

D. 6 minutes at 68°F

120. The recommended fixing time for radiographs is:
  A. 8 minutes
  B. 6 minutes
  C. 9 minutes
  D. 10 minutes

121. Radiographs may be safely viewed after _____ of fixing time.
  A. 1 minute
  B. 2 minutes
  C. 3 minutes
  D. 4 minutes

122. Which one of the following is the correct sequence in which X-rays are processed?
  A. Wash, fix, and develop
  B. Develop, fix, wash, and dry
  C. Develop, wash, fix, and wash
  D. Fix, wash, develop, and wash

123. If an unexposed film is processed, it will appear:
  A. White
  B. Black
  C. Blue
  D. Clear

124. Films are rinsed after developing to:
  A. Remove the film emulsion
  B. Speed up the developing process
  C. Wash off the developing solution
  D. Remove the fixer solution

125. A film will turn black if it is exposed to:
  A. Safelight
  B. Whitelight
  C. Daylight
  D. Only B and C

126. Soiled uniforms with developer or fixer stains require a soak of:
  A. 2 ounces of bleach and 2 ounces of vinegar to 1 gallon of water
  B. 3 ounces of bleach and 3 ounces of vinegar to 1 gallon of water
  C. 1 ounce of bleach and 1 ounce of vinegar to 1 gallon of water
  D. 1/2 ounce of bleach and 1/2 ounce of vinegar to 1 gallon of warm water

127. Films should be rinsed in the water bath after they have been developed and prior to being fixed for _____ seconds.
  A. 10
  B. 15
  C. 20 to 30
  D. 40

128. Dental films should be stored in a cool, dry area that is shielded from radiation in a(n):
  A. Lead container
  B. Aluminum container
  C. Tungsten container
  D. Paper dispenser

129. The function of fixing dental films during darkroom processing is to:
  A. Stop the action of the developer
  B. Give contrast to the film
  C. Reduce silver salts
  D. Keep the silver compound suspended evenly on the film

130. Processing solutions should be changed every:
  A. 2 weeks
  B. 1 week
  C. 4 weeks
  D. 4 months

131. A test that can be used to determine the quality control in manual processing includes a:
  A. Stepwedge device
  B. Photoplate image
  C. Time/temperature analysis
  D. All of the above

132. Which one of the following is impervious to the penetration of X-rays:
  A. Copper
  B. Tungsten
  C. Lead
  D. Quartz

133. The temperature of the developing solution should be:
    A. 80°F
    B. 60°F
    C. 65°F
    D. 68°F

134. The safelight should be:
    A. 4.5 watts
    B. 3.5 watts
    C. 7.5 watts
    D. 9 watts

135. When the developing solution becomes exhausted, how do processed films appear?
    A. Dark
    B. Blurred
    C. Light
    D. Brown or gray

136. Automatic processing of films has advantages that include:
    A. Less time in the darkroom
    B. Dry film viewed in approximately 5 minutes
    C. Roller marks on the film
    D. Only A and B
    E. Only C

137. The lead foil backing shields the film from:
    A. Moisture
    B. Fogging
    C. Backscatter
    D. Film emulsion

138. Rapid processing procedures are "ideally" utilized for _____ procedures.
    A. Endodontic
    B. Oral surgical
    C. Orthodontic
    D. Only A and B
    E. All of the above

139. The purpose of the fixing process is to:
    A. Not affect silver salts that have been exposed to radiation
    B. Remove the silver salts that have been exposed to radiation
    C. Remove silver salts that have not been exposed to radiation
    D. None of the above

140. The recommended procedure for the final rinse cycle when processing exposed films is to wash in:
    A. Running water for 20 minutes
    B. Running water for 40 minutes
    C. Still water for 15 minutes
    D. Still water for 25 minutes

141. The larger grains of crystals in the film emulsion determine:
    A. Film size
    B. Film type
    C. Film speed
    D. Film names

142. Use of high-speed film:
    A. Increases exposure time
    B. Decreases exposure time
    C. Has no effect on exposure time

143. A light image caused by inadequacy of the time/temperature cycle is due to a:
    A. Too long developing time
    B. Too short developing time
    C. Too long fixing time
    D. Too short fixing time

144. A black image on a film is due to an inadequate time/temperature cycle that is caused by:
    A. Safe light exposure
    B. White light exposure
    C. Overdevelopment
    D. Overfixing

145. A partial image is caused by an error in processing technique due to:
    A. Excessively high temperature of solutions
    B. Extreme low temperature of solutions
    C. Low level of solutions
    D. High level of solutions

146. If the film is moved from one bath at a high temperature to another at a

lower temperature, the result will be:
A. Fog
B. Latent image
C. Reticulation
D. Double exposure

147. During dark room processing procedures, white blotches on the radiograph are due to:
A. Developer splashes
B. Fixer splashes
C. Rough handling of the film rack
D. Static

148. Low optical density of the processed film results in a:
A. Thin image
B. Herringbone pattern
C. Blackened image
D. None of the above

149. A radiograph that is in the developing solution for a longer period of time than recommended according to time and temperature standards will appear:
A. Lighter
B. Darker
C. The same
D. Herringboned

150. Dark films are the result of:
1. Underdeveloping
2. Overdeveloping
3. Underexposing
4. Overexposing
5. Overfixing
A. 1, 3, and 5
B. 2, 4, and 5
C. Only 2 and 4
D. Only 2 and 5

151. Films not fixed for the proper amount of time will appear:
A. To have black lines running through them
B. To be brittle
C. To have a brown tint
D. White

152. Too short a fixing time can result in:
A. Partial loss of the image
B. Slow film drying
C. Improper hardening of the emulsion
D. All of the above

153. Fogged films are caused by:
A. White light leaks
B. Fixer splash
C. Aged or outdated films
D. Only A and C
E. All of the above

154. When only part of the film shows an image, it is due to:
A. Low level of developer
B. High level of developer
C. Low level of water
D. High level of water

155. Pulling an X-ray too rapidly from its paper causes:
A. Air bubbles
B. Fog
C. Static electricity
D. Double exposure

156. The safe light may be checked for accuracy by the:
A. Time test
B. Step wedge test
C. Observation coin test
D. None of the above

157. The stepwedge device is utilized for quality control in determining:
A. X-ray machine errors
B. Manual processing errors
C. Both A and B
D. None of the above

PART I. Radiographic Exposure and Processing Exercise

DIRECTIONS (Questions 158-168): Identify the radiographic exposure and processing errors in the following numbered films. Match the identified error with the correct film.

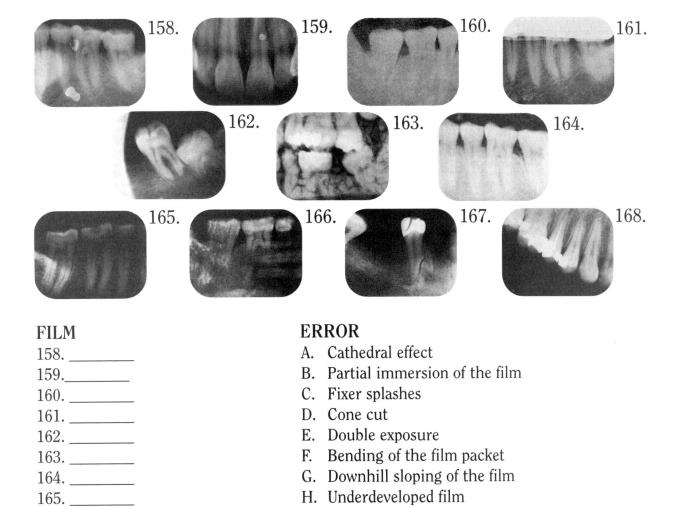

FILM

158. _____

159. _____

160. _____

161. _____

162. _____

163. _____

164. _____

165. _____

166. _____

167. _____

168. _____

ERROR

A. Cathedral effect

B. Partial immersion of the film

C. Fixer splashes

D. Cone cut

E. Double exposure

F. Bending of the film packet

G. Downhill sloping of the film

H. Underdeveloped film

I. Overdeveloped film

J. Light film and incorrect film placement

K. White spot caused by an air bubble

DIRECTIONS (Questions 169-179): In each of the following questions, select the one choice that answers the question or completes the sentence best.

B. Chairside exposure techniques and errors

169. Overlapping in radiographs is the result of an error in:
A. Horizontal angulation
B. Vertical position
C. Horizontal lines
D. Vertical angulation

170. A dental film that has double placement and exposure of X-radiation will show a:
A. Loss of contrast
B. Blackened area
C. Herringbone pattern
D. Dual image
E. All of the above

171. If the periapical radiograph of the maxillary premolars or molars shows

the lingual cusps, the problem is caused by:

A. Elongation
B. Foreshortening
C. Horizontal overlapping
D. Cone cutting
E. None of the above

172. Assuming the film placement is correct, the central beam of the X-ray tube head cylinder should be directed toward the:

A. Long axis of the tooth
B. Contact area of the teeth to be exposed
C. Center of the film
D. Only C
E. All of the above

173. A ½-inch margin above the occlusal surface and no apical structure in view on a mandibular periapical radiograph indicates that the film was placed:

A. Too high in the arch
B. Too low in the arch
C. Vertical to the occlusal surface
D. Perpendicular to the occlusal surface

174. A dark area between the teeth at the occlusal plane on a posterior bitewing indicates that the:

A. Patient bit too hard on the tab
B. Patient moved during exposure
C. Patient did not bite hard enough on the tab
D. Tab was placed on the occlusal

175. The elongation of the radiographic image is due to _____ of the PID.

A. Too little angulation
B. Too much angulation
C. Improper horizontal angulation mesially
D. Improper horizontal angulation distally

176. Foreshortening of the radiographic image is due to _____ angulation.

A. Too little verticle
B. Too much vertical
C. Too little horizontal
D. Too much horizontal

177. A periapical film that has been placed in the mandibular premolar area shows the absence of the mesial structures of the premolar teeth. The film should be repositioned:

A. More distally
B. More mesially
C. Toward the occlusal
D. Toward the lingual

178. A film that is positioned too low in the patient's maxillary arch and has more than a ¼-inch margin below the crowns of the teeth of interest will result in the absence of the _____ structures.

A. Coronal
B. Mesial
C. Distal
D. Apical

179. Placing a film backward in the oral cavity will cause _____ to occur.

A. Reticulation
B. Herringbone pattern
C. Latent image
D. Fog

DIRECTIONS (Questions 180-184): Match the exposure problems in Column A with the probable cause in Column B.

Column A

180.___ Cone cutting
181.___ Bent film

182.___ Slanting

183.___ Herringbone
184.___ Embossed dot

Column B

A. Due to reversed film placement
B. The edge of the film was not positioned parallel to the occlusal plane
C. The primary beam not aimed at the center of the film
D. Due to excessive finger pressure
E. A circular indentation on the film that is positioned toward the incisal or occlusal plane of the teeth

DIRECTIONS (Questions 185-193): In each of the following questions, select the one choice that answers the question or completes the sentence best.

VI. Anatomical landmarks

185. The type of film that provides a detailed examination of the entire tooth and the surrounding tissues is:
    A. Interproximal bitewing
    B. Panoramic film
    C. Periapical film
    D. Occlusal film

186. The radiolucent structure that appears as a line between the central incisors at midline is the:
    A. Incisive foramen
    B. Nasal fossa
    C. Nasal septum
    D. Median palatine suture

187. The structure that gives the typical "Y" formation in the canine area is the:
    A. Lateral fossa
    B. Incisive foramen
    C. Anterior wall of the sinus
    D. Zygoma

188. The radiolucent oval area between the maxillary central incisors is the:
    A. Nasal fossa
    B. Median palatine suture
    C. Incisive foramen

D. Maxillary sinus

189. The genial tubercles are found in film of the:
    A. Maxillary central incisors
    B. Mandibular central incisors
    C. Maxillary canine
    D. Mandibular molar

190. The hamular process is a:
    A. Radiopaque horizontal band
    B. Radiolucent shadow
    C. Radiopaque hooklike bony projection
    D. Radiolucent line

191. The maxillary sinus may be seen in the:
    A. Central lateral incisor area
    B. Canine area
    C. Premolar area
    D. Molar area
    E. Only B, C, and D

192. The maxillary six-year molars have _____ roots.
    A. One
    B. Two
    C. Three
    D. None of the above

193. The mandibular second molars have _____ roots.
    A. One
    B. Two
    C. Three
    D. None of the above

Part II: Radiographic Mounting Exercise

DIRECTIONS (Question 194): All radiographs are positioned labially. Place the number of the radiograph next to the letter of the proper mount window.

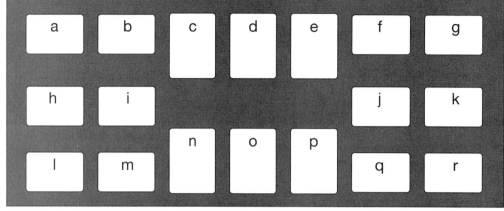

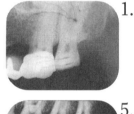 1.
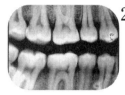 2.
 3.
 4.

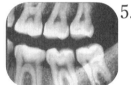 5.
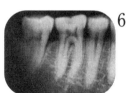 6.
 7.
 8.

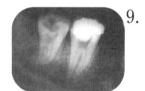 9.
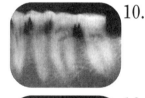 10.
 11.
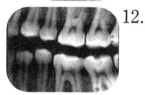 12.

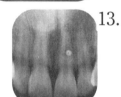 13.
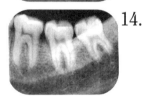 14.
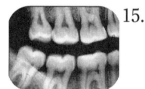 15.
 16.

194. Place the correct number in the space provided:

a. _____   g. _____   m. _____

b. _____   h. _____   n. _____

c. _____   i. _____   o. _____

d. _____   j. _____   p. _____

e. _____   k. _____   q. _____

f. _____   l. _____   r. _____

DIRECTIONS (Questions 195-219): In each of the following questions, select the one choice that answers the question or completes the sentence best.

VII. Radiation protection: operator and patient

195. The dental X-ray tube machine head limits the size of the primary beam by regulating the:
    A. Size of the tube
    B. Number of electrons
    C. Diameter of the collimator
    D. Length of the cylinder

196. The recommended position for the operator during X-radiation exposure is:
    A. Behind a leaded door at a distance of at least 6 feet from the central beam
    B. At a 135° angle from the central beam at the side of the head of the patient, you must be at least 6 feet from this central beam
    C. At a 90° angle from the central beam at the side of the door, you must be at least 6 feet from this central beam
    D. Behind the gypsum wall
    E. Only A and B

197. The maximum permissible dose of radiation for each member of the dental staff must not exceed _____ per year.
    A. 4 rem
    B. 5 rem
    C. 6 rem
    D. 7 rem

198. The major reason for reduction of exposure time when producing diagnostic radiographs is to protect the patient from:
    A. Gamma radiation
    B. Primary radiation
    C. Secondary radiation
    D. Scatter radiation
    E. Only C and D

199. Scatter radiation occurs as a result of exposing a dental film on a patient and can be defined as:
    A. Primary radiation moving off in all directions
    B. Tertiary effect of the primary beam of radiation
    C. Electronic impulses needed to conclude the process
    D. Confining the focal spot of the primary beam

200. An aluminum filter located in the X-ray unit functions to:
    A. Limit the size of the X-ray beam
    B. Increase the intensity of the beam
    C. Eliminate unnecessary X-radiation of longer wavelengths
    D. None of the above

201. The Sievert is the unit that is utilized to measure the equivalent to the:
    A. Rad
    B. Rem
    C. Roentgen
    D. Absorbed dose

202. Coulomb per kilogram is a unit of exposure, and its equivalent measurement is the:
    A. Rad
    B. Roentgen
    C. Rem
    D. Maximum permissible dose

203. The X-ray beam should be collimated at the patient's skin and should not exceed:
    A. $1\frac{1}{2}$ inches
    B. $2\frac{3}{4}$ inches
    C. $3\frac{5}{8}$ inches
    D. $4\frac{1}{4}$ inches

204. The maximum radiation dosage for pregnant women is:
    A. 5/Rems
    B. 50 millisievert
    C. 0.05 Rems
    D. None of the above

205. Temporary redness of the skin caused by an overexposure to radiation is known as:
    A. Threshold
    B. Erythema
    C. Dermatitis
    D. Phlebitis
    E. None of the above

206. The aluminum material that is placed in the path of the beam of radiation to remove many soft rays or longer wavelengths that are undesirable is the:
    A. Collimator
    B. Filter
    C. Ionizing shield
    D. Only A and B

207. A monitoring badge is a device that will measure how much radiation the _____ is receiving.
    A. Patient
    B. Operator
    C. Dental lab technician
    D. None of the above

208. Which speed range number of a dental film indicates a lesser amount of exposure needed to produce a radiograph?
    A. A
    B. E
    C. C
    D. D

209. The maximum permissible dose of radiation for each member of the dental staff must not exceed:
    A. 2 R every 3 months
    B. 1.25 R every 3 months
    C. 4 R every 4 months
    D. 3 R every 4 months

210. The cervical (lead) collar is used in dental radiographic procedures to protect the patient's:
    A. Gonadal tissue
    B. Thyroid gland
    C. Spleen and liver

    D. Digestive tissue

211. The tissue most sensitive to X-radiation is:
    A. Bone
    B. Blood
    C. Muscle
    D. Skin

212. The effect of X-radiation on human tissue is harmful because it is:
    A. Momentary
    B. Temporary
    C. Cumulative
    D. None of the above

213. Which one of the following positions will give adequate protection for the operator?
    A. Standing 3 feet from the primary beam
    B. Standing at the side of the lead barrier
    C. Standing 6 feet from the primary beam
    D. Standing 4 feet from the primary beam

214. The most sensitive facial tissue is the:
    A. Cheek
    B. Lip
    C. Eye
    D. Nostril

215. The beam of X-ray photons that originates from the focal spot of the tube within the X-ray unit is known as the:
    A. Secondary radiation
    B. Scatter radiation
    C. Primary beam
    D. None of the above

216. The portion of the primary beam that is limited by the collimator inside the position-indicating device is known as the:
    A. Secondary beam
    B. Long wavelength
    C. Scatter beam
    D. Useful beam

217. The ALARA (as low as reasonably achievable) concept states that the radiation dose be kept to a minimum.
   A. True
   B. False

218. Safety specifications that are mandated by the federal government as well as by individual states require X-ray units to have:
   A. Leaded X-ray heads
   B. Aluminum filtration
   C. Tubeheads sealed in oil-immersed protective casings
   D. Electronic timer exposure switches that automatically cut off the electrical current
   E. All of the above

219. Federal legislation requires dental auxiliaries to:
   A. Investigate regulations mandated by the State Board of Dentistry
   B. Successfully pass a radiology course as required by the individual's State Board of Dentistry
   C. Be technically skilled as a dental radiographer
   D. Maintain a current status as a Certified Dental Assistant as it pertains to the individual's State Board of Dentistry requirements
   E. All of the above

....

DIRECTIONS (Questions 220-224): Match the following anatomical landmarks in Column A to the respective dental radiographic regions in Column B.

VIII. Radiographic interpretation

Column A

220. _____Sinus cavity
221. _____Incisive foramen
222. _____Mental foramen
223. _____Internal oblique line
224. _____Genial tubercule

Column B

A. Maxillary central incisors
B. Mandibular molar
C. Maxillary pre-molar
D. Mandibular anterior
E. Mandibular premolar

DIRECTIONS (Questions 225-229): Match the following dental materials in Column A to their respective radiographic images in Column B.

Column A

225. _____Amalgam restoration
226. _____Gutta-percha
227. _____Cavity liner
228. _____Stainless steel crown
229. _____Acrylic crown

Column B

A. Appears as radiopaque
B. Appears as radiolucent

DIRECTIONS (Questions 230-234): Match the following pathological findings in Column A with their respective radiographic appearances in Column B.

Column A

230. _____Abscess

231. _____Carie

Column B

A. Radiopaque circled border within a radiolucent area
B. Encapsulated radiographic image of a developing structure

232. _____Cyst
233. _____Impaction
234. _____Periodontal bone disease

C. Circular radiolucent area
D. May be viewed as a loss of depth and width of supporting structures.
E. Radiolucency appearing in the enamel and dental portions of the tooth

DIRECTIONS (Questions 235-245): In each of the following questions, select the one choice that answers the question or completes the sentence best.

IX. Infection control protocol

235. Gloves must be worn by all dental staff members when in contact with:
    A. Blood and saliva
    B. Blood, saliva, or mucous membranes
    C. Blood, saliva, mucous membranes or contaminated surfaces
    D. Blood, saliva, mucous membranes, contaminated surfaces or soiled items

236. Instruments that penetrate soft tissue and/or bone should be:
    A. Disinfected
    B. Sterilized

237. Instruments that contact oral soft tissue should receive:
    A. Sterilization
    B. High-level disinfection
    C. Both A and B
    D. None of the above

238. Dental film packets can be disinfected for:
    A. 1 hour
    B. ½ hour
    C. 40 minutes
    D. 15 minutes

239. An infection control aid for film packets is known as a:
    A. Bacteria aid
    B. Decontaminate aid
    C. Leaded slip
    D. Barrier envelope

240. The exposure button is:
    A. Covered
    B. Covered and changed between patients
    C. Not necessary to cover
    D. Sprayed directly with a disinfectant

241. Exposed radiographs:
    A. May be contaminated with blood and or saliva
    B. Are opened without touching the contaminated dental film with ungloved hands
    C. Are opened in the darkroom using disposable gloves
    D. Only B and C
    E. All of the above

242. When opening film in the darkroom allow the film to drop:
    A. In the cup
    B. On a paper towel
    C. On a paper towel; then discard the packets, and process the film
    D. On a paper towel and keep gloves on while processing the film

243. Films protected with a barrier should be:
    A. Wiped off to remove excess fluids
    B. Stored in a paper cup
    C. Opened without gloves
    D. All of the above
    E. Only A and B

244. Films protected with a barrier require:
    A. Removal of the protection barrier before film processing
    B. Removal of the protection barrier and placing the film in a clean

paper cup

C. Carrying films (with protective barrier removed) to the darkroom

D. All of the above

E. Only A and C

245. The infection control protocol for handling patients who are receiving

radiographs should include:

A. Protective wear including a regu lation lab coat, a facial mask, eye wear, and gloves

B. Sterilization of the film-holding device

C. Operatory disinfection

D. All of the above

E. None of the above

Answers

1. C. Professor Wilhelm Roentgen discovered the X-ray in 1895, when he experimented with a primitive cathode ray tube. An activated electric current passed through the tube and a glow appeared on a fluorescent screen, which led to the discovery of the unknown ray.

2. A. Xeroradiography is an advanced method in radiology that utilizes the principle of copying. Electrically charged plates are used to make radiographic exposures instead of conventional X-ray film.

3. E. Energy forms are both natural and man-made and share common characteristics that are part of the electromagnetic spectrum.

4. A. Photons are defined as "pure bundles of energy." X-rays are referred to as photons.

5. C. Soft radiation is also referred to as grenz rays, which have low frequency and low energy and are incapable of penetrating tooth tissue. (See Figure 3-1.)

6. E. Man is exposed to background radiation from all the aforementioned sources.

7. A. Ionizing radiation produces ions that pass through our tissues and body. The change that occurs in cell structure due to the cumulative effect of X-rays in a lifetime is a primary concern.

8. E. Common characteristics of radiation forms include all the aforementioned properties.

9. C. Hard radiation is utilized for diagnostic purposes in dentistry. This type of radiation has short wavelengths and higher energy or penetrating power, which is suitable for taking dental radiographs.

10. D. An electron is the negatively charged particle of an atom.

11. D. The fuzzy outline that can occur around the tooth is due to an increase in the recording plane (the film) and the object (the tooth). To improve the sharpness of the image, the film and the object should be close to one another.

12. D. The electromagnetic spectrum represents the range of energy forms based on frequency and wavelength.

13. E. Ionizing radiations produce ions and include gamma rays, X-rays, and cosmic rays that are capable of penetrating tissue.

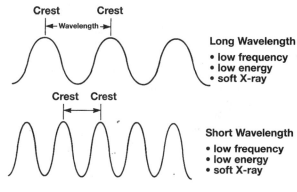

Figure 3-1

14. D. X-rays are categorized in the electromagnetic spectrum according to their wavelength.

15. D. Frequency is a measurement of the amount of energy of the wavelength. The shorter the wavelength, the more penetrating the power of the energy form.

16. E. All the aforementioned characteristics describe the various forms of energy.

17. C. A roentgen is defined as the X-radiation that passes through a volume of air.

18. B. A rem is defined as "roentgen equivalent man," which measures the effect in humans from exposure to ionizing radiation.

19. D. Free electrons are attracted to the tungsten target, which is located in the anode of the Coolidge tube. (See Figure 3-2.)

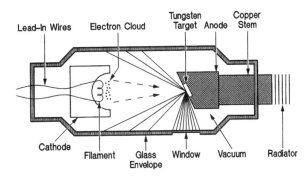

Figure 3-2

20. E. Dense structures absorb more X-rays and therefore will appear more radiopaque on film.

21. D. The converted energy in the X-ray tube produces 99 percent heat within the X-ray tube and 1 percent radiation.

22. E. The electrical circuits in the dental X-ray unit are known as the low-voltage and high-voltage circuits. (See Figure 3-3.)

23. B. The heating of the cathode filament is produced by the filament circuit and controlled by a rheostat

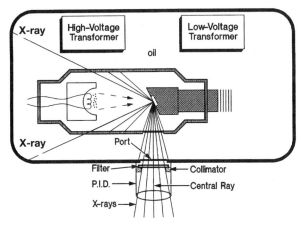

Figure 3-3

in the circuit. This is the function of the milliamperage setting.

24. B. The anode is the positive terminal in the electric circuit in the Coolidge tube where X-rays are created. (See Figure 3-4.)

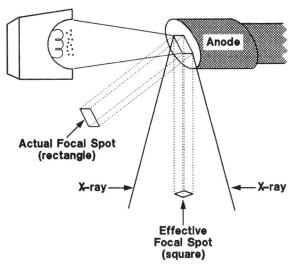

Figure 3-4

25. B. Thermionic emission occurs when the tungsten filament located on the cathode is heated to incandescence by an electric current within the X-ray Coolidge tube.

26. B. The anode is the positive terminal located in the Coolidge tube.

27. D. The focal spot is an area located on the anode. The smaller the spot, the better or the more improved the sharpness of the radiograph.

28. C. The electric current is directed from the filament wire to the target of the anode.

29. A. The amperage controls the number of electrons produced. An increase or decrease in the control on the unit determines the production of more or less X-rays.

30. B. When increased, the amperage control will produce more X-rays.

31. A. The kilovoltage control determines the speed of the electrons produced and, therefore, results in more penetrating power of the X-rays when increased.

32. C

33. E

34. D

35. B

36. A

37. C

38. A

39. E

40. B

41. D

42. A. If the intensity of the X-ray beam is reduced, there should be an increase in exposure factors to maintain the maximum density of the film.

43. C. When the target film distance is doubled, the exposure time is increased fourfold based on the application of the inverse square law, which is:

$$\frac{\text{Original mAs}}{\text{New mAs}} = \frac{(\text{Original distance})^2}{(\text{New distance})^2}$$

44. D. Milliamperage seconds determine the total radiation generated by multiplying mA times the exposure time equals mAs.

45. A. Decreasing the milliamperage will result in a lighter density film

because the number of electrons produced is decreased.

46. A. Long-scale contrast differences in a radiograph appear with density differences that are small and are differentiated by many shades of gray.

47. B. Short-scale contrast differences in a radiograph appear with large areas of density differences.

48. A. Too much vertical angulation will result in a foreshortened image on the radiograph. In order to correct the problem, decrease the angulation vertically.

49. A. The central ray must be aimed at the teeth of interest. Also, the entire PID must cover the radiograph or cone cutting will result.

50. C. Horizontal overlapping results when the central ray is not aimed in a perpendicular manner between the interproximal areas of the teeth of interest. The result on the radiograph is overlapped interproximal structures.

51. C. The periapical film shows the entire root, the root apex, and the surrounding anatomical structures.

52. C. The ideal position for the patient is to be seated upright and have the occlusal plane parallel to the floor.

53. B. The vertical edge of the PID should be parallel to the long axis of the teeth being radiographed. (See Figure 3-5.)

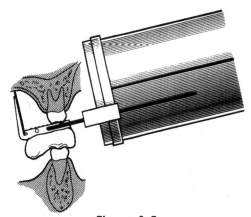

Figure 3-5

54. B. The film should be positioned parallel to the long axis of the tooth. This will enable the X-rays to strike the film at right angles in a perpendicular relationship to the teeth and the film.

55. B. Elongation of the image results when the PID is insufficiently angulated. To correct the problem, the PID should be increased.

56. D. All the aforementioned statements are true.

57. D. The advantage of the parallel technique is to reduce the distortion of the image, especially in the maxillary molar region, and to prevent penumbra.

58. D. The rectangular cone or PID effectively limits the size of the X-ray beam that strikes the patient's face.

59. C. The intensity of the radiation is decreased when the target-film distance is increased, which results in an improved radiograph.

60. D. The XCP (extension cone paralleling) instruments are utilized to align the X-ray into position with a 12- to 16-inch target-film distance. (See Figure 3-6.)

61. C. When the target-film distance is doubled, the intensity of the radiation is diminished which is based on the inverse square law. Such factors as exposure time, milliamperage, and kilovoltage must be increased. Therefore, doubling the target-object distance requires the exposure time to be increased fourfold.

62. D. All the aforementioned conditions are important regarding the oral examination prior to the exposure procedure.

63. A. When exposing radiographs on children, the exposure time is reduced about one-third because of the relative size difference in bone structure and density.

64. A. The standard number of X-ray films in a full mouth series ranges between 18 and 20.

65. C. The embossed dot on the film is positioned toward the occlusal or incisal edge of the film in order not to interfere with the anatomical structure in the region of interest.

66. E. All the aforementioned modifications are required for pedodontic film surveys.

67. E. Exposure modifications for the edentulous patient requires the use of cotton rolls or blocks to provide ease of film retention and a replacement for the missing tooth or teeth. A decreased exposure time of approximately 25 percent should be utilized for the edentulous patient.

68. A. The panoramic film provides an overview of the maxillary and mandibular jaws, teeth, and surrounding structures.

69. C. Cephalometric film is utilized as a diagnostic record for orthodontic and oral surgery clinical evaluations.

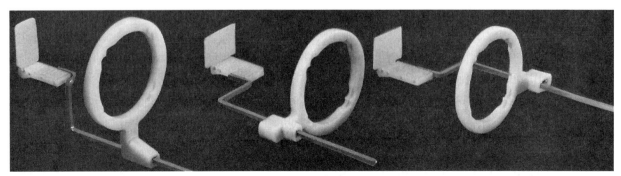

Figure 3-6

70. B. Xeroradiography produces a photographic image that will reduce exposures by approximately two-thirds. The exposures are made on an electrically charged plate.

71. E. Extraoral films are clinically valuable for diagnosing pathological findings and abnormalities caused by trauma and developmental factors.

72. D. Rotational panoramic radiography involves the movement of the film cassette and the tube head in opposite directions.

73. C. The focal trough represents the entire area to be examined and radiographed during rotational panoramic radiography, which includes dental arches, sinuses, and area anatomical structures.

74. A. The panoramic film is loaded into a cassette in the darkroom with the safe light on. A special GBX filter is utilized for the light-sensitive film.

75. D. The Frankfort plane is determined by establishing a horizontal line which extends from the ala of the nose to the external auditory meatus on the patient's face. The line is parallel to the horizontal plane of the floor.

76. B. A split image indicates that the X-ray machine stopped during the exposure cycle, which is more common among the older panoramic models.

77. C. Panoramic film provides an overview of the entire dentition.

78. C. Panoramic film provides an overview of the dental arches; however, loss of detail, inherent magnification, and image distortion are problems.

79. C. Malpositioning of the patient's head and exposure errors contribute to problems during panoramic radiography.

80. B. Tomograph is the term that applies to a panoramic radiograph.

81. C. The cassette is a metal-encased device that retains panoramic film during exposure.

82. A. The intensifying screen reduces the radiation for the patient because it fluoresces and enables the latent image to form at a faster rate.

83. D. A lead marker is utilized to mark panoramic film.

84. E. Panoramic film is sensitive to violet, blue, and green fluorescent light, which is created within the extraoral cassette when the radiation penetrates the emulsion of the intensifying screen.

85. B. Panoramic film can be developed in conventional processing tanks. Special attention to proper time and temperature guidelines should be followed.

86. A. The patient is draped with a lead apron during panoramic radiography. The thyroid collar will interfere with the rotating cassette.

87. C. The maxillary and mandibular teeth are held in position with a bite block, which serves to stabilize the correct edge-to-edge relationship required during panoramic radiography.

88. A. When the patient is positioned correctly, it is essential that the spine and the back should be erect to minimize diminution and blurring of the image.

89. E. The patient is instructed to remove all eye wear, jewelry, and metal wear, such as zippers, hair ornaments, and removable dental prostheses and appliances.

90. E. All of the aforementioned factors affect the exposure setting; however, the kilovoltage and milliamperage should be set according to the manufacturer's recommendations.

91. D. Chin rests and head-positioning devices are utilized to position the patient's head during panoramic radiography.

92. E. All the aforementioned problems can occur when the patient is positioned too far forward. The patient should be positioned with the anterior teeth occluding in the bite block groove and the chin correctly positioned in the chin rest device. (See Figure 3-7.)

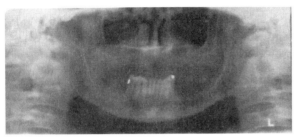

Figure 3-7

93. B. The problem of a ghostlike appearance of the mandible which is wide and blurred is due to the patient being positioned too far backward and the chin not resting correctly in the chin rest. (See Figure 3-8.)

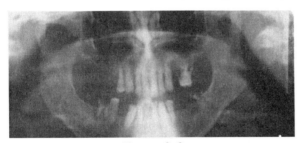

Figure 3-8

94. A. A blurred portion of the image is due to patient movement. Instruct the patient not to move during the procedure. (See Figure 3-9.)

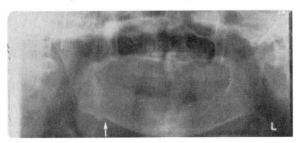

Figure 3-9

95. A. If patient is not positioned erectly, the spinal column appears as a opaque pyramid shape in the middle of the panoramic film. (See Figure 3-10.)

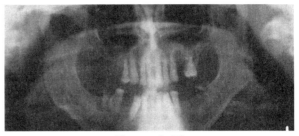

Figure 3-10

96. C. A light leak caused by an open seam of the cassette during exposure will cause a dark area to appear on the film when it is processed. (See Figure 3-11.)

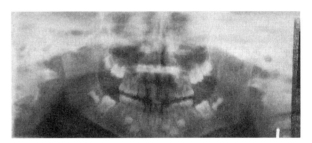

Figure 3-11

97. E. The film will appear both fogged and overexposed because of a cassette that is not completely closed.

98. B. Releasing the exposure button for a brief moment will result in a vertical opaque line on the processed image. (See Figure 3-12.)

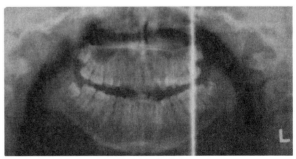

Figure 3-12

99. B. Ideally, an extraoral projection may be appropriate for the handicapped patient with TMJ for an overview

evaluation, and the ease of the technique may be most suitable for patient cooperation.

100. D. Extraoral films are placed in a metal cassette under darkroom conditions and are tightly closed and positioned until exposed.

101. A. The intensifying screen is comprised of crystal salts, including calcium tungstate, rare earth phosphors, and barium strontium sulfate, which have the ability to fluoresce when they are penetrated with X-radiation. This results in a shorter exposure time.

102. D. The lateral skull survey provides a lateral view of the entire skull.

103. B. The lateral oblique survey is commonly referred to as the lateral jaw survey and is most suitable for patients who require evaluations of pathological traumatic conditions.

104. A. The Water's view projects the posterior-anterior view of the sinuses.

105. A. The cross-sectional projection requires the application of the parallel or right-angle technique.

106. B. Radiographic films should be rinsed in a circulating bath of water for 20 to 30 seconds in order to remove the alkaline developer.

107. C. Stirring rods are utilized to stir the developing and fixing solutions prior to processing. Care should be taken not to contaminate the rods by thoroughly rinsing with water and drying before stirring each solution.

108. C. The coin test aids in determining if the darkroom is light-tight for safe film processing. A coin is placed on an unexposed film and exposed to the safe light for 4 minutes and processed. If the film shows the coin outline, this indicates the safe light is not adequate.

109. D. The 7.5 watt bulb is required for darkroom utilization and should be located 4 feet from the work surface.

110. B. Water and a commercial cleaning solution (hydrochloric acid) are utilized to clean the processing tanks each time the solutions are changed to remove residual deposits on the tank walls.

111. C. The latent image is the invisible image produced when the film is exposed to radiation but not processed.

112. C. OSHA standards require proper labeling of the old fixer solution and adherence to proper disposal procedures with a reputable waste disposal company.

113. A. The reducing agent actively affects the contrast of the film during the developing process.

114. E. It is essential for the automatic processor to be maintained with routine care for optimum performance and processing results.

115. D. Ideally, a duplicating unit or double film can be used to provide records for insurance companies and protection against malpractice.

116. D. An angulation of 65° of the central ray should be directed toward the teeth of interest for the topographic projection.

117. D. The occlusal projection is especially useful in detecting pathological conditions or objects when a periapical film will not be adequate for full viewing.

118. C. The thermometer is always placed in the developer as the films will be processed in this solution first.

119. C. The recommended developing time and temperature is 5 minutes at 68° Fahrenheit. It is most important to follow the manufacturer's recommendation of the time/temperature guidelines for processing films, especially when adjustments are made.

120. D. The recommended fixing time is 10 minutes. However, the film can be read after 2 minutes of fixation.

121. B. To accommodate a need for viewing the film in less than 10 minutes, a wet reading can be done after 2 minutes.

122. C. The proper sequence for processing radiographic films is initially developing and then washing, fixing, and finally washing.

123. D. The unexposed film will appear clear if it is processed.

124. C. Rinsing the film in the circulating water bath removes the developer and enables the fixer solution to retain its acidity.

125. D. Both white light and daylight will cause the film to turn black when it is processed.

126. D. A commercial stain-removing product or the aforementioned solution will effectively clean soiled clothing. Usually a soaking of 5 to 10 minutes will be adequate prior to laundering.

127. C. It is recommended that the films be rinsed in the circulating water bath for at least 20 to 30 seconds prior to being placed in the fixing solution.

128. A. Dental films can be stored safely in a lead container in a refrigerator set at 50° to 70°F.

129. A. The fixing process stops the developing process and enables the image to become visible.

130. C. It may be adequate to change the processing solutions every 4 weeks. It is important to determine more frequent solution changes based on use.

131. A. A stepwedge device is utilized to test the quality of the processing solutions.

132. C. Lead provides a barrier to the penetration of radiation.

133. D. Ideally, the developing solution should be 68°F. A thermometer is placed in the developing tank for accurate temperature reading.

134. C. The safe light wattage should be determined by the type of films utilized. A wattage of 7.5 is routinely utilized.

135. C. Light films may clearly indicate that the developing solution is exhausted and requires replacement with new solution.

136. D. Automatic film processing enables the dentist to quickly view a dry film and reduces darkroom time.

137. C. The lead foil backing protects the film from scatter radiation that strikes the film emulsion during exposure.

138. D. Ideally, the endodontic specialist and the oral surgeon may benefit from the rapid processing technique for clinical evaluation and treatment planning.

139. C. The fixing solution allows the unexposed silver bromide crystals to become separated from the film emulsion.

140. A. A minimum amount of washing time of 20 minutes in circulating water is recommended for adequately fixed films.

141. C. The film emulsion is comprised of silver halide crystals, which determine the film speed. The larger grains result in a faster film speed.

142. B. The utilization of high-speed film reduces the exposure time for the patient.

143. B. Too short a developing time or too low a temperature will result in a light radiographic image.

144. C. An overdeveloped film is caused from a too high developing temperature or a too long developing time. A thermometer and timer should be utilized to monitor the

developing process.

145. C. A low level of solution causes the film to be partially submerged, and therefore a partial image results.

146. C. Reticulation is caused from the film being placed from one solution at a high temperature to the water bath at a lower temperature.

147. B. Careless handling of the fixer, such as careless spillage or splashing, can cause white blotches on the film.

148. A. A thin image appears light and is caused from insufficient darkroom processing or exposure errors.

149. B. A radiograph that is overdeveloped will appear dark and may be impossible to interpret.

150. C. Dark films result from overdevelopment and overexposing.

151. C. Inadequate fixing of the film will result in an appearance that is fogged and stained with a brown tint.

152. D. All the aforementioned results can occur.

153. E. Fogged films appear cloudy and provide a poor clinical diagnostic aid. Fogged film can be the result of various causes that must be determined by the radiographer/clinician.

154. A. When the radiograph is partially submerged under the developing solution, the level may have been depleted. It is necessary to make sure that all radiographs attached to the film rack are completely immersed in the developer.

155. C. Using too rapid a motion when removing an X-ray can result in static electricity, especially if the air is dry.

156. C. The coin test is performed by placing a coin on a film that is unexposed in the darkroom with no lights on. The safe light is then turned on for 4 minutes, and the film is processed. If the coin outline is detected on the film, the safe light must be examined for problems.

157. C. The stepwedge is utilized for quality control in determining errors in both manual processing and the X-ray unit.

158. C

159. K

160. I

161. B

162. D

163. A

164. J

165. H

166. E

167. F

168. G

169. A. Horizontal overlapping is due to the central ray of X-rays not being aimed in a perpendicular relationship to the teeth of interest.

170. D. A dental film that has been mistakenly double-placed in the region of interest will appear to be double exposed.

171. A. The elongated image will show the lingual cusps of the premolars and molars. The vertical angulation of the PID will have to be corrected.

172. E. All the aforementioned directions are necessary regarding the correct film placement procedure.

173. A. A film that is placed too high in the mandibular arch will cut off the apical structures, which will result in a poor diagnostic visual aid.

174. C. A dark area between the teeth at the occlusal plane is evidence that the patient did not occlude completely on the tab or block of the bitewing film. Consequently, the crestal bone and a portion of the crown may be absent from the film.

175. A. Too little angulation vertically of the PID results in an elongated radiographic image. Proper alignment of the PID in relationship to the film and the tooth is essential.

176. B. Too much vertical angulation causes the radiographic image to appear foreshortened.

177. B. When the mesial structures of the mandibular premolar teeth are missing, the film should be adjusted more mesially to cover the distal half of the canine in order to include the first and second premolar teeth.

178. D. The apical structures will be missing because the film did not adequately cover the tooth and surrounding structures.

179. B. A herringbone pattern appears on the processed film as a result of placing the film backward in the oral cavity.

180. C

181. D

182. B

183. A

184. E

185. C. The periapical film provides a view of the teeth of interest, including the crown, root, and surrounding structures.

186. D. The median palatine suture appears as a radiolucent line between the maxillary central incisor areas. (See Figure 3-13.)

187. C. The inverted "Y" formation that is present in the canine area is formed by the lateral wall of the nasal fossa and the anterior wall of the sinus.

188. C. The incisive foramen appears as a radiolucent oval area above the median palatine suture. (See Figure 3-13.)

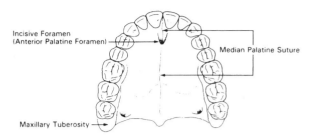
Figure 3-13

189. B. The genial tubercles are seen in the mandibular central film and are bony protuberances found on the lingual surface of the mandible. (See Figure 3-14.)

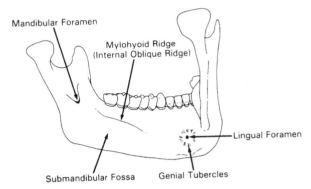
Figure 3-14

190. C. The hamular process, a hooklike structure, is seen in the posterior area of the maxillary molar film.

191. E. The maxillary sinus is a radiolucent area which may be seen in the maxillary canine, premolar, and molar areas.

192. C. The maxillary six-year molars have three roots.

193. B. The mandibular second molars have two roots.

194. a. 16

    b. 7

    c. No radiograph

    d. 13

    e. 3

    f. 11

    g. 1

    h. 15

i. 2

j. 12

k. 5

l. 9

m. 6

n. No radiograph

o. 4

p. 8

q. 10

r. 14

195. C. The collimator, which is comprised of lead and has an opening, restricts the size of the useful beam.

196. E. The operator should stand at a distance of 6 feet or more from the central beam in the minimum scatter area or behind a leaded door.

197. B. The operator is permitted to receive a maximum permissible dose of 5 rem or 50mSv (millisieverts) per year.

198. B. The patient is exposed to primary radiation during radiographic exposures. Protective measures provide quality control standards for the patient as well as the operator when X-radiation is utilized.

199. A. Scatter radiation occurs when primary radiation passes through the patient's head and tissues and deflects in all directions during the exposure process.

200. C. The aluminum filter wards off the long wavelengths of X-rays that are incapable of penetrating tooth tissue.

201. B. The sievert is comparable to the rem equivalent. The equivalent is expressed as 1 sievert equals 100 rems.

202. B. The International System of units of radiation includes the unit coulomb per kilogram whose equivalent is the roentgen, which mea-

sures the exposure to radiation.

203. B. The X-ray beam diameter should not exceed 2.75 inches on the patient's face.

204. C. The pregnant woman should be limited to an exposure of 0.5 millisievert or 0.05 rem per month.

205. B. An overdose of radiation exposure can cause erythema, which causes redness of the skin.

206. B. The aluminum filter provides a barrier to the undesirable long wavelengths that are incapable of penetrating tissue.

207. B. The operator should wear a monitoring radiology badge to measure the amount of exposure received during a period of time. The badge insert is sent to the manufacturer for readings.

208. B. The E-speed or Ekta speed film requires less exposure time for the patient.

209. B. This is the MPD (Maximum Permissible Dose) for an adult over a three-month period.

210. B. The thyroid collar is worn to protect the thyroid area, which is considered sensitive to radiation.

211. B. The tissue that is considered to be the most radio-sensitive to X-radiation is blood cells. Specifically in order of sensitivity they are: white blood cells, red blood cells, reproductive cells, epithelial cells, endothelial cells, connective tissue, bone, nerve, brain, and muscles.

212. C. X-radiation is cumulative in the human tissue. Ionizing radiation exposure can alter the structure of the cell and damage it. It is imperative to employ protective measures for the patient and operator during the exposure process.

213. C. The operator is protected from scatter radiation by standing at least 6 feet or more away from the

primary beam.

214. C. The eye is considered to be the most radiosensitive facial tissue.

215. C. The X-ray beam that originates from the focal spot of the anode is the primary beam, which radiates through the aperture of the tubehead.

216. D. The useful beam is the portion of the beam that is limited by the collimator and passes through the aperture of the tubehead.

217. A. The ALARA principle denotes "as low as reasonably achievable" with regard to the exposure of X-radiation for the dental patient. The risk versus benefit philosophy is considered by the dentist in determining the need for dental radiographs for clinical diagnosis and treatment planning.

218. E. All the aforementioned requirements pertain to safety specifications mandated by the federal government.

219. E. All the aforementioned requirements are necessary to comply with federal regulation of dental auxiliaries.

220. C

221. A

222. E

223. B

224. D

225. A

226. A

227. B

228. A

229. B

230. C

231. E

232. A

233. B

234. D

235. D. All the aforementioned contact situations require dental personnel to wear gloves.

236. B. All instruments that penetrate soft tissue and/or bone are always sterilized.

237. C. In this situation, both sterilization and high-level disinfection are acceptable.

238. D. Disinfection for 15 minutes is acceptable when exposing dental film packets.

239. D. A barrier envelope is utilized when exposing dental film. It fits over the film as an effective infection control aid when exposing radiographs.

240. B. In order to ensure infection control, the exposure button should be covered with a barrier and changed between patients.

241. E. All the aforementioned statements are correct.

242. D. In order to maintain infection control, hands should be gloved during the processing procedure.

243. E. Both statements are true regarding the correct radiographic processing procedure.

244. D. All the aforementioned precautions are used when handling exposed films during the processing procedure.

245. D. All the aforementioned precautions are used when handling patients receiving radiographs.

4

Medical Emergencies in the Dental Office

CHAPTER OUTLINE

I. Emergency drugs and equipment

II. Medical management

III. Life-threatening emergencies

IV. Safety in the dental office

V. Infection control protocol

DIRECTIONS (Questions 1-135): In each of the following questions, select the one choice that answers the question or completes the sentence best.

A. Emergency drugs and equipment

1. The dental management of a medically compromised patient should include the following:
   A. Health history
   B. Clinical lab testing
   C. Medical consultation
   D. Only B and C
   E. All of the above

2. Physical Status 3 classification for the medically compromised dental patient would determine the following consideration during dental management:
   A. Routine dental therapy
   B. Routine dental therapy with modifications
   C. Dental therapy with severe limitations
   D. None of the above

3. When a drug is administered, dispensed, or prescribed in the dental office, it should be:
   A. Dispensed only in liquid form
   B. Noted on the patient's chart in pencil
   C. Noted on the patient's statement
   D. Not the responsibility of the dental assistant
   E. Noted on the patient's chart in ink

4. Which of the following are effective measures for preventing emergencies in the dental office?
   1. Monitoring vital signs preoperatively
   2. Monitoring the patient during therapy
   3. Completing and evaluating an adequate health history preoperatively
   4. Maintaining an up-to-date medical kit
   A. 1, 2, and 3
   B. 1, 3, and 4
   C. 2, 3, and 4
   D. 1, 2, 3, and 4

5. Life-threatening emergencies can occur in the dental office because there is:
   A. Advanced therapeutic treatment for the medically compromised patient
   B. A large population of elderly patients
   C. A tendency to appoint patients for a longer duration of time
   D. Only B and C
   E. All of the above

6. The question "Have you taken any medicine or drugs during the past two years?" is important because it:
   A. Identifies the medical disorder being treated
   B. Identifies the potential side effects
   C. Indicates the potential for drug interaction
   D. Only a and b
   E. All of the above

7. In 1970, the Federal Comprehensive Drug Abuse Act was established to categorize drugs according to abuse potential, drug dependency, and medical utilization.

   Match the five categories for drug classification with the corresponding descriptions:
   Schedule I _____

   A. Drugs with a low potential for abuse that are acceptable for medical treatment; Abuse may lead to limited physical or psychological dependence (stimulants and barbituates).

Schedule II _____
Schedule III _____
Schedule IV _____
Schedule V _____

B. Drugs that have a high potential for abuse and are acceptable for medical use; may lead to moderate physical and psychological dependence (codeine or morphine).

C. Drugs with a high potential for abuse (heroin and LSD) are not used for medical purposes.

D. Drugs with a low potential for abuse and are acceptable for medical use (over-the-counter drugs).

E. Drugs with a low potential for abuse that are acceptable for medical use. (some depressants).

8. Deterioration of medicine is the result of:
   A. Exposure to air
   B. Temperature changes
   C. Exposure to light
   D. All of the above
   E. None of the above

9. The parenteral route for administration of drugs is:
   A. Oral
   B. Rectal
   C. Sublingual
   D. By injection

10. The route of administration of drugs under the skin is known as:
    A. Subcutaneous
    B. Sublingual
    C. Intramuscular
    D. Inhalational

11. Drugs that act together and have an undesirable effect are defined as:
    A. Synergistic
    B. Hypersensitive
    C. Antagonistic
    D. Intolerant

12. An allergic reaction due to a previous exposure to an agent is known as:
    A. Overdose
    B. Drug dependence
    C. Acquired drug tolerance

D. Hypersensitivity

13. A drug which lessens the sensation of pain is an:
    A. Anticoagulant
    B. Antidote
    C. Analgesic
    D. Antihistamine

14. The dose that will cause death in a person who abuses drug substances is known as the:
    A. Overdose
    B. Toxic dose
    C. Lethal dose
    D. Antidote

15. A drug which is administered to cause vomiting is known as an:
    A. Emetic
    B. Aspirin
    C. Antidote
    D. Antipertussive

16. The majority of drugs utilized in the dental practice are:
    A. Local anesthetics
    B. Antibiotics
    C. Sedatives
    D. All of the above
    E. Only A and B

17. The most common adverse drug reaction is due to:
    A. Overdose

B. Allergy

C. Patient pathology

D. Only A and B

E. All of the above

18. What preventive measure can be employed to prevent a possible allergic response in a patient?

A. Obtaining a medical history

B. Obtaining a medical history and talking with the patient

C. Obtaining a medical history, talking with the patient, and consulting with a physician

D. None of the above

19. The route of administration of drugs into the gastro-intestinal tract is known as:

A. Enteral

B. Parenteral

C. Muscular

D. Sublingual

20. The most common allergic manifestation to a local anesthetic is:

A. Vasodepressor syncope

B. Anaphylactic shock

C. Allergic dermatitis

D. Only A and C

E. All of the above

21. The side effects of nitrous oxide and oxygen are:

A. Headaches

B. Dizziness

C. Nausea and vomiting

D. Cough and cold

22. Nitroglycerin is administered to a patient who has:

A. Heart failure

B. Pericarditis

C. Myocardial infarction

D. Angina pectoris

23. The drug of choice that is utilized to treat the patient who is afflicted with long-term seizures is:

A. Dilantin (phenytoin sodium)

B. Insulin

C. Aspirin

D. Sulphur

24. The drug of choice that is utilized to treat the patient afflicted with diabetes is:

A. Dilantin (phenytoin sodium)

B. Codeine

C. Insulin

D. Aspirin

25. Use of sedatives or tranquilizers may indicate a disorder associated with:

A. Seizures

B. Allergies

C. Anxieties

D. All of the above

26. A patient who takes antihistamines most probably has a history of:

A. Heart disease

B. Allergy

C. Arthritis

D. Angina pectoris

27. Use of anticoagulants may indicate:

A. Allergy

B. Pregnancy

C. Seizures

D. Myocardial infarction

28. Inflammatory changes of the mucous membranes beneath a denture may be due to:

A. Heat-cured acrylic resins

B. Cold-cured acrylic resins

C. Metal framework

D. None of the above

29. A rash that is hard, edematous, dry, and scaly is a clinical manifestation of:

A. Urticaria

B. Contact dermatitis

C. Hives

D. Angioedema

30. A long-acting barbiturate that is used in dentistry is known as:

A. Aspirin

B. Phenobarbital

C. Demerol

D. Codeine

31. An agent that is used to relieve pain and reduce fever and inflammation is a(n):

A. Barbiturate

B. Narcotic

C. Analgesic

D. Antibiotic

32. An organic substance produced by microorganisms and capable of destroying bacteria is known as a(n):

A. Analgesic

B. Narcotic

C. Barbiturate

D. Antibiotic

33. Narcotics, prescribed in moderate doses:

A. Relieve pain

B. Produce sleep

C. Produce unconsciousness

D. Only A and B

E. Only A and C

34. _____ is most effectively used to combat infections caused by streptococci.

A. Nitroglycerine

B. Antihistamine

C. Penicillin

D. Aspirin substitute

35. The function of a hemostatic agent is to:

A. Increase the flow of blood near a lacerated blood vessel

B. Arrest the flow of blood near a lacerated blood vessel

C. Centrifuge whole blood

D. None of the above

36. The major cause of drug-related incidents is the:

A. Potential single action of a drug

B. Frequency of drug reactions

C. Indiscriminate utilization of drugs

D. Drugs devoid of toxicity

37. Most serious and frequent drug reactions are due to drugs administered:

A. Orally

B. Sublingually

C. Topically

D. Parenterally

38. An antihypertensive is prescribed to a patient with:

A. Bronchial asthma

B. Hypertension

C. Vasodepressor syncope

D. Postural hypotension

39. A patient with arthritis may have a history of utilizing:

A. Antihistamines

B. Narcotics

C. Salicylates

D. Nitroglycerin

40. The chronic use of salicylates (aspirin) may alter an individual's:

A. Anxiety levels

B. Clotting ability

C. Stress level

D. Susceptibility to infection

41. The result of a patient having exhibited a severe sensitivity reaction to a drug may be:

A. Hypertension

B. Hypotension

C. Anaphylaxis

D. Urticaria

II. Medical management

42. Angina pectoris is a(n):

A. Cancer of the heart

B. Spasm of the alveoli

C. Painful condition of the heart

D. External condition of the lung

43. Predisposing factors that will initiate angina are:

A. Vasodilator drugs

B. Low altitudes and light meals

C. Emotional tranquility

D. Caffeine ingestion and high altitudes

44. It is possible for a patient who experiences angina pain to have discomfort in the:
A. Left shoulder
B. Upper epigastric region
C. Neck and jaw
D. None of the above
E. All of the above

45. A patient who is experiencing angina pain during dental treatment should be managed by:
A. Moving the patient to an upright position
B. Moving the patient to a supine position
C. Administering nitroglycerine
D. Only A and B
E. Only A and C

46. An acute myocardial infarction can be more prevalent for:
A. Persons with a history of atherosclerosis
B. Males in the fourth decades of life
C. Males in the fifth to seventh decade of life
D. Only B and C
E. Only A and C

47. A person experiencing a heart attack will exhibit the following clinical manifestations:
A. Nausea and vomiting
B. Palpitations
C. Knifelike pain in the shoulders and jaw
D. Only C
E. All of the above

48. A person whose physical findings include cyanotic nailbeds and mucous membranes that are ashen gray may be experiencing:
A. Angina pectoris
B. Acute myocardial infarction

C. Hyperglycemia

D. Hypoglycemia

49. The risk of mortality for the patient who has an acute myocardial infarction is _____ hours.
A. 8 to 10
B. 3 to 6
C. 3 to 4
D. 4 to 6
E. 2 to 3

50. Management of a patient who has an acute myocardial infarction includes:
A. Providing basic life support
B. Summoning medical assistance
C. Monitoring vital signs
D. Only B and C
E. All of the above

51. Dental treatment should be postponed for a patient with myocardial infarction for _____ months.
A. 3
B. 4
C. 5
D. 6

52. Symptoms of congestive heart failure include the following:
A. Undue fatigue and weakness
B. Hyperventilation
C. Cardiac asthma
D. Only A and C
E. All of the above

53. A condition characterized by weakness, breathlessness, abdominal discomfort, and edema in the lower portion of the body resulting from reduced outflow of blood is known as:
A. Pulmonary edema
B. Heart failure
C. Congestive heart failure
D. Acute myocardial infarction

54. A patient with severe congestive heart failure may require:
A. Postoperative antibiotics
B. Referral to the physician

C. Positioning in an upright manner

D. Supplemental oxygen

E. All of the above

55. A patient with rheumatic heart disease may be susceptible to:

A. Angina

B. Cardiac asthma

C. Bacterial endocarditis

D. Viruses

56. A patient with a history of congenital heart disease may be susceptible to:

A. Infective endocarditis

B. Prolonged bleeding after surgery or prophylaxis

C. Congestive heart failure

D. Only A and B

E. All of the above

57. Patients with artificial heart valves or prosthetic valves may have potential problems relating to routine dental care, which may be prevented by:

A. Medical consultation

B. Antibiotic coverage

C. Reduced dosage of anticoagulant medication prior to prophylaxis and surgery

D. Only A and C

E. All of the above

58. A patient who has had a heart transplant could have potential problems relating to dental care, which may include:

A. Infection from immune suppression

B. Excessive bleeding due to anticoagulant therapy

C. Bacterial endocarditis

D. Only A and B

E. All of the above

59. Antibiotic prophylaxis is recommended for patients with:

A. Prosthetic cardiac valves

B. Previous history of bacterial endocarditis

C. Systemic pulmonary shunts

D. Only A and C

E. All of the above

60. Antibiotic prophylaxis is not recommended for patients with:

A. Ventricular septal defects

B. Cardiac pacemakers

C. Previous rheumatic fever without valvular dysfunction

D. Only A and B

E. All of the above

61. Antibiotic prophylaxis is recommended for patients with rheumatic fever and/or prosthetic cardiac replacements when performing:

A. Prophylaxis

B. Incision and drainage

C. Surgical operations

D. Only B and C

E. All of the above

62. Dental manipulations for a patient receiving kidney dialysis treatment are safely performed:

A. Two days after treatment

B. One day after treatment

C. Three days after treatment

D. Four days after treatment

63. Patients receiving kidney dialysis require precautions with dental care to eliminate:

A. Overdosing of medication

B. Bacteria entering into the shunt devices

C. Bacteria entering into the heart valves

D. Only B and C

E. All of the above

64. The standard oral antibiotic prophylaxis regimen for adult patients at risk for bacterial endocarditis is amoxicillin, which is dispensed:

A. 4 grams 1 hour before the procedure and 1 gram 4 hours after the initial dose

B. 6 grams 1 hour before the procedure and 1 gram 6 hours after the initial dose

C. 3 grams 1 hour before the procedure and 1.5 grams 6 hours after the initial dose

D. 8 grams 1 hour before the procedure and 1.5 grams 6 hours after the initial dose

65. Alternative antibiotics for patients allergic to amoxicillin or penicillin:
A. Erythromycin stearate
B. Erythromycin ethylsuccinate
C. Clindamycin
D. Only A and B
E. All of the above

66. Patients not able to take oral medications must use an alternative route of administration, which includes:
A. Intravenous (IV)
B. Intramuscular (IM)
C. Subcutaneous
D. All of the above
E. Only A and B

67. A patient who is diagnosed antibody-positive for HIV (AIDS) should be managed by the attending dental personnel to prevent:
A. Needle stick injury of the dental personnel
B. Instrument wounding of the dental personnel
C. HIV infection transmission
D. Only A and B
E. All of the above

68. A patient diagnosed with AIDS can have potential problems when being treated for routine dental care. Preventive measures can include:
A. Universal infection control procedures
B. Possible antibiotic coverage
C. Bleeding time testing
D. All of the above

69. An AIDS patient may have oral complications, including:
A. Kaposi's sarcoma

B. Oral moniliasis
C. Xerostomia
D. Only A and C
E. All of the above

70. Patients treated with radiation to the head and neck may experience oral complications such as:
A. Candidiasis
B. Loss of taste
C. Xerostomia
D. Cervical caries
E. All of the above

71. A patient suffering from a behavioral or psychiatric disorder may be difficult to manage for routine dental care because of:
A. Difficulty in communication
B. Uncooperative behavior
C. Aggressive behavior
D. Only B and C
E. All of the above

72. If a patient suffering from hepatitis needs emergency dental care, dental personnel should:
A. Use an isolated operatory and adhere to strict aseptic techniques
B. Wear rubber gloves, gown, face mask, and protective eyewear
C. Use a rubber dam, if possible, to minimize contact with oral secretions
D. Minimize aerosol production by utilizing a low-speed handpiece and reducing the use of the air syringe
E. All of the above

73. A patient with active sputum-positive tuberculosis should be treated with hospital dental care if the patient is over the age of 6.
A. True
B. False

74. A patient who has chronic active hepatitis may have an oral complication such as:
A. Bleeding

B. Poor wound healing

C. Oral ulcerations

D. Tonsillitis

E. Pharyngitis

75. Alcoholic liver disease, known as cirrhosis, may show oral complications such as:

A. Bleeding

B. Glossitis

C. Angular cheilosis

D. Only A and C

E. All of the above

76. Patients with venereal disease such as syphilis, gonorrhea, and genital herpes require the dentist to:

A. Postpone dental treatment

B. Use protective barriers

C. All of the above

D. None of the above

77. Patients with genital herpes who have oral herpetic lesions have potential problems related to routine dental care. The treatment plan should include:

A. Avoidance of elective dental care

B. Unnecessary protective eyewear

C. Elective dental care

D. Only B and C

E. All of the above

78. A pregnant patient in the last trimester can experience problems related to dental care such as:

A. Supine hypotension

B. Nutritional deficiencies

C. Pregnancy gingivitis

D. Only B and C

E. All of the above

79. A patient who has a joint prosthesis should be managed for dental care by:

A. Completing a medical/dental history

B. Consulting a physician

C. Determination of antibiotic coverage

D. Only A and C

E. All of the above

80. A patient with a replacement of the hips, knees, or elbows with a prosthetic device should require the dentist to:

A. Consult with the patient's surgeon

B. Administer high blood pressure medication

C. Provide additional therapy

D. None of the above

81. A patient who has undergone a renal transplant should be managed for dental care by:

A. Consulting with a physician

B. Possible supplemental steroids

C. Antibiotic coverage

D. Only A and C

E. All of the above

82. A patient who has a permanent pacemaker may experience electromagnetic interference, which may temporarily alter its function. Such interference may come from:

A. Microwaves

B. Cavitron

C. Pulp testers

D. Only B and C

E. All of the above

83. Which one of the following describes a condition in which there is a deficiency to a blood vessel due to functional constriction or actual obstruction?

A. Infarction

B. Thrombosis

C. Ischemia

D. Embolism

84. How much time should ideally elapse between a cerebral vascular accident and elective dental therapy?

A. 1 week

B. 6 weeks

C. 3 months

D. 6 months

85. Most frequently, CVAs (cerebral vascular accidents) are caused by:

A. Cerebral infarction

B. Diabetic coma

C. Hypotension

D. Convulsions

86. Which one of the following is a major risk factor in the development of CVAs?

A. Anticoagulant therapy

B. Hypotension

C. Hypertension

D. Diabetes

87. The most common tonic/clonic convulsion is known as:

A. Petit mal

B. Grand mal

C. Psychomotor

D. Seizure

88. During the management of the convulsing patient, the operator or assistant should:

A. Hold the patient's tongue between the thumb and forefinger

B. Place padded tongue depressors between the patient's teeth

C. Not place any object in the oral cavity during the seizure

D. Seat the patient in an upright position

89. A predisposing factor that may trigger convulsive behavior is:

A. Stable physical condition

B. Emotional stability

C. Flickering lights

D. Euphoria

90. A condition in which there is an increase of blood glucose levels is known as:

A. Hypoglycemia

B. Hyperglycemia

C. Hyperinsulation

D. Cell stimulation

91. Chronic complications of diabetes include:

A. Large blood vessel disease

B. Small blood vessel disease

C. Infection

D. Only A and B

E. All of the above

92. Loss of consciousness, hunger, nausea, sweating, anxiety, tachycardia, bizarre behavior, and convulsions are clinical manifestations of:

A. Hypoglycemia

B. Hyperglycemia

C. Thyroid disease

D. Angina

93. The management of a patient who exhibits symptoms of hypoglycemia in the dental office may include:

A. Administration of oral carbohydrates

B. Termination of the dental procedure

C. Basic life support

D. Only A and B

E. All of the above

94. An unconscious patient who manifests symptoms of hyperglycemia should be managed by:

A. Terminating the dental procedure

B. Placing the patient in a supine position

C. Administering an intravenous line of 5% dextrose and water

D. Only A and C

E. All of the above

95. Hyperthyroidism is clinically manifested by symptoms of:

A. Weight loss

B. Palpitations

C. Nervousness

D. Only A and B

E. All of the above

96. Hypothyroidism is clinically manifested by symptoms of:

A. The loss of energy

B. Muscle and joint pain

C. Intolerance to cold

D. Only A and B

E. All of the above

97. Vasodepressor syncope is usually

caused by:

A. Bradycardia

B. Airway obstruction

C. Increase in cerebral blood flow

D. Decrease in cerebral blood flow

98. The most frequently encountered psychogenic factor leading to vasodepressor syncope is:

A. Distrust

B. Anxiety

C. Fatigue

D. Disease

99. Which one of the following is the precipitating factor of vasodepressor syncope in the dental office?

A. Sitting upright

B. Air conditioning

C. Blood and instruments

D. Heated room

100. Syncope is best described as a(n):

A. Symptom

B. Disease

C. Acute respiratory attack

D. Allergic reaction

101. Generally, the most frequently encountered cause of postural hypotension in the dental office is:

A. Administration of a particular drug

B. Physical exhaustion

C. Prolonged recumbency

D. Only A and C

102. Which one of the following is a clinical example of inadequate delivery of oxygen to the brain?

A. Hyperglycemia

B. Hyperventilation

C. Epilepsy

D. Orthostatic hypotension

103. Unconsciousness would most likely be reversed by placing the patient in the supine position when caused by which of the following?

A. Hypoglycemia

B. Diabetes

C. Vasodepressor syncope

D. Hypotension

104. A higher rate of vasodepressor syncope is noted in which one of the following groups?

A. Children under 15

B. Women under 35

C. Men under 35 or 40

D. Infants

105. The type of drug that could be administered to treat vasodepressor syncope is a(n):

A. Narcotic

B. Antihistamine

C. Ammonia

D. Depressant

106. A patient with acute adrenal insufficiency may be in immediate danger of death because of:

A. Infection and shock

B. Congestive heart failure

C. Coma and shock

D. Shock and cardiac arrest

107. Predisposing factors that may lead to adrenal insufficiency include:

A. Removal of an adrenal tumor

B. Injury to the adrenal gland

C. Destruction of the pituitary gland

D. Only A and B

E. All of the above

III. Life-threatening emergencies

108. The major cause of loss of consciousness in the dental office by the normal patient under the age of 40 is:

A. Related to psychogenic reactions

B. Precipitated by cardiovascular difficulty

C. Due to hypoglycemia

D. Brought about by epilepsy

109. A hyperventilating patient will usually be most comfortable in what position?

A. Prone

B. Supine

C. Trendelenburg's

D. Upright

110. The type of drug that could be administered to treat a hyperventilating patient is a(n):

A. Vasodilator

B. Antihistamine

C. Aspirin

D. Tranquilizer

111. The medical emergency *least* likely to occur in the dental office is:

A. Vasodepressor syncope

B. Hyperventilation

C. Bronchial asthma

D. Acute adrenal insufficiency

112. The term syncope refers to:

A. Loss of consciousness

B. Low oxygen content

C. Lack of oxygen

D. None of the above

113. The sight of blood on surgical dental instruments may lead to a "sight or fright" response, which is known as:

A. Syncope

B. Psychogenic reaction

C. Vasodepressor syncope

D. All of the above

114. Hyperventilation syndrome may include the following signs:

A. Faintness and rapid breathing

B. Sharp pain substernally

C. Indigestion

D. None of the above

115. In managing hyperventilation syndrome, supplying carbon dioxide-enriched air to the patient may be done with a:

A. Funnel

B. Brown paper bag

C. Head band

D. Hat

116. Those patients predisposed to hyperventilation syndrome are:

A. Patients who grin and bear it

B. Patients aged 15 to 40

C. Both A and B

D. None of the above

117. Acute asthmatic attacks range in severity with acute episodes of:

A. Radiating pain down the left arm

B. Wheezing and coughing

C. Edema

D. None of the above

118. A bronchodilator is used for:

A. Hyperventilation syndrome

B. Acute asthma

C. Heart failure

D. Pulmonary edema

119. A common cause of acute asthma is:

A. Drugs

B. Stress

C. Fatigue

D. Rest

IV. Safety in the dental office

120. Side effects of inhalation sedation are:

A. Angioedema

B. Vomiting and nausea

C. Headache and bradycardia

D. None of the above

121. According to the federal Food and Drug Administration, nitrous oxide tanks are always what color?

A. Red

B. Green

C. White

D. Blue

122. The control measures for the prevention of nitrous oxide leakage include:

A. Scavenging nasal mask

B. Air monitoring program

C. Venting vacuum system

D. Only A and C

E. All of the above

123. Accordingly, nitrous oxide analgesia is not recommended for:
    1. Pregnant women
    2. Mouth breathers
    3. Individuals with infectious diseases
    4. Individuals with cardiovascular problems
    A. 1 and 2
    B. 1 and 3
    C. 1, 2, and 3
    D. 4

124. Nitrous oxide units have a flow meter that:
    A. Indicates the pressure of gas within the cylinder
    B. Provides the operator with an accurate measurement of the flow of gases the patient receives
    C. Controls the volume of gases administered
    D. Transports gases from the unit to the mask

125. The oxygen tank is always color-coded:
    A. Green
    B. Blue
    C. Yellow
    D. Red

126. Leakage from anesthesia or analgesia units is due to:
    A. Defective fittings
    B. Defective breathing bags
    C. Worn connectors
    D. Worn hoses
    E. All of the above

127. Recommendations for proper utilization of nitrous oxide include:
    A. Adequate ventilation
    B. Proper fit of the face mask
    C. Regular maintenance and service of all equipment
    D. Only A and C

E. All of the above

128. The adverse effects of occupational exposure to nitrous oxide can include an increase in:
    A. Spontaneous abortions
    B. Liver diseases
    C. Kidney diseases
    D. Neurologic diseases
    E. All of the above

129. Oxygen is considered an essential component of an emergency kit in the dental office. It is identified as a(n) _____ drug.
    A. Noninjectable
    B. Injectable
    C. Diluted
    D. Contraindicated

130. An emergency kit for the dental office should be composed of the following items:
    A. Injectable drugs
    B. Noninjectable drugs
    C. Emergency equipment
    D. Only A and B
    E. All of the above

131. Chronic occupational exposure to nitrous oxygen can result in:
    A. Spontaneous abortion
    B. Mental difficulty
    C. Liver disease
    D. Only A and C
    E. Only A and B

132. Effective ways to reduce exposure to nitrous oxide and oxygen are through:
    A. Infrared analysis
    B. Scavenging systems
    C. Mercury dosimeters
    D. All of the above
    E. Only A and B

133. Preventing an unfavorable reaction to local anesthetics requires a:
    A. Thorough, updated medical history
    B. Nonaspirating system

C. Fast injection

D. None of the above

V. Infection control protocol

134. The oral thermometer should be properly cared for prior to and after it is utilized to take a patient's temperature. It is disinfected by immersion in:

A. Soap and water

B. Iodophor

C. Quaternary ammonium compounds

D. Isopropyl alcohol

135. Prior to the utilization of a stethoscope, the ear pieces should be disinfected with:

A. Soap and water

B. Isopropyl alcohol

C. Ethyl alcohol

D. Iodophor

E. Only B and C

Answers

1. E. Today, because of the increase of medically compromised patients seeking dental care, it is essential for the dentist to be apprised of the physical evaluation and health history of patients in order to properly manage their dental needs.

2. B. Physical status 3 of the medically compromised patient requires modification of dental treatments during management.

3. E. Any drug or medication prescribed for a dental patient should always be noted in ink on the patient's clinical dental record.

4. D. All the aforementioned procedures are essential in order to prevent medical emergencies in the dental office.

5. E. All the aforementioned are key elements regarding life-threatening emergencies in the dental office.

6. E. All the reasons listed contribute to the knowledge obtained by the dentist regarding patient disorders and illnesses.

7. C. Schedule I

   B. Schedule II

   A. Schedule III

   E. Schedule IV

   D. Schedule V

8. D. Proper storage is essential for maintaining drug potency. Exposure to air, moisture, light, and temperature can cause deterioration of drugs.

9. D. Administration of drugs by injection is known as the parenteral route.

10. A. An injection administered subcutaneously is given underneath the skin.

11. C. The undesirable result of the action of combined drugs is known as antagonism.

12. D. An allergic response by an individual to an agent is known as hypersensitivity.

13. C. An analgesic is administered to relieve pain.

14. C. A lethal dose of a drug will cause death.

15. A. An emetic is an agent that produces vomiting in an individual.

16. D. In dentistry, the most common drugs utilized on a daily basis are local anesthetics, antibiotics, and sedatives.

17. E. All the aforementioned factors can produce an adverse drug reaction in an individual.

18. C. In order to prevent a possible aller-

gic response in a patient, all these measures are necessary.

19. A. The enteral route of administration is within the gastrointestinal tract.

20. E. There has been a marked decrease in allergic reactions to local anesthetics. However, manifestations such as vasodepressor syncope, allergic dermatitis, and anaphylaxis can occur.

21. C. Nausea and vomiting are two side effects of nitrous oxide and oxygen.

22. D. The drug of choice for a patient who is experiencing angina is nitroglycerine.

23. A. Phenytoin is an effective agent to treat central long-term seizures when managing epileptic patients.

24. C. Insulin is the drug that functions to properly metabolize blood sugar and maintain the correct blood sugar level.

25. C. Sedatives and tranquilizers are effective agents to control anxiety in a patient.

26. B. Antihistamines indicate a patient has a sensitivity to a specific antigen.

27. D. Anticoagulants are effective agents to prevent blood clots in a patient who has a history of myocardial infarction. These agents are blood thinners.

28. B. Acrylic resins that are cold-cured or self-cured can cause allergic response in the patient and should be avoided. Heat-cured resins are less likely to cause an allergic reaction.

29. B. Contact dermatitis can be caused by an individual coming into contact with an irritating or sensitizing chemical.

30. B. Phenobarbital is used for sedation to induce sleep and calmness.

31. C. An analgesic effectively relieves pain and reduces fever and inflammation.

32. D. An antibiotic inhibits the growth of or destroys microorganisms and is used to treat infectious diseases.

33. D. When narcotics are prescribed in moderate doses, they are effective agents in relieving pain and producing sleep. However, if they are utilized in excessive doses, they will cause unconsciousness, stupor, coma, and in some instances, death.

34. C. Penicillin is bacteriocidal. It suppresses the growth of most gram-positive and some gram-negative forms of bacteria. Streptococci are gram-positive bacteria that are destroyed by penicillin.

35. B. A hemostatic agent is defined as any agent that stops bleeding.

36. C. The indiscriminate use of drugs is the major cause of drug-related incidents.

37. D. Parenteral routes of administration of a drug can cause adverse drug reactions based on the speed of absorption.

38. B. Antihypertensive medication is prescribed to manage high blood pressure.

39. C. Salicylates or aspirins are commonly prescribed for patients to relieve the pain of arthritis.

40. B. Salicylates or aspirin can cause blood thinning and delay blood clotting in a patient who routinely takes the medication.

41. C. Anaphylaxis is the most severe and life-threatening allergic reaction to drugs.

42. C. Angina is caused by an insufficient supply of oxygen to the heart muscle and causes substernal pain.

43. D. These factors can stimulate an anginal episode in a patient.

44. E. All the aforementioned locations are sites where angina pain can occur in a patient.

45. E. These are the two procedures that should be followed during the management of patients experiencing an angina episode.

46. E. Acute myocardial infarction can be more prevalent in the male population aged 50 to 70 as well as in individuals having a history of atherosclerosis.

47. E. All the aforementioned manifestations can be exhibited by a person having a heart attack.

48. B. A person experiencing an acute myocardial infarction may exhibit physical findings which include cyanotic or blue-tinged nailbeds and ashen mucous membranes as well as cool, pale, moist skin.

49. D. The risk for mortality of a patient who has an acute myocardial infarction is 4 to 6 hours with the most threatening period being 1 to 2 hours post infarction.

50. E. The management of a patient with acute myocardial infarction requires all of these steps. Dental treatment should be terminated immediately.

51. D. The protocol requires a 6-month waiting period for the resuming of routine dental care for a patient who has suffered a myocardial infarction.

52. E. Clinical manifestations of heart failure include all the aforementioned symptoms.

53. C. Congestive heart failure is a complex disease that involves the failure of the left and right ventricles. Commonly, congestive heart failure can be caused by cardiac valvular disease, coronary atherosclerotic heart disease, and hypertension.

54. E. Dental management considera-

tions for a patient with congestive heart failure require consultation with the patient's physician, a review of the medical history and medications, and an evaluation of the patient's health status. These steps will enable the dentist to modify dental management accordingly.

55. C. Patients diagnosed with rheumatic heart disease can be susceptible to infective endocarditis and should be evaluated medically to determine antibiotic coverage.

56. E. A patient with a history of congenital heart disease requires a complete medical/dental history and medical consultation with the physician prior to dental treatment. Careful determination of dental management, including antibiotic coverage before dental procedures, avoidance of dehydration, and bleeding time and prothromb in time tests, is required for this medical problem.

57. E. All these preventive measures may be undertaken by the dentist upon consultation with the physician to avoid medical complications.

58. D. Usually, antibiotic coverage is recommended for a heart transplant patient to prevent local infection but not bacterial endocarditis.

59. E. All the aforementioned medical conditions would require an antibiotic regimen.

60. E. None of the aforementioned conditions require an antibiotic regimen.

61. E. All of the procedures listed are invasive and therefore require antibiotic regimen.

62. B. Patients receiving kidney dialysis should follow precautions that include waiting for a period of 8 to 24 hours after dialysis treatment for dental care.

63. D. Pre- and postoperative antibiotic

prophylaxis should be prescribed for a patient with chronic kidney disease that involves dialysis.

64. C. The recommended antibiotic regimen conforms with standards established by the American Heart Association.

65. E. All the aforementioned drugs can be prescribed for patients who are allergic to amoxicillin or penicillin.

66. D. Patients unable to take oral prophylactic antibiotics may have an alternative route of administration which includes intravenous, intramuscular, or subcutaneous.

67. D. Universal precautions for infection control procedures should be followed for all patients receiving dental care, as well as avoidance of needle stick and instrument injuries.

68. D. All the aforementioned measures should be followed regarding the prevention of medical complications for an AIDS patient.

69. E. All the oral complications listed can be manifested in the AIDS patient, as well as non-Hodgkin's lymphoma, squamous cell carcinoma, lymphadenopathy, progressive periodontal disease, hairy leukoplakia, and condyloma acuminatum.

70. E. All the complications listed can be manifested in a patient treated with radiation to the head and neck.

71. E. Patients diagnosed with behavioral or psychiatric disorders may be difficult to manage during routine dental care. A review of the medical/dental history and physician consultation will enable the dentist to understand and deal with the patient's dental needs.

72. E. All the aforementioned procedures should be followed strictly to prevent medical complications and possible transmission to dental personnel.

73. A. True. A patient with active sputum-positive tuberculosis can transmit the disease to the dentist, patients, and staff. Dental treatment should be performed in a hospital setting.

74. A. Patients with viral hepatitis type B, delta type non-B can have bleeding. The prothrombin time and bleeding time should be determined prior to preoperative procedures.

75. E. All the aforementioned are commonly manifested as oral complications in the patient with cirrhosis.

76. B. The dentist should practice protective and preventive measures while treating a patient with such disorders.

77. A. Patients with oral herpetic lesions should not be treated for elective dental care because there is the chance of possible transmission to the dentist or staff.

78. E. All of the problems listed can occur in a pregnant patient. Prevention of such problems will help to avoid medical complications.

79. E. A patient with a joint prosthesis may require antibiotic coverage, which would be planned by the attending physician and orthopedic surgeon to prevent infective endocarditis.

80. A. A consultation with the surgeon will affirm antibiotic regimen requirements for a patient with replacement devices.

81. E. All these preventive measures should be followed for a renal transplant patient to avoid medical complications such as infection, stress, poor healing, hypertension, and hepatitis.

82. E. All the aforementioned devices may interfere with the function of a pacemaker.

83. C. The statement correctly describes the condition known as ischemia.

84. D. Medically, it is recommended that patients who have suffered a cerebral vascular accident postpone elective dental care for 6 months.

85. A. Cerebral infarction is the leading cause of CVAs.

86. C. Cerebral vascular accidents (CVAs) occurs most frequently in patients who exhibit hypertension, or high blood pressure.

87. B. During grand mal or major epilepsy, the individual exhibits the tonic/clonic type of seizure, which is characterized by intermittent muscular contractions and relaxation.

88. C. During the tonic/clonic phase of a seizure, the operator should try to prevent the patient from injury and make sure an adequate airway is maintained. Nothing should be placed in the patient's mouth at this time.

89. C. Flickering lights may be an acute trigger that may actively precipitate a seizure.

90. B. In the condition known as hyperglycemia, there is an increase of sugar in the blood.

91. E. All the aforementioned conditions are chronic complications of diabetes.

92. A. Hypoglycemia signals a condition known as low blood sugar in a patient.

93. E. All the aforementioned steps should be followed during management of the hypoglycemic condition.

94. E. The management procedure for hyperglycemia includes all the aforementioned steps.

95. E. Hyperthyroidism may include each of the symptoms listed.

96. E. Hypothyroidism is a condition that includes all the aforementioned symptoms.

97. D. A decreased cerebral flow causes a patient to experience vasodepressor syncope.

98. B. Anxiety is the most common psychogenic factor that leads a patient to develop vasodepressor syncope in the dental office.

99. C. The sight of blood and/or instruments may be the precipitating factor that leads the patient to develop vasodepressor syncope. Instruments should be placed so they are not visible to the patient.

100. A. Syncope, or the sudden loss of consciousness, is only a symptom. Syncope may occur in healthy individuals; however, sometimes this occurrence indicates that there is an underlying, undiagnosed medical condition.

101. D. Both of these conditions are the most frequent reasons for a patient to exhibit signs of postural hypotension.

102. D. When the patient is positioned in the upright position for a long period of time, there will be a decrease of blood flow to the brain.

103. C. Vasodepressor syncope rarely occurs when the patient is in the supine position. This position allows blood to flow to the brain as the feet are positioned higher than the head.

104. C. Men between 16 and 35 display a higher rate of vasodepressor syncope than do infants, children under the age of 15 or the female who is under the age of 35.

105. C. Ammonia is a respiratory stimulant. An ampule is crushed between the operator's fingers and gently placed underneath the patient's nose.

106. D. A patient with acute adrenal insufficiency may be in serious danger of death due to an insufficiency of (cortisol) glucocorticoid, which can cause shock and cardiac arrest.

107. E. All the aforementioned predisposing factors may lead to adrenal insufficiency.

108. A. Psychogenic reactions most commonly occur in patients under the age of 40 and can be caused from a "sight and fright" syndrome.

109. D. The upright position is usually the most comfortable for the conscious hyperventilating patient.

110. D. Tranquilizers are the drug of choice to treat the patient who is hyperventilating.

111. D. Vasodepressor syncope, hyperventilation, and bronchial asthma are medical emergencies that may arise in the dental office. Both primary and secondary acute adrenal insufficiency are not common medical emergencies in dentistry.

112. A. Syncope is defined as the loss of consciousness caused by a lessened amount of blood reaching the brain.

113. B. The psychogenic response is directly related to a patient's sight and fright of blood on dental and surgical instruments, which can lead to vasodepressor syncope.

114. A. Faintness and rapid breathing are two signs of hyperventilation syndrome, which is usually precipitated by acute anxiety in the dental office.

115. B. In order to correct hyperventilation the individual may rebreathe exhaled air, which is enriched with carbon dioxide, through a brown paper bag, full face mask, or hands that are cupped over the face.

116. C. Young patients, those older than 15 and younger than 40, and individuals who do not inform dental personnel that they are anxious about their dentistry usually are prone to suffer from hyperventilation syndrome.

117. B. Wheezing and coughing are symptoms of acute asthma.

118. B. A bronchodilator is used to manage an acute asthmatic attack. It contains drugs that relax or dilate bronchial smooth muscle.

119. B. Stress is a contributing factor in acute asthma.

120. B. Vomiting and nausea are side effects that are associated with inhalation sedation.

121. D. Nitrous oxide tanks are always blue.

122. E. All the aforementioned control measures are essential for the prevention of nitrous oxide leakage.

123. C. Pregnant women, mouth breathers, and individuals with infectious diseases should not be administered nitrous oxide to achieve analgesia.

124. B. The flowmeter measures the nitrous oxide gases the patient receives during general anesthesia.

125. A. Oxygen tanks are always green.

126. E. All the aforementioned items will allow leakage to occur from the anesthesia or analgesia units.

127. E. Adequate ventilation, proper fit of the mask, and regular maintenance and servicing of equipment are recommended in order to properly utilize nitrous oxide in the dental office.

128. E. All the aforementioned conditions may occur as a direct result of occupational exposure to nitrous oxide.

129. A. Oxygen is administered by inhalation.

130. E. All the aforementioned items should be included in a dental office emergency kit.

131. D. Chronic exposure to nitrous oxygen can lead to spontaneous abortion and liver diseases in those individuals who are employed in areas where this anesthetic is utilized on a regular basis.

132. E. Reduction in the exposure for those individuals who work with nitrous oxide and oxygen is effectively monitored by infrared analysis and a scavenging system.

133. A. A patient medical history provides detailed information regarding allergic responses.

134. B. An iodophor is utilized to disinfect an oral thermometer prior to and after taking a patient's temperature.

135. D. Prior to and after taking a patient's blood pressure, the ear pieces should be disinfected with an iodophor.

5

Occupational Safety

CHAPTER OUTLINE

I. OSHA standards related to dentistry

DIRECTIONS (Questions 1-10): For each of the items in this section, one or more of the numbered options is correct. Choose answer:

    A. If only 1, 2, and 3 are correct
    B. If only 1 and 3 are correct
    C. If only 2 and 4 are correct
    D. If only 4 is correct
    E. If all are correct

1. A federal agency that was created by Congress in 1970 for the purpose of protecting employees from hazards in the workplace is referred to as:
    1. Environmental Protection Agency
    2. American Dental Association
    3. Better Business Bureau
    4. Occupational Safety and Health Administration

2. Universal precautions for bloodborne diseases in dentistry prompted regulatory action for the prevention of the transmission of the following:
    1. Hepatitis B
    2. Measles
    3. AIDS
    4. Mumps

3. In the dental office, who is covered by the bloodborne pathogens standard?
    1. Part-time employees
    2. Full-time employees
    3. Temporary and probationary employees
    4. Dentists

4. Occupational exposure is defined by OSHA as contact with:
    1. Blood
    2. Saliva
    3. Infectious materials
    4. Hazardous waste

5. An exposure central plan that complies with OSHA's standards includes the following:
    1. Exposure determination with regard to individual job descriptions
    2. Implementation of universal precautions
    3. Handling regulated waste
    4. Operating computer systems

6. Personal protective equipment refers to:
    1. Gloves
    2. Gowns
    3. Masks
    4. Eyewear

7. When treating patients in the dental office, gloves are required when dental personnel anticipate hand contact with:
    1. Blood
    2. Infectious materials
    3. Saliva
    4. Urine

8. Gloves must be replaced when:
    1. Contaminated after each patient use
    2. Torn
    3. Punctured
    4. Prior to handling the patient's record

9. Exposure control precautions require certain types of gowns to be worn based on the types or degree of exposure. These gowns include:
    1. Lab coats
    2. Clinic jackets
    3. Long-sleeved gowns
    4. Short-sleeved gowns

10. Masks and protective eyewear provide adequate protection from contamination from blood, saliva, and infectious materials in the form of:
    1. Splashes
    2. Droplets
    3. Splatters
    4. Spraying

DIRECTIONS (Questions 11-27): In each of the following questions, select the one choice that answers the question or completes the sentence best.

11. Laundering and caring for personal protective clothing include the following standards:
    A. Personal protective clothing may not be worn in eating areas and outside the office
    B. Protective personal clothing may be laundered in the employee's home
    C. Employees are prohibited from taking personal protective clothing to their home for laundering
    D. Only A and C
    E. Only B and C

12. What is the responsibility of the dental employer with regard to handwashing facilities?
    A. Readily accessible areas should be available to the employee for this purpose
    B. If handwashing facilities are not readily available, the employer must provide the employee with antiseptic hand cleanser or towelettes for this purpose, until the employee is able to wash with soap and running water
    C. Employees are not required to wash hands on a regular basis
    D. Only A and B

13. How does the auxiliary properly handle contaminated sharps within the dental office setting?
    A. Recapping by utilizing a one-handed technique or mechanical device is acceptable
    B. Contaminated sharps must be placed in a red or biohazard-labeled, puncture-resistant, leak-proof container
    C. Any puncture-resistant container must be closed for handling purposes

    D. Only A and B
    E. All of the above

14. Sharps must be properly disposed of:
    A. In accordance with waste disposal laws in your geographic location
    B. By placing them in the wastepaper basket in the operatory
    C. By disposing of them in any type of waste receptacle
    D. None of the above

15. If an employee refuses to obtain the hepatitis B vaccination, the employer is required to:
    A. Dismiss the employee
    B. Have the employee sign an informed refusal and/or declination form
    C. Ask the employee not to participate in surgical procedures
    D. None of the above

16. Housekeeping responsibilities of dental personnel require special attention to contaminated:
    A. Work surfaces
    B. Bins, pails, and receptacles
    C. Equipment
    D. All of the above

17. What is considered regulated waste within the dental office?
    A. Blood, saliva, and infectious materials
    B. Gauze that has been saturated with blood
    C. Teeth that have been extracted
    D. Biopsied tissue samples
    E. All of the above

18. The following symbol indicates the universal _____ symbol.
    A. Waste
    B. Radiation
    C. Sharps
    D. Biohazard

19. The protocol that should be followed by dental employees if they have an exposure incident includes:

A. Written statement that includes the route of the exposure and details of the incident, including the source individual, if feasible

B. Test results of the source individual's blood, if available

C. Drawing and testing of the employee's blood

D. Medical evaluation of the employee's illnesses after the exposure incident has occurred

E. All of the above

20. A dental employer must provide a training program for all employees that includes:

A. Copy of the OSHA standards in the federal register that address occupational exposure to bloodborne pathogens

B. Exposure control plan

C. Explanation of biohazard labels utilized in the dental office

D. All of the above

21. Employee training programs must be provided to dental personnel:

A. On a monthly basis

B. Initially at the time of employment if the employee is assigned to duties that involve exposure to blood, saliva, or infectious materials

C. Only if the employee's duties change so that he or she is at greater risk for exposure to blood, saliva, or infectious materials

D. Only B and C

E. All of the above

22. Dental employers are required to maintain a medical record for all employees whose job description states that they are exposed to blood, saliva, and other potentially infectious materials. These records should include the following information:

A. Name of the employee and his or her social security number

B. Documented copy of the hepatitis B

vaccination history of the employee, including dates of administration of the series and respective medical records

C. Any results of previous tests the employee may have had

D. Documentation and narration with regard to exposure incidents

E. All of the above

23. Dental employees are prohibited from eating, drinking, smoking, or performing personal grooming tasks in areas where they may be exposed to blood, saliva, and infectious materials.

A. True

B. False

24. What is the OSHA requirement as far as a fire safety policy in the dental office is concerned?

A. Maintenance of a fire extinguisher

B. Maintenance of a written safety policy

C. Training sessions that instruct employees about the utilization of the fire extinguisher

D. Dental office may be exempted from developing a training program if its policy states that employees evacuate the premises immediately

E. All of the above

25. The "Employee Right to Know Law" is an OSHA hazards communication regulation that informs the dental auxiliary with regard to:

A. Potential dangers of hazardous chemicals in the dental office

B. Injury due to sharps

C. Radiation exposure

D. None of the above

26. Specified guidelines for handling hazardous chemicals require the following precautions:

A. Adhere to the manufacturer's recommendations

B. Wear personal protective equipment such as face masks, gloves, and protective clothing

C. Clean hazardous spills or splashes immediately
D. Only A and B
E. Only B and C

27. Proper labeling of all hazardous materials utilized in the dental office must

include the following:
A. Chemical identification
B. Name of the product
C. Hazardous material warning
D. All of the above
E. Only A and C

Answers

1. D. Occupational Safety and Health Agency (OSHA).

2. B. OSHA is also regulating standards for hepatitis B as well as other bloodborne disease.

3. E. All employees, including the dentist, are covered by OSHA standards. The owner of an unincorporated practice is not an employee.

4. E. OSHA defines contact with blood, infectious materials, hazardous waste, and saliva as potential occupational exposure.

5. A. OSHA standards for an exposure plan includes exposure determination with regard to individual job descriptions, implementation of universal precautions, handling regulated waste in addition to other critical elements of implementation as listed in the federal register (29 CFR — Part 1910.1030)

6. E. All these barrier protective wear items are examples of personal protective equipment.

7. A. Hand contact with blood, infectious materials, and saliva requires the use of gloves.

8. E. Gloves are replaced when contaminated after each patient use, if they are torn or punctured, and prior to handling patient's records.

9. A. Gowns or clinic-type jackets are acceptable personal protective equipment that will protect clothing from blood, saliva, and infectious materials. Surgical procedures that involve exposure to

large amounts of blood require dental personnel to wear fluid-resistant long-sleeve gowns.

10. E. Masks and protective eyewear are required to prevent injury and contamination to the eyes, nose, or mouth from splashes, droplets, sprays, or splatters of potentially infectious materials such as blood and saliva. A face shield is also an acceptable form of barrier protection.

11. D. Personal protective clothing is not to be worn in areas where food is present or outside the dental office. Employees should not take protective clothing home for laundering purposes.

12. D. Employers are required to provide adequate facilities for handwashing. If facilities are not available, then the employee may wash with antiseptic hand cleanser and clean cloth/paper towels, or antiseptic towelettes until appropriate handwashing facilities can be utilized.

13. E. Sharps are properly handled by utilizing the recapping technique with a one-handed method or a mechanical device. Sharps must be placed in a puncture-resistant, leakproof container that is properly labeled "biohazard" or red in color and capable of being closed.

14. A. Sharps should be properly disposed of by adhering to the waste disposal laws pertinent to the geographic location.

15. B. A hepatitis B vaccination declina-

tion/refusal form should be signed by the employee and retained as a record by the employer.

16. D. Housekeeping responsibilities require the decontamination of contaminated work surfaces, equipment, bins, pails, and receptacles.

17. E. Regulated waste includes blood, saliva, and infectious materials; items that are saturated with blood and or infectious materials that would be capable of releasing these materials under compression; and contaminated sharps and pathological and microbiological waste containing blood, saliva, or infectious materials.

18. D. This illustration shows the universal biohazard symbol.

19. E. All the aforementioned are requirements of the protocol. In addition, the employee can receive counseling as well as medically prescribed prophylaxis treatment.

20. D. All the aforementioned must be included as part of the employee's training program.

21. D. Training must be provided to a new employee who has direct contact with bloodborne pathogens and for employees whose duties change and will now be at a greater risk for exposure to blood, saliva, or infectious materials.

22. E. The dental employer is required to maintain medical records for all employees that must include the aforementioned information. Additionally, the employer must keep these records for the duration of the employee's employment plus 30 years. All records are considered confidential.

23. A. In addition, food and drinks are not to be stored in a refrigerator, freezer, or any other container where blood, saliva, or infectious materials are present.

24. E. The fire safety policy that is mandated by OSHA for the dental office includes all the aforementioned procedures.

25. A. The "Employee Right to Know Law" protects the rights of the employees by informing them of potentially dangerous chemicals that are utilized in the dental office.

26. D. Guidelines for handling hazardous chemicals should be in compliance with OSHA's recommendations.

27. D. Proper labeling of hazardous materials includes the aforementioned procedures.

6

Dental Education and Oral Physiotherapy

CHAPTER OUTLINE

I. Plaque control and oral hygiene

II. Fluoride

III. Vitamins and minerals involved with bone and tooth formation

IV. Lipids

V. Nutrition counseling

VI. Community dentistry

QUESTIONS (Questions 1-67): In each of the following questions, select the one choice that answers the question or completes the sentence best.

I. Plaque control and oral hygiene:

1. The specific microorganism involved in the dental disease triad is:
   A. Staphylococci
   B. Diplococci
   C. Cocci
   D. Streptococcus

2. Immediately following the ingestion of sucrose, there is a rapid drop in the pH of plaque. The saliva becomes _____ and, therefore, the patient is said to be _____ susceptible to dental caries.
   A. Neutral/least
   B. Basic/less
   C. Acidic/more
   D. None of the above

3. Sugar in solution is more cariogenic than solid and sticky forms of sweets.
   A. True
   B. False

4. In order for dental caries to occur, the following items must be present:
   A. Susceptible tooth surface
   B. Specific microorganism
   C. Carbohydrate food source
   D. All of the above

5. Large amounts of sucrose ingested at mealtimes are less cariogenic than small amounts of sucrose ingested at frequent intervals throughout the day.
   A. True
   B. False

6. Dental plaque occurs in the oral cavity within _____ of tooth brushing and flossing.
   A. Hours
   B. Seconds

C. Minutes
D. Days

7. A thorough toothbrushing and flossing may be required only _____ time(s) per day to prevent dental caries.
   A. One
   B. Two
   C. Three
   D. Four

8. Brushing and flossing the teeth disorganizes plaque that has accumulated on the tooth surfaces.
   A. True
   B. False

9. The material that is applied to the dentition and shows the patient that plaque is present is known as:
   A. Fluoride
   B. Etching solution
   C. Disclosing solution or tablets
   D. Jeweler's rouge

10. A nylon filament toothbrush:
    A. Effectively cleans the cervical area
    B. Causes less trauma to the gingival tissues
    C. Is able to effectively cleanse orthodontic appliances and/or fixed appliances
    D. Can be directed interproximally
    E. All of the above

11. A natural bristle toothbrush is not recommended as it:
    A. Absorbs water
    B. May harbor microorganisms because the bristles are hollow tubes
    C. Is stiff and does not conform to the tooth surface, making plaque removal difficult
    D. All of the above
    E. Only A and C

12. The Fone's method of brushing advocates utilization of the ____ method of

toothbrushing, which is especially good to teach _____.

A. Circular/children
B. Side-to-side/children
C. Up-and-down/teenagers
D. Sweeping/adults

13. Hydrotherapy allows the patient to apply a forced intermittent stream of water in order to remove food debris from the oral cavity.

A. True
B. False

14. Microorganisms get trapped in the papillae of the tongue; therefore, you should brush this area once or twice a day to remove debris and plaque.

A. True
B. False

15. Dental floss is available in waxed and unwaxed varieties. As far as plaque removal is concerned, waxed floss is the better choice.

A. True
B. False

16. Your toothbrush should be replaced every _____ months and/or after illness.

A. 1 to 2
B. 2 to 3
C. 3 to 4
D. 3 to 6
E. 3 to 8

COLUMN A
Match the following:

17. _____ Daily brushing and flossing

18. _____ Nylon filament toothbrush

19. _____ Powered/automatic toothbrushes

20. _____ Toothpick

21. _____ The Bass method of tooth-brushing

COLUMN B

A. Rinses clean, dries rapidly, and maintains its form over a longer period of time

B. The earliest method devised for the care of teeth

C. Allows the patient to direct the bristles into the gingival sulcus

D. Ideal for patients with limited dexterity

E. The most effective method to remove plaque

COLUMN A
Match the following:

22. _____ Interdental stimulator

23. _____ Proxybrush

24. _____ Floss threader

25. _____ End tuff brush

COLUMN B

A. Device utilized to insert dental floss or tape

B. Rubber-tipped aid utilized for interproximal massage and plaque removal

C. Device for removing plaque from difficult or malaligned teeth

D. Device for removing plaque from interproximal spaces as well as bi- or tri-furcated root areas

E. Device for removing calculus from hard-to-reach areas

II. Fluoride

26. Fluoride can be added to a domestic water supply at the rate of:
    A. 1 ppm
    B. 10 ppm
    C. 100 ppm
    D. 1000 ppm

27. A combined fluoride program includes the following:
    A. Utilizing a fluoridated dentifrice
    B. Rinsing with a fluoridated mouthwash
    C. Applying fluoride topically at regular intervals
    D. Ingesting fluoridated water
    E. All of the above

28. Sodium fluoride is administered in a series of four applications spaced 2 days to 1 week apart at intervals throughout childhood that correlate with tooth eruption patterns.
    A. True
    B. False

29. During the mineralization stage, fluoride is available to the tooth surface through the bloodstream.
    A. True
    B. False

30. Acidulated phosphate fluoride is applied _____ time(s) annually during the recall appointments.
    A. One
    B. Two
    C. Three
    D. Four

31. An 8 to 10% solution of stannous fluoride is applied to a child's teeth in single applications at 4-to-6 month intervals, beginning at approximately age 3.
    A. True
    B. False

32. If properly applied, regular applications of stannous fluoride at specific intervals of time will reduce caries.
    A. True
    B. False

33. Before a topical application of fluoride can be applied to the teeth, the patient must have:
    A. Thorough prophylaxis
    B. Teeth flossed
    C. Teeth dried
    D. Teeth isolated
    E. All of the above

34. To receive the maximum benefit of a topical fluoride treatment, the fluoride must remain in contact with the tooth surface for approximately ____ minutes.
    A. 1 to 2
    B. 2 to 3
    C. 3 to 5
    D. 6 to 8

35. After a topical fluoride treatment, the patient must be instructed not to eat or drink anything for at least:
    A. 1 hour
    B. 10 minutes
    C. 30 minutes
    D. 3 minutes

III. Vitamins

36. The minerals that participate in tooth and bone formation are:
    A. Calcium
    B. Phosphorus
    C. Potassium
    D. Only A and B
    E. Only A and C

37. Vitamin _____ is made available to the skin in the presence of sunlight.
    A. A
    B. D
    C. E
    D. K

38. One of the primary sources of calcium is _____.

A. Meat

B. Milk and milk products

C. Fish

D. Dark-green leafy vegetables

39. In order for calcium to be absorbed in the body, there has to be an adequate amount of _____ in the diet.

A. Phosphorus

B. Iron

C. Vitamin A

D. Vitamin D

40. Milk is a food that has been _____ with vitamins _____.

A. Enriched/A and D

B. Fortified/A and D

C. Refined/A and C

D. Fortified/A and C

IV. Lipids

41. A function of lipids in the body is to:

A. Provide energy

B. Regulate body processes

C. Build muscle tissue

D. Protect vital organs

E. Only A and D

42. Which one of the following does *not* describe a function of lipids?

A. Carrier of fat-soluble vitamins

B. Essential constituent of body tissues

C. Best source of energy for the brain

D. Storage form of energy

E. Adds flavor to foods

43. One gram of fat yields:

A. 4 calories

B. 5 calories

C. 6 calories

D. 9 calories

44. The term "unsaturated fat" means that the fat:

A. Lacks glycerol

B. Has one or more bonds between carbons in the molecule that are

not saturated with hydrogen

C. Is a solid at room temperature

D. Is not saturated with kilocalories

45. Animal fats contain more _____ than vegetable oils.

A. Triglycerides

B. Saturated fat

C. Unsaturated fat

D. Bile

E. Kilocalories per gram

46. Saturated fatty acids are:

A. Found abundantly in plant oils

B. Found abundantly in animal fats

C. Related to a high incidence of heart disease

D. Usually liquids at room temperature

E. Only B and C

47. Cholesterol is found in plant and animal foods.

A. True

B. False

48. Dietary saturated fats tend to _____ serum cholesterol, and polyunsaturated fats tend to _____ it.

A. Increase/increase

B. Decrease/decrease

C. Decrease/increase

D. Increase/decrease

49. Saturated fats seem to be capable of increasing blood levels of _____. This is unfortunate because high levels of this compound are associated with _____.

A. Glucose/diabetes

B. Uric acid/gout

C. Cholesterol/heart disease

D. Glycerol/cancer

50. Hardening of the arteries or atherosclerosis is:

A. Thickening of the blood, slowing its movement throughout the body

B. Accumulation of cholesterol and calcium along the inner surfaces of blood vessels

    C. Another term for high blood pressure

    D. Caused by the death of red blood cells

51. Mounds of lipid material, mixed with smooth muscle cells and calcium, which are lodged in the artery walls are:

    A. Aortas

    B. Aneurysms

    C. Plaques

    D. Embolisms

52. A myocardial infarction is:

    A. Stroke

    B. Heart attack

    C. Deterioration of the heart muscle

    D. Another name for an atherosclerotic plaque

V. Nutrition counseling

53. The best type of food diary is one that charts the patient's diet for:

    A. 5 days

    B. 7 days

    C. 3 days

    D. 14 days

54. The interviewing and counseling visit should take place at least _____ days after the food diary is given to the patient to complete.

    A. 3

    B. 4

    C. 5

    D. 7

55. The first step in diet counseling is to:

    A. Explain the potential effects of the six food groups on dental and general health

    B. Make a judgement on the patient's eating habits

    C. Complete a sample diet form with the help of the patient

    D. Define the objective of the diet counseling program

56. The saliva flow test reveals the:

    A. Acid-producing organisms and carbohydrate food stuffs retained on the teeth

    B. Acidogenic potential of the total oral flora

    C. Dietary sucrose intake

    D. None of the above

57. The function of the Snyder test is to:

    A. Establish a lactobacillus count

    B. Identify the bacteria present in dental plaque

    C. Measure the rate of salivary flow or secretion

    D. Measure the acidogenic potential of the total oral flora

58. A nutrition case history is written in _____ style.

    A. Outline

    B. Objective

    C. Narrative

    D. Subjective

59. The patient should be allowed to delete from the diet plaque-forming foods and sugar-sweetened foods. In addition, the patient is encouraged to select non-plaque-promoting snack substitutes.

    A. True

    B. False

60. By multiplying the number of sugar exposures by _____, the counselor can determine the number of _____ that the oral cavity has the potential for acid production.

    A. 20/hours

    B. 20/minutes

    C. 60/seconds

    D. 60/hours

61. The number of minutes that the oral cavity has potential acid production can be recalculated into hours by:

    A. Multiplying by 60

    B. Dividing by 60

C. Multiplying by 20

D. Dividing by 20

62. Which one of the following is true concerning the caries-producing factor of foods?

A. Honey is less harmful than other sugars

B. Both honey and brown sugar contribute less to caries production

C. From a caries-producing standpoint, natural and refined sugars are equally detrimental

D. Natural sugars are significantly more nutritious than other forms

63. When planning a revised diet for the patient, the counselor may substitute one cup of nonfat milk for:

A. One cup of buttermilk

B. One cup of nonfat plain yogurt

C. One-half cup of evaporated non-fat milk

D. All of the above

E. Only A and C

VI. Community dentistry

64. When treating the handicapped or the elderly patient in the dental office, special consideration of the following factors should be emphasized:

A. Review of the patient's drug regimen

B. Avoidance of the supine position

C. Appoint the patient at a time that meets his or her needs

D. Cardiac patients are usually scheduled in the morning

E. All of the above

65. Preventive dental services available in the community are:

A. Fluoridated water

B. Fluoride rinse programs

C. Fluoride supplement programs

D. School sealant programs

E. All of the above

66. Patients who have pacemakers should not be treated with the following techniques:

A. Cleaning the teeth with an ultrasonic scaler

B. Drilling with a high-speed handpiece

C. Taking impressions with hydrocolloid

D. Taking impressions with alginate

67. A child who is a minor requires written parental consent in order for operative dentistry to be performed?

A. True

B. False

Answers

1. D. Streptococcus is the specific microorganism that must be present in the oral cavity in order to initiate the decay process.

2. C. Prior to eating, an individual's plaque pH is 6.2 to 7.0, which is within the neutral zone. When a carbohydrate food source is ingested, the pH of the plaque drops. Enamel decalcification can occur with a pH reading of 5.0 or lower. A patient who exhibits a lower pH level is said to be more susceptible to developing dental caries.

3. B. Sugar that is in a solid, sticky form such as a cookie or a candy bar is retained in and on the tooth surface. A sugar that is in a liquid form, such as in sweetened soda, washes over the surfaces of the teeth and has less chance of being retained on and between the teeth.

4. D. All the aforementioned items must be present in order for the decay process to begin.

5. A. When sugar is ingested frequently throughout the day, the pH level of

the plaque continually drops to the acidic range. Thus, the individual is said to be at a greater risk for the initiation of dental decay.

6. B. Plaque begins to form immediately after an individual has thoroughly brushed and flossed his or her teeth.

7. A. If the patient brushes and flosses his or her teeth thoroughly once per day, dental caries may be prevented.

8. A. Toothbrushing and flossing disorganize colonies of plaque and renders them unable to cause decay. If plaque is allowed to accumulate on and between the tooth surfaces, it becomes organized and has the potential to decalcify the tooth surface and initiate dental decay.

9. C. Disclosing liquid or tablets is a vegetable-based dye that stains tooth surfaces red to show the patient that plaque has formed on and between these areas. It can be easily removed by brushing and flossing the teeth.

10. E. All the aforementioned are desirable characteristics of a nylon filament toothbrush.

11. D. All the aforementioned are undesirable characteristics of a natural bristle toothbrush.

12. A. The Fone's method of toothbrushing is recommended for the pediatric patient as it employs a circular motion which is ideal for children who are lacking gross coordination skills.

13. A. Hydrotherapy allow the patient to remove food debris from the gingival sulcus areas.

14. A. The patient should be instructed to brush the tongue every time he or she brushes the teeth in order to remove debris and plaque from this area.

15. B. Waxed and unwaxed dental floss are equally effective in removing plaque from the interproximal tooth surfaces.

16. D. The patient should be instructed to replace his or her toothbrush every 3 to 6 months or after an illness. Children's toothbrushes should be replaced in the same manner.

17. E

18. A

19. D

20. B

21. C

22. B

23. D

24. A

25. C

26. A. In an area that has a temperate climate, fluoride can be added to a domestic water supply at the rate of 1 ppm. This rate can be adjusted from 0.6 to 1.2 ppm in warmer or colder climates.

27. E. All the aforementioned are methods utilized by the individual to receive the benefits of a combined fluoride program.

28. A. Sodium fluoride is administered to the patient in a series of four applications spaced 2 days to 1 week apart in intervals throughout childhood that correlate with tooth eruption patterns.

29. A. During the mineralization stage of tooth development, the teeth acquire fluoride through the bloodstream. At this point in time, the teeth are not erupted; however, the enamel is being formed.

30. B. Acidulated fluoride is administered to the patient twice a year during recall appointments.

31. A. An 8 to 10% solution of stannous fluoride is administered to a child

in single applications at 4-to-6-month intervals beginning at age 3.

32. A. Stannous fluoride, administered on a regular basis adhering to the specific time sequence and correct application procedures, will significantly reduce caries.

33. E. All the aforementioned steps must be followed before administering a topical application of fluoride.

34. C. In order to receive maximum absorption, topical fluoride should remain in contact with the tooth surface for 3 to 5 minutes.

35. C. The patient who has had a topical application of fluoride should not eat or drink anything for 30 minutes.

36. D. Calcium and phosphorus work together to encourage bone and tooth formation.

37. B. Vitamin D is frequently referred to as the "sunshine" vitamin, as it is available to the skin in the presence of sunlight.

38. B. Milk and milk products supply the body with calcium.

39. D. Vitamin D enhances the uptake and absorption of calcium from the intestine.

40. B. Milk is a food which has been fortified with vitamins A and D.

41. E. Lipids function in the body to provide energy and protect vital organs.

42. C. Lipids are slowly metabolized by the body to provide long-term energy; however, carbohydrates have the ability to be absorbed quickly and ensure that the brain is supplied with an adequate amount of energy.

43. D. One gram of fat will yield 9 calories.

44. B. An unsaturated fat has one or more bonds between carbons in the molecule that are not saturated with hydrogen.

45. B. An animal fat contains more saturated fat and calories than a vegetable fat.

46. E. Saturated fat is derived from animal sources such as whole milk, beef, cheese, and organ meats. Unsaturated fat is found in plant oils which include corn oil, saffron oil, and peanut oil.

47. B. Cholesterol is not made by the body; however, it is supplied to the body by foods that are of an animal origin.

48. D. Saturated fats increase serum cholesterol, while polyunsaturated fats tend to decrease it.

49. C. A high serum blood level of cholesterol may be indicative of a patient with increased risk of heart disease.

50. B. Cholesterol is not made by the body. It is derived from the foods we eat that are high in saturated or animal fats. Cholesterol accumulates on the walls of blood vessels and, over a period of time, decreases their diameter and causes the heart to work harder to pump blood to the body.

51. C. Plaque accumulates on the inner walls of blood vessels. It is made up of lipids, smooth muscle cells, and calcium.

52. B. A heart attack is also known in medical terminology as a myocardial infarction.

53. A. A 5-day food diary is the best way to get an accurate history of the patient's dietary habits. In addition, a weekend should be included in this 5-day period.

54. C. The interviewing and counseling visit should be scheduled 5 days after the food diary is completed.

55. A. The diet counselor should begin the session by explaining the potential effects of the six food groups on the patient's dental as well as general health.

56. B. The saliva flow test tells the diet counselor about the acidogenic potential of the bacteria in the patient's oral cavity.

57. C. The Snyder test measures the rate or amount of salivary flow that occurs in the patient's oral cavity.

58. C. The nutrition case history is documented by utilizing a narrative style format.

59. A. The patient is encouraged to participate in deleting and adding foods to his present diet.

60. B. If the counselor multiplies the number of sugar exposures by 20, the resulting figure will inform the patient of the number of minutes that his oral cavity has the potential to produce acid.

61. B. If the counselor multiplies the number of sugar exposures by 20 and divides the resulting figure by 60, the patient's hourly potential for acid production may be determined.

62. C. From a nutritional point of view, natural and refined sugars have an equally detrimental effect on the tooth surface. Both types of sugars contribute to an increased rate of dental caries in the oral cavity.

63. B. On the patient's revised diet, the counselor may substitute one cup of nonfat milk for one cup of plain, nonfat yogurt. Both of these foods contain approximately the same amount of nutrient values.

64. E. All the aforementioned factors should be considered when treating the handicapped and/or elderly patient in the dental office.

65. E. All the aforementioned dental services are available to individuals residing in the community.

66. A. Patients who have pacemakers should have their teeth cleaned by utilizing a manual scaling method rather than an ultrasonic scaling technique. Electromagnetic interferences, such as an ultrasonic scaling device, may alter the performance of a pacemaker.

67. A. This is a true statement pertaining to parental/guardian consent when treating a minor.

7

Dental Office Management

QUESTIONS

DIRECTIONS (Questions 1-92): In each of the following questions, select the one choice that answers the question or completes the sentence best.

I. Communication and reception protocol

1. In a dental office, a business assistant can encounter pressure, frustration, and interruption. She or he can easily manage this situation by:
   A. Assigning tasks to others
   B. Taking the phone off the hook
   C. Remaining calm and completing tasks
   D. Taking a personal day off

2. The office procedural manual provides:
   A. Guide for all office activities
   B. Informational guide for operating equipment
   C. Instruction for operating the dental unit
   D. Records that the business assistant keeps

3. An office manual is effective when it is:
   A. Prepared by a supply company
   B. Organized by a consultant
   C. Organized by the dentist and staff
   D. Prepared by the staff manager

4. The Dentist(s) that recognizes each staff member as a person whose goals are unified for that dental office is an example of _____ leadership.
   A. Free-reign
   B. Authoritative
   C. Participatory
   D. None of the above

5. The person who is assigned supervisory responsibilities in the dental office is known as the:
   A. Chairside assistant
   B. Bookkeeper
   C. Staff manager

   D. Dental hygienist

6. Barriers to communication in the dental office include:
   A. Age, health, and education
   B. Status, prejudice, and impatience
   C. Humor, empathy, and sincerity
   D. All of the above

7. Management can be defined as:
   A. Ordering and directing
   B. Motivating and guiding
   C. Demanding and intimidating
   D. Overshadowing leadership

8. An important link for a meaningful relationship between members of the dental office and the patient is:
   A. Prejudgement
   B. Dictatorship
   C. Impatience
   D. Communication

9. Some examples of sample letters that should be kept on file for reference in the dental office include the following:
   A. Recall letter
   B. Referral letter
   C. Birthday letter and holiday greeting
   D. Only A and B
   E. All of the above

10. The various classifications of computers include the:
    A. Mainframe
    B. Minicomputer
    C. Microcomputer
    D. Only B and C
    E. All of the above

11. The basic operations for a computer include:
    A. Input
    B. Processing
    C. Output
    D. Storage
    E. All of the above

12. The rights of a patient during the treatment phase do not include the following:
    A. Be informed about his or her condition
    B. Refuse treatment
    C. Confidential records
    D. Dictate the course of treatment

13. Before proceeding with treatment, the patient should be notified of the:
    A. Cost
    B. Time needed to accomplish the procedure
    C. Any risks the treatment may entail
    D. All of the above

14. If the dentist is delayed, patients who are waiting should be:
    A. Kept busy as a distraction
    B. Ignored
    C. Notified of the delay
    D. Told to leave

15. Nonverbal communication in the dental office includes:
    A. Hand signals
    B. Dress
    C. Facial expressions
    D. All of the above

16. Distortions in communication may occur with dental patients because of such factors as:
    1. Clarity of the stated information
    2. The patient not understanding the language or dialogue
    3. Fear and anxiety
    4. A summary of the dental treatment
    5. Background noise and interference
    6. Exchange of questions and answers
       A. 1, 4, and 5
       B. 2, 3, and 5
       C. 3, 4, and 6
       D. 4, 5, and 6

17. The business assistant may have responsibilities that include:
    A. Greeting patients
    B. Maintaining a neat and professional appearance
    C. Maintaining an orderly reception area
    D. Only B and C
    E. All of the above

18. The word "pain" may be rephrased as:
    A. Discomfort
    B. Hurt
    C. Trouble
    D. Sore

19. A patient who is nervous when he or she enters the dental office will often display behavior that may appear:
    A. Confident and smiling
    B. Embarrassed and fidgety
    C. Calm and relaxed
    D. None of the above

20. The reception area may make a favorable impression on a patient when the office reflects a(n):
    A. Austere background
    B. Plain and simple motif
    C. Friendly and cheerful atmosphere
    D. Dull or dark blue atmosphere

21. The office policy contains information that includes:
    1. Auxiliary utilization
    2. Office hours
    3. Office philosophy
    4. Employment benefits
       A. 1, 3, and 4
       B. 2, 3, and 4
       C. 1, 2, and 3
       D. 2, 1, and 4

22. A cordial and responsive telephone technique are characteristics of a _____ personality in the dental business office.
    A. Photogenic
    B. Phonogenic
    C. Photographic
    D. Phonographic

23. An example of words and phrases that should not be utilized during telephone conversations with patients include the following:
   A. Hurt, drill, filling, and pull teeth
   B. Investment, restoration, dentures, and dentistry
   C. Injection, instrument, uncomfortable, and confirm
   D. Fee, prepare, treat, and extract

24. Outgoing calls will be placed by the business assistant. The following techniques should be followed:
   A. State your reason for calling
   B. Preplan the call by having the correct telephone number available
   C. Identify yourself when your call is answered
   D. All of the above
   E. Only B and C

25. If you need to place the caller on hold so that you may procure information, you should:
   A. Indicate that you will return
   B. Return to the telephone to assure the caller that you are still involved with the task
   C. Thank the caller for holding when you return
   D. Only A and B
   E. All of the above

26. When answering the telephone in the dental office, the assistant should:
   A. Determine the reason for the call, terminate politely, and answer politely
   B. Answer promptly, determine the reason for the call, and terminate politely
   C. Terminate politely, answer promptly, and determine the reason for the call
   D. None of the above

27. The preferred professional telephone greeting that would be utilized in the dental office by the business assistant is:
   A. "Hello. This is Grace speaking. May I help you?"
   B. "Hi. My name is Susie. What can I do for you?"
   C. "Good morning. Dr. Jones's office. May I help you?"
   D. "Good morning, Dr. Jones's office. This is Sue. How may I help you?"

28. A patient calls and insists on speaking with the doctor. The correct way to handle this situation would be:
   A. Indicate that the dentist is with a patient
   B. Tell the patient that the dentist would like the patient's name, phone number, and purpose of the call
   C. Document the correct spelling of the patient's name and record the phone number
   D. All of the above

II. Appointment control and patient recall:

29. A day sheet in each treatment room provides the following data:
   A. Patient's medical problems
   B. Patient's occupation
   C. Procedure to be performed and the length of the appointment
   D. Number of visits

30. The patient should be informed of the fee for the dental treatment:
   A. Prior to treatment
   B. After treatment
   C. During treatment
   D. None of the above

31. The patient's clinical chart:
   A. Is maintained for each patient and contains a record of treatment that has been performed
   B. Does not protect the patient
   C. Does not protect the dentist
   D. None of the above

32. "Reg flag phrases" regarding communication in dentistry refer to:
    A. Unfavorable words and phrases
    B. Verbal communication
    C. Patient's fee schedule
    D. Patient's treatment plan

33. In the dental office, who controls the appointment book?
    A. Dentist
    B. Chairside assistant
    C. Receptionist
    D. Dental hygienist

34. Which appointments should be scheduled for the early morning hours?
    A. Appointments for adults
    B. Appointments for young children
    C. Appointments for the auxiliaries
    D. None of the above

35. "Prime time" in the dental office refers to the following block:
    A. Before 10:00 a.m.
    B. At 11:30 a.m.
    C. At 12:00 p.m.
    D. After 3:00 p.m.

36. The call list refers to a:
    A. Treatment plan
    B. Time box
    C. Variety of patients who need appointments
    D. None of the above

37. Rules for efficient appointment management require that:
    1. One person be in charge of the appointment book
    2. A treatment plan for the patient be well-defined
    3. All patients be scheduled for short appointments
    4. The patient's needs be accommodated while control of the appointment book be maintained
    5. Entries be made in ink
       A. 1, 2, and 4
       B. 1, 2, 4, and 5

C. 2, 4, and 5
D. 3, 4, and 5

38. A young child is being scheduled for an appointment. It is wise to schedule an appointment that:
    1. Avoids nap time
    2. Is of long duration
    3. Is of short duration
    4. Is in the early morning
    5. Is shortly after lunch
       A. 1, 2, and 4
       B. 1, 3, and 4
       C. 2 and 5
       D. 2 and 4

39. A patient calls his or her dental office with an emergency caused by an unexpected accident. The person answering the phone should:
    A. Schedule the patient for the earliest appointment next week
    B. Tell the patient you are "all booked up" and that perhaps someone else might be available
    C. Tell the patient to come in during your first available time that day, at which time the emergency will be treated and another appointment scheduled if the dentist is unable to complete the treatment on that day
    D. Express your sympathy, and tell the patient that the dentist will phone in a prescription to the pharmacist
    E. Refer the patient to the emergency room of a local hospital

40. If patient requires a series of appointments for treatment over several weeks, the best appointment scheduling for the patient would be:
    A. Variety of days and times
    B. Same day and time each week
    C. Alternate days, Monday the first week, Tuesday the second week, etc.
    D. Only Thursday and Friday

41. The most efficient format for an appointment book is the:
    A. Dual column appointment book

B. Multiple column book

C. Week-at-a-glance appointment book

D. Dated appointment book

42. A buffer period is a(n):

A. Appropriate date

B. Regular period of time twice a month

C. Unit increment of time for mornings or afternoons

D. All of the above

43. _____ patients require a routine exam and prophylaxis on a 6-month basis.

A. Emergency

B. Recall

C. Both A and B

D. None of the above

44. Which patient would likely pose a scheduling problem?

A. Patient arriving early

B. Patient behind in his payment

C. Drop-in emergency

D. All of the above

45. A patient who does not show up for his or her appointment should be handled in the following manner, which includes:

A. Closing the patient's file

B. Taking no action

C. Overlapping the patient's next appointment

D. Contacting the patient

46. A patient cancels an appointment an hour before he or she is due. A good course of action is to:

A. Close the office during the appointment time

B. Allow the dentist to solve the problem

C. Call a patient who is available on short notice

D. Announce that the entire staff can take a coffee break

47. A patient arrives at the office for his appointment on the wrong day. This

situation should be handled in the following way:

A. Reschedule the appointment

B. If there is an opening in the schedule, the patient may be treated

C. Inform the patient of the error and make a new appointment

D. Only A and B

E. All of the above

48. The types of recall systems utilized in the dental office include:

A. Advanced appointment

B. Telephone

C. Mail

D. Only A and C

E. All of the above

49. The advanced appointment system for recalling patients has an advantage in that it is:

A. Cost-effective

B. Time-saving

C. Simplified

D. Only A and B

E. All of the above

50. The disadvantages of the telephone system for recalling patients include:

A. Person may not be home

B. It is time-consuming

C. It may disturb the individual

D. All of the above

51. The recall mail system informs the patient that he or she should contact the office to make an appointment. The advantages include:

A. Patient assumes the responsibility

B. Message is sent directly to the patient

C. Patient may ignore the notice

D. Only A and B

E. All of the above

52. Failure to maintain a recall system will result in:

A. Neglect of the patient's oral health

B. Diminished activity in the appointment book

C. Decreased accounts receivable

D. All of the above

53. The success of a recall system depends on:
   A. Dental health education
   B. Motivation
   C. Consistent follow-up
   D. All of the above

III. Business records/bookkeeping and accounts receivable

54. The recording, classifying, and summarizing of business records is referred to as:
   A. Accounting
   B. Financial auditing
   C. Bookkeeping
   D. Data systems

55. A heavy plastic or metal precision constructed board used for bookkeeping procedures is called a:
   A. Daily journal board
   B. Pegboard
   C. Ledger card
   D. Fiber board

56. A check and balance system for the accuracy of financial computations is known as:
   A. Bank deposit
   B. Daily cash paid
   C. Proof of posting
   D. Total accounts receivable

57. A record of the financial information for each patient is found on the:
   A. Ledger card
   B. Receipt/charge slip
   C. Payment slip
   D. Clinical record

58. A professional courtesy to a patient is entered in the:
   A. Fee column
   B. Received on account column
   C. Adjustment column
   D. Special treatment column

59. A patient is seen for treatment for a total fee of $80. The previous balance on the account was $200. The patient paid $60. The new balance is:
   A. $280
   B. $140
   C. $220
   D. Credit of $20

60. Which one of the following groups is the correct computation for the totals given in columns D, A, B, and C?

Previous Balance (Column D)	+ Charges (Column A)	- Credits (Column B)	Current Balance (Column C)
$ 0	$ 75	$ –	$ 75
$ 300	$ 100	$ –	$ 400
$ 475	$ 125	$ 100	$ 500
$ 0	$ 200	$ 150	$ 50

A. D = $500, A = $480, B = $150, and C = $1025
B. D = $775, A = $500, B = $250, and C = $1025
C. D = $700, A = $600, B = $250, and C = $1025
D. D = $775, A = $500, B = $250, and C = $1125

61. The formula used in pegboard book-keeping to determine the proof of posting is:
   A. Previous balance + credits – charges = new balance
   B. Previous balance + charges – credits = new balance
   C. New balance – charges + credits = previous balance
   D. Previous balance + charges – cash received – insurance charges = new balance

62. Each employee's earnings records should provide the following information:
   1. Name of employee, address, social security number, and rate of pay
   2. Withholding status, marital status, and deductions
   3. Regular earnings as well as over-time earnings
   4. Quarterly and annual earning totals
   A. 1 and 2
   B. 1 and 3
   C. 2 and 3
   D. All of the above

63. The management of financial arrange-ments for a patient should include:
   1. Incorporation of sound business concepts
   2. Presentation of payment options
   3. Convenience only to the patient
   4. Standardization within the geo-graphic area
   5. Account management written poli-cies for the patient
   A. 1, 2, 4, and 5
   B. 1, 3, 4, and 5
   C. 2, 3, 4, and 5
   D. 1, 2, 3, and 4

IV. Dental insurance

64. The _____ is the person who represents the family unit in relation to the dental plan.
   A. Beneficiary
   B. Dependent
   C. Spouse
   D. Subscriber

65. The insurance company that pays the benefits claimed under a dental plan is

known as the:

A. Beneficiary
B. Subscriber
C. Insured
D. Carrier

66. A statement listing services rendered, date of services, and an itemization of the fees is a:

A. Claim form
B. Certificate of eligibility
C. Purchase order
D. Table of allowances

67. Third-party precertification (or prior authorization) will inform the:

A. Dentist and patient of the obligation assumed by the third party
B. Dentist of the correct treatment plan
C. Dentist that prepayment is available
D. Patient of the dentist's skills

Match the following:

68. _____ Coordination of benefits
_____ Deductible
_____ Pretreatment estimate
_____ Subscriber
_____ Assignment of benefits

A. Amount the patient pays toward treatment
B. Insured
C. Dual coverage
D. Subscriber authorizes payment to dentist
E. Information submitted prior to treatment

V. Patient records

69. Patient records are:

A. Public information
B. Available only to relatives
C. Confidential
D. Released at the assistant's discretion

70. What patient records are placed in an inactive file?

A. Records of all patients who have completed treatment
B. Records of patients who will return in 1 year
C. Records of patients who are no longer seeking treatment at the office
D. Records of patients who receive treatment at a discount

71. The patient's records include information such as:

A. Study models
B. Clinical charts
C. Radiographs
D. All of the above

72. The clinical record is an important document in the dental office because it provides:

A. Patient's past dental history
B. Information about productivity
C. Accurate data concerning the patient's past and present dental treatment
D. Messages to dental assistant

73. The reasons patient records may be transferred may include:

A. Patient changing dentist
B. Patient moving
C. Consultation with a referring dentist
D. Only B and C
E. All of the above

VI. Banking procedures

74. A _____ is used to pay minor office expenses.

A. Night deposit
B. Petty cash fund
C. Voucher check
D. Bank draft

75. The types of checks that a business assistant handles in the business office may include:
A. Certified check
B. Cashier's check
C. Money order
D. Only A and B
E. All of the above

76. A credit bureau is an agency that assists the dental office in the following way:
A. Lends money
B. Denies credit
C. Reports information about a person's payment habits
D. Collects money

VII. Inventory control

77. The system that utilizes control cards for inventory control is known as the:
A. Tag system
B. Card-file inventory system
C. Purchase quantity card system
D. Generic card system
E. All of the above

78. A supply company informs the office that an item that has been ordered is not available and will be shipped when it arrives. This is known as:
A. Bad order
B. Back-order item
C. Extra supply
D. Deficit spending

79. The purchase quantity of an item is determined by the:
A. Delivery time
B. Rate of use and shelf life of the item
C. Size of storage space
D. Only B and C
E. All of the above

80. When supplies are stored the storage area should be:
A. Cool, dry, and clean
B. On a shelf

C. Small in size
D. At the end of the wall
E. None of the above

81. When an order is received and unpacked, all of the contents are checked against the:
A. Invoice
B. Credit card
C. Requisition number
D. Stock

82. The main advantage of purchasing a large quantity of a particular supply at one time is to:
A. Make storage easier
B. Save money when buying in bulk
C. Make billing easier
D. None of the above

83. Dental supplies that are constantly being utilized in the office are known as:
A. Expendables
B. Disposables
C. Deductibles
D. Nonexpendables

84. When supplies are stored during inventory control, narcotics should be placed:
A. Away from heat
B. Away from radiation
C. In a locked cabinet
D. In a refrigerator

85. When you are stocking newly received supplies, they should be:
A. Dated
B. Stacked neatly
C. Checked against the invoice
D. All of the above

VIII. Infection control protocol

86. _____ provide information about hazardous materials utilized in the dental office.
A. Waste disposals
B. Back orders

C. EPA regulations

D. Material safety data sheets

87. The _____ makes the arrangements for disposing hazardous waste products from the dental office.

A. Hygienist

B. Dental assistant

C. Business assistant

D. Dentist

88. The _____ summarizes the classifications of regulated waste and compliance guidelines for the dental office.

A. Local dental society

B. American Dental Association

C. Environmental Protection Agency

D. Occupational Safety and Health Administration

89. Sharps are considered a _____ product.

A. Medical waste

B. Disposable

C. Puncture-resistant

D. Rigid

90. Blood-soaked items should be disposed of by:

A. Segregation into separate containers

B. Noting the weight of the items

C. Correct labeling of the container

D. Only A and B

E. All of the above

91. Recordkeeping for medical waste disposal should be retained for:

A. 2 years

B. 3 years

C. 4 years

D. 5 years

92. Label outer containers containing medical waste for shipping with a:

A. Water-resistant label

B. Pencil

C. Paper tag

D. Masking tape

Answers

1. C. The business assistant should maintain organization and management skills in business and dentistry.

2. A. An office procedural manual provides guidelines relating to office policy, philosophy, communications, employment policy, office records, infection control policy, clinical procedures, inventory systems, and professional organizations.

3. C. The office manual should be written under the dentist's direction and additionally developed by members of the dental team for input and coordinated effort.

4. C. Participatory leadership encourages all staff members and the dentist to contribute to decision making and responsibilities relating to their jobs.

5. C. The staff manager is the individual delegated to assume the responsibility of supervisor or manager of the dental office.

6. B. Barriers such as prejudice and preoccupation can be detrimental to the patients' dental needs and negate a positive dental staff and patient relationship.

7. B. Management provides the network for dental personnel to be motivated and guided as a professional team.

8. D. Communication is the key to establishing a positive relationship as a dental team.

9. E. Each of the aforementioned sample letters provides a reference file for

the business assistant who assumes the responsibility for written communication.

10. E. The classification of computers is general in nature and includes (1) the mainframe, which is a large system for storing and processing large amounts of data; the (2) minicomputer, which offers a compact version for processing and storing data; and the (3) microcomputer, which is a small personal computer commonly used in dental offices.

11. E. Computer operation includes input, processing, output, and storage.

12. D. The rights of a patient are considered inherent, and the dental professionals should always be considerate of the patient as a person. The patient can refuse treatment or request treatment but cannot dictate the course of treatment.

13. D. All this information should be communicated to the patient prior to treatment.

14. C. It is always considerate and honest to explain to the patient that the dentist may have had a delay or is treating a patient with an emergency.

15. D. Nonverbal communication provides the dental team with recognition and awareness of a patient's feelings through gestures and cues.

16. B. Communication in the dental office requires open discourse between the staff and patients as well as elimination of background noise.

17. E. It is important for the business assistant to greet patients, maintain a professional appearance personally, and establish order in the office reception area.

18. A. The word "discomfort" may be less offensive to a patient, especially if he or she is anxious or fearful.

19. B. A nervous patient may overtly communicate reactions such as embarrassment and fidgeting.

20. C. The reception area often reflects the atmosphere of the office. A professional and cheerful waiting area makes the patient feel comfortable.

21. C. The office policy is an excellent way to have a written statement of essential information pertaining to the philosophy of the practice and facts relative to the dental team and the patient.

22. B. A phonogenic personality is a key quality for the business assistant primarily responsible for telephone management.

23. A. The aforementioned phrases should not be expressed during telephone procedures. Professional phrases can be substituted which include discomfort, restore, restoration, and extract.

24. D. All the aforementioned procedures are essential when placing an outgoing call.

25. E. It is businesslike to indicate to the patient that you will return and to assure the caller you are engaged in a specific task. Once you have returned to the phone, politely thank the caller for holding.

26. B. The correct telephone protocol requires the business assistant to answer promptly, determine the reason for the call, and terminate the call in a polite and professional manner.

27. D. The telephone greeting should be professional, prompt, and express willingness to assist the patient.

28. D. All the aforementioned responses are important regarding the manner in which patients should be handled when the dentist is unable to talk with an insisting patient. A polite but firm approach is appropriate.

29. C. The day sheet details the dentist's and/or hygienist's schedule of patients and appointment time.

30. A. The patient should be informed of the fee prior to the dental treatment.

31. A. The patient clinical chart is a documented record of the patient's dental treatment.

32. A. Communication in the dental office with patients should be professional and appropriate. Red flag phrases are unfavorable and should be avoided or rephrased.

33. C. The receptionist has the responsibility for handling and controlling the appointment book.

34. B. Usually, young children tend to be more cooperative and responsive during morning appointments and tire by the early afternoon.

35. D. "Prime time" in the dental office occurs after 3:00 p.m.

36. C. A list of patients who can be contacted for a dental appointment.

37. A. All the aforementioned rules are essential for efficient appointment management.

38. B. All the aforementioned considerations are essential when scheduling an appointment for a child.

39. C. It is important to schedule an appointment as soon as possible for a patient with an emergency.

40. B. Usually the same day and time each week works out the best for the patient who requires a series of appointments.

41. C. In order to maintain effective and efficient appointment control, a week-at-a-glance appointment book is ideal.

42. C. A buffer period is a unit of time either for the morning or afternoon marked off in the appointment book.

43. B. Typically, a recall patient is scheduled for a routine exam and prophy-laxis on a bi-annual basis.

44. C. Usually a drop-in emergency will pose a scheduling problem and would require adjustment into the regular daily schedule.

45. D. The patient should be contacted regarding failure to keep an appointment.

46. C. A patient who cancels an appointment an hour before he or she is due may cause an unfortunate void in the schedule. The receptionist may contact a patient on the call list who would be available on short notice.

47. E. Each of these solutions is an appropriate response to this situation.

48. E. All the aforementioned systems are utilized in the dental office as a method of recalling patients.

49. E. All of these stated factors are advantageous regarding the employment of the advanced appointment system in the dental office.

50. D. The telephone system can present a time consuming recall method that may result in the inability to reach the patient at an appropriate time.

51. D. The patient has the responsibility of contacting the dental office upon due notice of appointment recall.

52. D. All the aforementioned results may occur with the failure to maintain a recall system.

53. D. The success of a recall system is dependent on the continuous follow-up of patient contact, as well as the positive motivation for patient dental health education.

54. A. Accounting is required in the business management of the dental office to record, classify, and summarize business records.

55. B. A pegboard is a precision construction board that contains the daily journal sheets needed to record financial computations.

56. C. Proof of posting enables the business assistant to verify daily financial transactions.

57. A. The ledger card is a record of the patient's financial information.

58. C. A professional courtesy will be entered as a debit adjustment and deducted from the total balance.

59. C. $220.

60. B. Column D = $775, column A = $500, column B = $250, and column C = $1025.

61. B. Previous balance (column D) + charges (column A) − credits (column B) = current balance (column C).

62. D. All the aforementioned information should be reflected in each employee's earnings records.

63. A. Financial arrangements for patients should include all the aforementioned principles.

64. D. Subscriber.

65. D. The carrier is the insurance company that pays for the claimed benefits offered under the group or private dental plan.

66. A. The claim form includes information such as type and date of services rendered as well as the fees.

67. A. Prior authorization informs both the dentist and the patient of the financial coverage by the third party.

68. C, A, E, B, and D.

69. C. Patient records are treated as confidential documents, which are comprised of the patient's clinical and financial data.

70. C. Patients who no longer seek dental treatment at the dental office have records that are placed in the inactive file.

71. D. All the aforementioned items are included in the patient's record.

72. C. The clinical record is a legal document containing patient data relative to the patient's past and present dental and medical history, as well as planned treatment.

73. E. All the aforementioned are reasons for transferring patient records.

74. B. Petty cash is a small amount of money that is kept in a dental office for minor expenses in addition to being utilized for change during business transactions.

75. E. The business assistant handles various types of checks including all the aforementioned in addition to travelers checks, bank drafts, and voucher checks.

76. C. For a nominal fee, the credit bureau provides the dental office with information concerning the patient's credit status.

77. B. The card-file system is a method for listing expendable and nonexpendable supplies and is marked for reorder when supplies are needed.

78. B. A back order indicates that the item was out of stock at the time of the order.

79. E. All the aforementioned factors are important in determining the quantity of an item that will be ordered.

80. A. Usually the storage area should be cool and dry and kept clean.

81. A. An invoice confirms the order date and shipping date as well as the product code, quantity ordered, and total amount due or paid.

82. B. It may be more economical to purchase items at a bulk rate if the item is used frequently.

83. A. Expendable supplies are utilized frequently in the dental office and need to be replaced often.

84. C. Narcotics should be stored in a locked cabinet.

85. D. Always check the invoice, date the new item, and store the item behind the remaining supply.

86. D. The material safety data sheet should be maintained in the dental office in compliance with OSHA standards. It provides important data concerning precautions in handling the product and other information.

87. D. The dentist is responsible for making decisions to properly dispose of hazardous waste products utilized in the dental office.

88. C. The EPA (Environmental Protection Agency) provides a summary of compliance guidelines for handling hazardous and medical waste in the dental office.

89. A. A sharp is a medical waste product and should be disposed of in a separate container labeled "infectious waste" or "medical waste."

90. E. All the aforementioned procedures should be followed when handling blood-soaked items.

91. B. Medical waste disposal records should be kept for 3 years to be in compliance with state and OSHA standards.

92. A. It is essential to utilize a water-resistant label when shipping containers with medical waste.

8

Comprehensive Diagnosis and Treatment Planning

CHAPTER OUTLINE

I. Collection and recording of clinical data

II. Medical/dental history

III. Oral examination

IV. Vital signs

V. Diagnostic aids

QUESTIONS

DIRECTIONS (Questions 1-50): In each of the following questions, select the one choice that answers the question or completes the sentence best.

I. Collection and recording of clinical data

1. A thorough dental examination is comprised of:
   A. Medical/dental history with accompanying patient data
   B. Vital signs
   C. Intra- and extraoral examination
   D. All of the above

2. The dentist develops a treatment plan for a patient based upon:
   A. Diagnostic patient records
   B. Thorough dental examination
   C. Medical and dental history with accompanying patient data
   D. Only A and B
   E. All of the above

II. Medical/dental history

3. When taking a medical history, the patient's height and weight should be documented on the medical history.
   A. True
   B. False

4. Upon entering the operatory, the dentist should observe the patient in terms of:
   A. Posture
   B. Gait or manner of walking
   C. Skin tone
   D. Only B and C
   E. All of the above

5. When is it necessary to update the patient's medical history?
   A. Each time the patient returns to the office for an appointment
   B. When a new patient joins the practice

C. Every 5 years
D. Only A and B
E. All of the above

6. The patient's dental history should include valuable information such as:
   A. Record of the patient's previous dental care
   B. Dates of the patient's last treatment
   C. Patient's recall history
   D. Only A and B
   E. All of the above

7. The patient chart includes the following:
   A. Documentation of the clinical examination
   B. Treatment history
   C. Financial statement
   D. Only A and B
   E. All of the above

III. Oral examination

DIRECTIONS (Questions 8-15): For each of the items in this section, one or more of the numbered options is correct. Choose answer:
   A. If only 1, 2, and 3 are correct.
   B. If only 1 and 3 are correct.
   C. If only 2 and 4 are correct.
   D. If only 4 is correct.
   E. If all are correct

8. The extraoral/intraoral examination involves the observation and palpation of the:
   1. Neck
   2. Face
   3. Lips
   4. Oral cavity

9. The armamentarium that is required for a complete oral examination includes:
   1. Gauze squares
   2. Mirror, explorer, and periodontal probe
   3. Dental floss
   4. Tongue depressors

10. When performing the extraoral/intra-oral examination, the patient's face and neck are examined for:
    1. Lumps
    2. Occlusion
    3. Pain, clicking, and tenderness of the temporomandibular joint
    4. Swelling

11. The oral tissues that are examined include the:
    1. Hard palate
    2. Uvula
    3. Buccal mucosa
    4. Soft palate

12. The gingival tissues are examined to determine the following:
    1. Epithelial attachment
    2. Pocket depth
    3. Generalized tissue color
    4. Appearance of the tissue

13. The lips are examined by observing the following:
    1. Texture
    2. Color
    3. Flexibility
    4. Size

14. The tongue is examined in the following manner:
    1. Ask the patient to extend the tongue
    2. Grasp the tip of the tongue with a 4 by 4 gauze square
    3. Observe the top and lateral borders of the tongue
    4. Request the patient to place the tip of the tongue to the palate and move it from side to side

IV. Vital signs

15. What constitutes the patient's vital signs?
    1. Pulse rate
    2. Respiration rate
    3. Blood pressure
    4. Temperature reading

16. Factors that will increase blood pressure include:
    A. Exercising and eating
    B. Fasting
    C. State of depression
    D. None of the above

17. Ventricular relaxation of the heart between contractions is known as:
    A. Systole
    B. Diastole
    C. Blood pressure
    D. None of the above

18. The contraction of the heart when the myocardial fibers tighten and shorten is known as:
    A. Systole
    B. Atrial
    C. Systema
    D. Diastole

19. The pressure of the blood against the walls of the blood vessels within the arteries is referred to as:
    A. Heart beat
    B. Vessel elasticity
    C. Blood pressure
    D. Systole

20. A blood pressure cuff connected to a glass tube containing a column of mercury is known as a:
    A. Spiroscope
    B. Thermometer
    C. Sphygmomanometer
    D. Aneroid gauge

21. A blood pressure cuff that is too small for the patient will give a(n) _____ reading:
    A. Falsely low
    B. Falsely high
    C. Inaudible
    D. Accurate

22. The correct sequence that should be followed when positioning the blood pressure cuff and stethoscope is:
    1. Place the stethoscope's diaphragm

under the cuff in the antecubital space.

2. Position the blood pressure cuff so that it encompasses the arm above the antecubital space.

3. Position the patient in an upright or supine position

4. The ear pieces of the stethoscope should be positioned toward the face and they should rest comfortably in the operator's ears.

5. Position the patient's left or right arm in an extended manner to assure that it is at heart level
   A. 3, 5, 2, 1, and 4
   B. 3, 2, 5, 1, and 4
   C. 1, 2, 3, 4, and 5
   D. 4, 2, 5, 3, and 1
   E. 2, 4, 3, 1, and 5

23. The sounds that are audible to the operator when taking blood pressure are known as:
   A. Korotkoff sounds
   B. Korticoid sounds
   C. Kork sounds
   D. None of the above

24. When a blood pressure reading is obtained, the first loud, sharp sound heard is known as the:
   A. Diastolic pressure
   B. Systolic pressure
   C. Systemic pressure
   D. Only B and C
   E. None of the above

25. When a blood pressure reading is obtained, the last sound of the audible heart beat is registered as the:
   A. Diastolic pressure
   B. Systolic pressure
   C. Systemic pressure
   D. Only B and C
   E. None of the above

26. The normal blood pressure reading in an adult is:
   A. 180/60

B. 135/80
C. 120/80
D. 140/80
E. 160/70

27. The procedure that should be followed when taking a blood pressure reading on a patient who has the blood pressure cuff and stethoscope in place is as follows:

1. Deflate and remove the cuff from the patient's arm and disinfect the stethoscope. Record the systolic and diastolic pressure readings on the patient's chart.

2. Unscrew the valve on the bulb and note the first loud sound, which will be the systolic pressure reading on the manometer, while listening with the stethoscope.

3. Slowly inflate the blood pressure cuff by squeezing the bulb until the radial pulse disappears, and observe this reading on the manometer.

4. Continue to release the bulb valve until the last audible sound is heard, which will be the diastolic pressure reading, and note the reading.

5. Locate the radial or brachial pulse on the patient's arm or wrist.
   A. 3, 2, 5, 4, and 1
   B. 1, 4, 2, 3, and 5
   C. 2, 3, 5, 4, and 1
   D. 5, 3, 2, 4, and 1

28. The heart rate should be evaluated for a minimum of:
   A. 5 seconds
   B. 30 seconds
   C. 45 seconds
   D. 2 minutes

29. The average pulse rate range for adults is:
   A. 130 to 160
   B. 80 to 100
   C. 60 to 80
   D. 50 to 60

30. The average pulse rate for children is:
   A. 130 to 160
   B. 80 to 100
   C. 60 to 80
   D. 50 to 60

31. Tachycardia is defined as:
   A. Unusually fast heartbeat
   B. Unusually slow heartbeat
   C. Heartbeat that is higher for women than men
   D. None of the above

32. A decreased pulse may be due to:
   A. Exercise
   B. Stimulants
   C. Strong emotions
   D. Depressants

33. When a pulse rate is obtained on a patient, the correct procedure should include the following:
   A. Position the index and third finger on inside of the wrist near the radius
   B. Note the number of heart beats in a 30-second unit of time and multiply the reading by 2 to obtain a 1-minute pulse reading
   C. Note the pulse reading and record in ink on the patient's record
   D. Only A and B
   E. All of the above

34. The normal respiratory rate for an adult is _____ breaths per minute.
   A. 10 to 15
   B. 5 to 10
   C. 16 to 18
   D. 20 to 25

35. When the respiration rate of a patient is recorded, the technique that is employed includes the following:
   A. Maintain the finger on the radial or brachial pulse
   B. Observe the rise and fall of the patient's chest as he or she inhales and exhales, noting that one com-

plete respiration includes one exhalation and one preinhalation
   C. Count the rate of respiration for 30 seconds and multiply by 2
   D. Only A and B
   E. All of the above

36. When the rate of respiration is taken on a patient, the procedure that is normally followed includes:
   A. Recording the rate of respiration in a 30-second unit of time and doubling the rate, or recording the rate for a full minute
   B. Noting any abnormal respiratory patterns
   C. Recording the data in ink on the patient's record
   D. Only A and B
   E. All of the above

37. A normal oral temperature reading for the majority of patients is:
   A. 98.6°F
   B. 96.8°F
   C. 37°C
   D. Only A and C
   E. Only B and C

38. The correct procedure for taking a temperature reading requires the following steps:
   A. Using a disposable thermometer or placing a disposable plastic sleeve over the thermometer
   B. Shaking the thermometer so the mercury reading is low
   C. Positioning the thermometer under the tongue for 3. 5 minutes, removing it from the oral cavity, and noting the reading
   D. Only A and C
   E. All of the above

39. The proper method of disinfection for an oral thermometer that has been encased in a plastic sleeve includes:
   A. Washing with soap and water
   B. Wiping with a germicidal or disinfecting agent

C. Wiping with cool water

D. None of the above

V. Diagnostic aids

40. If the vitalometer registers 10 and the patient has not reacted to the electrical stimulus, then it would appear that the pulp is:
    A. Hyperactive
    B. Hypoactive
    C. Necrotic
    D. Only A and C

41. In order to obtain an accurate reading of a tooth's vitality, the tip of the vitalometer should be in contact with:
    A. Enamel
    B. Dentin
    C. Composite restoration
    D. Amalgam restoration

42. When the excision method is used to obtain a biopsy the:
    A. Entire lesion is excised along with normal adjacent tissue
    B. Adjacent normal tissue plus abnormal tissue is taken for comparison, and surgery is indicated if the tissue is malignant
    C. Deep-seated tumors are examined by exploring and taking a specimen through deep-seated surgical excision; then the excision is closed and the patient is informed if further surgery is required
    D. None of the above
    E. Only A and C

43. The following situations warrant photographs of the patient's oral structures and face:
    A. Orthodontic treatment
    B. Reconstructive surgery
    C. Denture fabrication
    D. Cosmetic dentistry
    E. All of the above

44. When a root canal is performed, culture testing may be required to determine:
    A. If any resistant bacteria are present in the canal(s)
    B. Sterility of the canals
    C. Length of the canals
    D. Only A and B
    E. Only A and C

45. A culture tube may be read after 48 hours. A cloudy appearance of the tube indicates:
    A. Positive culture
    B. Bacteria are present in the culture
    C. Bacteria are not present in the culture
    D. Only A and B
    E. Only A and C

46. With the advent of antibiotics, culture testing may no longer be a part of the patient's intracanal treatment.
    A. True
    B. False

47. Which one of the following is considered a diagnostic aid when designing a treatment plan for a patient?
    A. Alginate impressions and gypsum models
    B. Radiographs
    C. Photographic slides
    D. Bite registration
    E. All of the above

48. Pain, pressure, and nausea are examples of _____ symptoms that may be felt by the endodontic patient.
    A. Objective
    B. Subjective
    C. Preoperative
    D. Postoperative

49. When the dentist is diagnosing an endodontic condition, the aids that may be utilized include:
    A. Percussion
    B. Thermal sensitivity
    C. Synder test
    D. Only A and B
    E. Only B and C

50. Transillumination fiber optic lights are utilized to detect:
   A. Fractures
   B. Different degrees of translucency from one tooth to another
   C. Alveolar bone density
   D. Only A and B
   E. Only B and C

Answers

1. D. All the aforementioned factors are essential to a thorough dental examination.

2. E. All of this information, including the patient's diagnostic records, histories, and personal data, is critical in formulating the treatment plan.

3. A. These statistics need to be assessed and documented in the patient's medical history.

4. E. All of these signs are indicative of the patient's general health.

5. D. New patients as well as returning patients need to have their medical histories updated or to complete a new medical history form.

6. E. All of the stated information is important regarding the patient's dental history and will assist the dentist in formulating his diagnosis and treatment plan.

7. D. The patient's chart serves as a permanent record of the individual's treatment history and clinical examination, which should be written in ink.

8. E. All of the aforementioned are included in the complete extraoral/intraoral examination.

9. E. All the aforementioned armamentarium is required in order to do a thorough oral examination.

10. E. All the aforementioned items are part of the examination procedure, in addition to the observation of the tongue, soft tissue, gingival tissues, lymph nodes, lips, oral habits and any difficulty in opening the mouth.

11. E. The oral cavity is examined to observe all tissues included within its borders.

12. E. The oral examination includes a general assessment of the gingival tissues.

13. E. The lips are examined for texture, color, flexibility, and general appearance of the tissue.

14. E. The tongue is thoroughly examined in the aforementioned manner to note any abnormal findings.

15. E. All the aforementioned parameters are measured, read, and recorded as patient vital signs.

16. A. Exercising and eating can contribute to increased or elevated blood pressure.

17. B. Diastole is the ventricular relaxation of the heart between contractions.

18. A. Systole is the contraction of the heart when the myocardial fibers tighten and shorten.

19. C. Blood pressure is defined as the pressure of the blood against the wall of the blood vessels within the arteries and is recorded in terms of its systolic and diastolic values. A normal blood pressure reading is 120/80 (systolic reading/diastolic reading).

20. C. The sphygmomanometer is the instrument utilized to obtain a blood pressure reading.

21. B. If the patient's blood pressure cuff is too small, the operator may obtain a falsely high reading.

22. A. This is the correct sequence for this procedure.

23. A. The Korotkoff sounds are audible to the operator when taking a blood pressure, and they range from strong and loud and descend to a soft disappearance.

24. B. The first audible sound detected with the stethoscope is the systolic pressure.

25. A. The last audible sound detected with the stethoscope is soft and disappearing and is referred to as the diastolic pressure.

26. C. The average adult blood pressure reading is approximately 120/80.

27. D. This is the correct sequence that should be followed when taking a patient's blood pressure.

28. B. The pulse or heart rate should be evaluated for at least 30 seconds or 1 minute.

29. C. 60 to 80 is the normal adult heart rate.

30. B. 80 to 100 is the average pulse rate for children.

31. A. An unusually fast heartbeat is commonly referred to as tachycardia.

32. D. A person who is taking depressants may exhibit a decreased pulse rate.

33. E. All the aforementioned are important regarding the correct procedure for obtaining a pulse recording.

34. C. The normal respiration rate for an adult is 16 to 18 breaths per minute.

35. E. This is the correct technique utilized when obtaining the patient's respiration rate.

36. E. All the aforementioned steps are required for counting the respiration rate of a patient.

37. D. 98.6°F or 37°C are comparable units of measure and represent a normal temperature.

38. E. All the aforementioned steps should be followed when obtaining the patient's temperature.

39. B. Wiping the thermometer with a germicidal or disinfecting agent will disinfect the thermometer if it has been covered with a plastic sleeve when taking an oral temperature.

40. C. A necrotic or nonvital pulp will not react to the vitalometer's stimulus and will register 10 on the dial.

41. A. The tip of the vitalometer should be in contact with the enamel portion of the tooth. If the tip is placed on a restoration or a prosthetic device, such as crown and bridge, the operator will get a false reading.

42. A. When the excision method is utilized, the entire lesion is excised as well as normal adjacent tissue so the pathologist can have comparable tissue samples to arrive at a diagnosis.

43. E. All the aforementioned situations warrant photographs of the patient's oral structures and face.

44. D. Culture testing is a useful diagnostic aid utilized to determine if bacteria remain in the canal and to check the sterility of the canal.

45. D. A cloudy appearance in the culture tube indicates that bacteria are present in the culture and that the resulting culture is positive.

46. A. Antibiotics destroy bacteria; therefore, it may not be necessary to take a culture of the patient's root canal to determine if the canal is bacteria-free.

47. E. All the aforementioned are considered to be valuable diagnostic aids

when designing a treatment plan for the patient.

48. B. Pain, pressure, and nausea are examples of subjective symptoms that would be felt by the patient who is experiencing endodontic disease.

49. D. Both percussion and thermal sensitivity are utilized to determine an endodontic diagnosis.

50. D. Transillumination with a fiber optic light allows the operator to visually compare translucency of the teeth. Additionally, the operator may be able to view fractures with this aid.